Development
of self in culture

Edited by Kristine Jensen de López and Tia G. B. Hansen

SELF IN CULTURE IN MIND, VOLUME 1
AALBORG UNIVERSITY PRESS

Development of self in culture
Self in culture in mind, volume 1
Edited by Kristine Jensen de López & Tia G. B. Hansen

© The authors & Aalborg University Press, 2011

Layout: akila v/ Kirsten Bach Larsen
Printed by Toptryk Grafisk ApS, 2011
ISBN: 978-87-7112-009-7
ISSN: 2245-1528

Cover painting: Casper Kjærsgaard Christensen
Language editor: Chris Cummins

Published by:
Aalborg University Press
Skjernvej 4A, 2nd floor
9220 Aalborg
Denmark
Phone: (+45) 99 40 71 40
Fax: (+45) 96 35 00 76
aauf@forlag.aau.dk
forlag.aau.dk

This book is financially supported by The Department of Communication and Psychology, Aalborg University, Denmark.

All rights reserved. No part of this book may be reprinted or reproduced or utilized in any form or by any electronic, mechanical, or other means, now known or hereafter invented, including photocopying and recording, or in any information storage or retrieval system, without permission in writing from the publishers, except for reviews and short excerpts in scholarly publications.

Contents

1 Self in culture in mind in development: Introduction   5
  Kristine Jensen de López, Tia G. B. Hansen

2 Self constructed in culture   25
  Jeremy I. M. Carpendale, Charlie Lewis

3 Child rearing in bicultural families: Socialisation goals   41
  and parental ethnotheories in West African-German families
  Astrid Kleis

4 Perceiving self through envy: A multi-culture comparison   65
  of preschool children
  Laura Quintanilla, Kristine Jensen de López

5 Developmental precursors of autonomy and relatedness: 89
  Discursive practices in childhood and autobiographical
  self-constructions in young adulthood
  Carolin Demuth, Heidi Keller, Helene Gudi, Hiltrud Otto

6 Development of self in an institutional context 121
   Mogens Jensen

7 Formal schooling, autobiographical memory and 145
   independent self-construal
   Manuel de la Mata Benítez, Andrés Santamaría Santigosa,
   Tia G. B. Hansen, Lucía Ruiz Ramos, Marcia L. Ruiz Cansino

8 Gender in three generations: Narrative constructions and 169
   psychological identifications
   Monica Rudberg, Harriet Bjerrum Nielsen

9 A social action learning approach to community resilience: 197
   "Our sharing of thoughts and feelings, our respect and
   trust should be passed on to the next generation"
   Peter Berliner, Line Natascha Larsen, Elena de Casas Soberón

Author list 223

Kristine Jensen de López
Tia G. B. Hansen

Self in culture in mind in development
Introduction

Some years ago we noticed an interesting convergence. While the mainstream media focused its interest on biological explanations of psychological phenomena – fuelled by new technological tools and the discoveries they yielded, but threatening to throw psychology into neo-reductionism – a vast range of psychological approaches were converging in a different way entirely. Within the wide range of possibilities that biological constraints leave open, a human being's culture, group, and individual agency assert their influence on the person that he or she becomes, and to most psychologists, we think, this is the level of analysis at which psychological phenomena can best be observed, understood and maybe explained.

The convergence that we saw in many recent psychological level approaches concerns the pivotal role of everyday practices as sites of mediation. Mind (and brain, and body) meets culture in everyday practices, human beings know and live culture through everyday practices, and a person's self develops through these sites of mediation. Often they are as invisible to the individual as water is to fish, but they exert their influence in very different ways than the biologically explicable way that water acts on fish.

This is no new discovery. We owe it to Michael Cole's (1998, p. 1) insistence that we "keep culture in mind" and Michael Tomasello's search for the cultural roots of human cognition (e.g., Tomasello, 1999), to Markus and Kitayama's (1991) seminal paper on self construal, and to other strong theorists in contemporary psychology, of whom some appear in this book and many others are referred to. It also dates back to prominent figures in the history of psychology such as George Herbert Mead, Sir Frederic Bartlett, Gregory Bateson, Lev Vygotsky and A. N. Leont'ev. What took our interest and started this book series was the observation that a surprising amount of recent and rigorously updated approaches also seemed to converge there, despite variations in their approach, focus of attention, and empirical method. That is, their findings could be interpreted as indicators of how selves are constituted through culture-mind-mediation during everyday practices.

Scientific communities

Several institutions and organisations take interest in psychological questions related to culture-mind-mediation. We particularly appreciate the work of two scientific societies in holding this torch: The *IACCP* (International Association of Cross-Cultural Psychology), and the *ISCAR* (International Society of Cultural and Activity Research). Conferences and readings from members of both societies have inspired the *Self in culture in mind* book series and in fact, the initial steps towards it were taken during a symposium dinner at the ISCAR conference held in San Diego in 2008.

IACCP defines its aim as facilitation of "communication among persons interested in a diverse range of issues involving the intersection of culture and psychology". It was founded in 1972 and comprises members from more than 65 countries (About IACCP, 2011). This society invites, collates and supports integration of research pertaining to issues of cross-cultural diversity, emphasising its global reach, and itself being cross-cultural in practice and effect as well as in theory.

Whereas *cross*-cultural is the core issue for IACCP, *culturalness* is the core issue for ISCAR (although we admit that this term for it is our own invention). ISCAR's membership also stretches throughout most of the world, with particular strength in the Americas and Scandinavia and strong bonds to Eastern Europe. ISCAR defines its aims as "developing multidisciplinary theoretical and empirical research on societal, cultural and historical dimensions of human practices" and "promoting mutual scientific communication and research cooperation among its members" (About ISCAR, n.d.). Historically, the society is an integration of two previous societies, the International Society for Cultural Research and Activity Theory and the Conference for Sociocultural Research. Based on a shared interest in historical and philosophical approaches and inspiration from Lev Vygotsky and his theoretical followers, these merged into ISCAR in 2002.

Methodologically speaking, IACCP theories are based on empirical evidence, which can take many forms but quantitative methods and hypothesis testing figure prominently (like mainstream psychology), whereas theories from ISCAR more often have a philosophical origin, empirical studies may not be included, and when they are, practice observations and other qualitative methods are preferred.

The *Self in culture in mind* (SICIM) book series, launched by the present volume, places itself in the intersection of these two societies; an intersection which we find deserves more attention. After all, culturalness, being an inevitable precondition of being human, should be at the core of any psychological theory; and cross-cultural variation is an inevitable premise of implemented culturalness. This begs the integration of insights from both perspectives. Or so we think. The SICIM series is one attempt to implement that thought.

The question of development

For developmental psychologists, core 'self in culture in mind' questions include the following. How do humans across the world and across different cultures come to develop a sense and understanding of self, and how is this process driven by their understanding of others and vice versa? In what sense is self-construal a part of human development, and what is the role of different styles of socialisations, as mediated by parents, peers and cultural institutions? These questions have been given consideration by contributors to this volume, each from their own perspective.

Developmental psychologists have traditionally approached the question of development from an individualist perspective, disregarding the role of interpersonal relations, human embodiment and the environment itself. More recently new technologies available for studying brain and genetic structures has led to a wave of interesting findings about the biological prerequisites for the human mind. However, these pay little attention to the fact that human brains reside inside persons, who in turn developed inside particular cultural environments and thus threaten to reinforce a traditional individualist (and sometimes reductionist) view of the person.

Nevertheless, over the past decades, there has also been an increased focus on the self as discursively constructed in everyday interactions (Ochs & Capps, 2001; Shotter, 1993), where self, culture, and autobiographical narrations are interrelated (Brockmeier & Carbaugh, 2001; Bruner, 1990), and on the question of how cross-cultural differences are mediated. It has been argued that, in order to understand the systematic role culture plays for the construction of self, it is crucial to take a developmental perspective within a socio-historic and eco-historical approach (Keller, 2007).

The authors of this book employ socio-cultural and interpersonal perspectives assuming that human beings' sense of self, their understanding of what that emplies and their self-construal, develop within the complexity of culturally embedded relationships. These emerge from the child's very first day of life and carry on expanding throughout the individual's life. This perspective differs from traditional developmental psychology, which mainly concentrates on development of self during childhood and adolescence, and which too rarely considers cross-cultural issues. Our attempt to unify life-span development with cross-cultural psychology is unique in this way.

Cultural models of the self provide essential frameworks for shaping socialisation goals and for shaping parental ideas about what constitutes effective child rearing (D'Andrade, 1984; Göncü, 1999; Harkness & Super, 1996; Keller, Voelker & Yovsi, 2005). The term 'cultural model', drawn from cognitive anthropology, indicates an organised set of ideas that are shared by members of a cultural group. Thus, parental ethnotheories are manifestations of socio-cultural orientation, that become converted into ideas about children, families and themselves as parents, as well as, ideas about good parenting and childcare practices. Although inter-individual differences are prevalent with respect to parenting goals and practices in every culture (e.g., Harkness & Super, 1996; LeVine et al., 1994), members of cultural communities can nevertheless be viewed as groups of individuals who co-construct a shared reality in different domains of life. In particular, concepts of individualism and collectivism as normative cultural dimensions (Hofstede, 1980; Kagitcibasi, 1997; Singelis, 1994; Triandis, 1995) and independent and interdependent construals of self as personal orientations (Markus & Kitayama, 1991) are now taken into account by developmental psychologists in order to explain how different developmental goals correlate with different socialisation contexts and parenting styles during different stages of development (Greenfield & Suzuki, 1998). Parental ethnotheories can thus be conceived of as the mediating link between these cultural meta-models, behavioural contexts and practices (Harkness, Super & van Tijen, 2000). It should therefore be expected that cultural communities that differ with respect to these value orientations may also differ with respect to the nature of parental ethnotheories.

Children's understanding of self is closely interconnected with their understanding of emotions. In particular, self-conscious emotions are argued to play an important role for a child's self-construal. While children's understanding of basic emotions such as happiness and sadness has received some attention by developmental psychologists, the set of complex and self-conscious emotions have rarely been investigated. Furthermore, the attention that has been given to children's development of emotional understanding is limited by an individualistic perspective on development. Self-conscious emotions are demanding to capture since they are truly embodied experiences, and hence cannot be identified through observations of bodily expressions displayed by the other. Coming to understand these emotions is by its nature an embodied activity tied to the child's prior experiences and understanding of complex interpersonal relationships. Because emotions such as envy do not have a bodily expression, in order to understand that a person is experiencing envy one must possess knowledge about the distinction between other and self. Following Bruner's theorising, children come to understand mental concepts such as self-conscious emotions through active use of these concepts in interpersonal contexts that promote meanings. The privileged role of interaction, where actions are allocated meanings and seen as the starting point of the child's comprehension of the mind, has recently gained strength in research on the social construction of the self (Carpendale & Lewis, 2004; Nelson, 2003). However, meanings may differ crucially across cultures. In order to understand relational meanings underlying self-conscious emotions, one additionally needs to rely on specific cultural practices and preconditions, e.g., access to goods.

This first volume of the new book series *Self in culture in mind* has been devoted to the very beginning of culture-mind-mediated selves. The beginning, in the sense that the volume includes discussions related to the evolutionary starting points for humans' development of self-construal, as well as to the emergence of and changes seen in self-construal during ontogenesis. The chapter sequence of the book roughly reflects a developmental sequence, i.e., studies of early self-construal precede studies of self-contrual during youth and adulthood.

Introduction to the chapters of this volume

The first contribution is by Jeremy Carpendale and Charlie Lewis, who echo Tomasello, Kruger and Ratner's (1993) notion of a 'ratchet effect' as well as Mead's (1934) notion of social interaction and attitudes. The authors argue that culture is a human niche and propose an account of how our biological natures make culture possible and how systems of behavioural practices are learned by children. While refuting the individualistic perspective, which takes the individual as a starting point, their theoretical proposal is a relational approach to self, where relations are primary and from which a sense of self and other gradually develops. Carpenter and Lewis stress that young infants gradually come to conceptualise their activity in terms of enduring and coherent individuality. Their point of departure is a phylogenetic and ontogenetic perspective, where they compare infants' development of intentionality and communication with that of closely related species, such as chimpanzees. Human infants engage in a specific type of human embodiment, which promotes the development of self and differs radically from the engagement of infant chimpanzees. One example of how early human activities of embodiment differ from those of chimpanzees and which consequently may scaffold the emergence of a self, is the fact that different modes are utilised by caretakers to carry their infants. Human parents walk upright and carry their infants in their arms or on their backs, while chimpanzee infants must hold on to their mother while she travels. Compared to chimpanzees, human infants hence have the possibility to direct a different type of interest towards the world, as indicated by leaning and reaching toward objects, which differs from the possibilities given to the chimpanzee infant, who simply must hold on. In this sense, the human infant's physical directedness towards the world may be seen as the root cause of their attraction to it. Although infants may not consciously be intending to communicate at this early stage, their actions still function to communicate to their caregivers. The authors point out that this embeddedness of infants within human interaction necessitates an early but simple grasp of the self in interaction (Reddy, 2008). Furthermore, infants' insignificant usage of pointing in their early interactions has implications for potential forms of social cognition and self-understanding in ontogenesis. Many developmental psychologists tend to look for genetic and neurological factors when explaining how human self-understanding becomes possible. Contrastingly, Carpenter and Lewis argue that culture provides a complex social environment for children's development to occur that is enduring but *not* encoded in genes. Importantly, the authors also argue that there must be adaptations that make culture possible. And despite these adaptations being accomplished in different ways across cultures, they must also be present in a general way to make culture possible at all.

The empirical contribution of Astrid Kleis sets out to disentangle the influence of culture and gender on parental ethnotheories with respect to views of autonomy and relatedness. German and West African families respectively can be seen as prototypes of the independent (autonomous) and interdependent (related) conceptions of parenting. These different socio-cultural orientations may easily come in conflict within each other in bi-cultural West African-German families living in Germany. Kleis' study provides evidence from a large sample of semi-structured interviews conducted with West African and German mothers and fathers in bicultural families with at least one child between the ages of 3 and 6 years. Each parent was asked to rank a set of aspects of family life, socialisation and relationships by how important these aspects were to them. The parents were also asked to describe similarities and differences in their attitudes to child rearing, family life and relationships. The study is very original and its results are discussed in relation to variance in the parental ethnotheories, the consequences of different parental ethnotheories for family life and parents' abilities to cope with as well as benefit from these differences in everyday family life.

In chapter four, taking a social-cultural, action-based and meaning-dependent approach to the emergence of mental concepts, Laura Quintanilla and Kristine Jensen de López discuss the role and influence of culture on preschool children's development of emotional comprehension within contexts of envy. They also explore the types of emotional attribution explanations and coping strategies children provide when witnessing contexts of envy across different age periods. Their investigation of the development of children's abilities to recognise and make attributions about the self-conscious emotion of envy is approached from a cross-cultural viewpoint, involving preschool children from three very different cultures (Danish, Spanish, and Zapotec, a Mexican Meso-American society). Their results demonstrate that preschool children from all three cultures display the understanding that another person can feel happy when witnessing the misfortune of another person – a core element in understanding the emotion of envy. Hence, the ability to comprehend the self-conscious emotion of envy seems to be universally present in preschool children and perhaps even generated by a general process, similar to what is suggested by Carpenter and Lewis (chapter 2). However, the age at which young children are able to express this ability and the strategies they suggest to decrease interpersonal conflicts arising from contexts of envy differ across cultures and societies. Zapotec children, compared to Spanish and Danish children, display a later onset of this ability, and also express a different developmental pattern when justifying the behaviour of the protagonists involved in the event causing the emotion to arise. Culture is taken to provide the child with a complex social environment within which development can unfold itself, and variations in cultural practices and socialisation may cause the children to proceed along different developmental trajectories (Jensen de López, 2006; Knüppel, Steensgaard & Jensen de López, 2007; Sinha & Jensen de López, 2001).

A particularly fruitful approach to the study of communicative practices in child socialisation is the study of family mealtimes (e.g. Larson, Wiley & Branscomb, 2006). Family mealtimes can be considered as "cultural sites for the socialization of children into competent and appropriate members of a society" (Ochs & Shohet, 2006, p. 35). The four authors of chapter five of this volume, Carolin Demuth, Heidi Keller, Helene Gudi and Hiltrud Otto, present a study of communicative practices in early family dinner conversations showing how these settings can be considered as developmental precursors of the narrative self in adulthood with regard to autonomy and relatedness. The authors studied videotaped dinner interactions of 20 middle class families with 3-year-old children in the southern part of Germany and analysed discourse expressions across the dimensions of autonomy and relatedness. In a follow-up study the participating children were recontacted in their late twenties, and asked to participate in an interview study on autobiographical remembering. The interview comprised an unstructured narrative part (Schütze, 1983) in which the participants were asked to tell the interviewer "the story of their life", as well as providing information through a semi-structured interview about the role of personal relations (family, friends, colleagues) and self-realisation (professional career, life planning) in their life. Analysis revealed systematic patterns with regard to the emphasis given to autonomy and relatedness in the participant's life accounts. Based on this typology, the findings from the interview were systematically related to the findings from the early childhood dinner conversations. They authors infer that the discursive constructions of early family interactions reveal broader cultural ideologies that can be seen later in the narrative self in adulthood. The study of discursive practices in the family can be said to provide us with valuable insights on how cultural worlds are constructed in everyday interactions and thus lay the foundations for the development of culture-specific understandings of a person's sense of self and of self in relation to others.

Moving on to the development of self during the period of adolescence, in chapter six Mogens Jensen introduces Barth's (2002) psychological concept of knowledge-forms in order to analyse and understand the interpersonal dynamics of pedagogical treatment of Danish adolescents in residential care. Knowledge-forms are seen as including values, possibilities of acting, and social hierarchies, and leave room for the individual adolescent to find his own way of handling his residence at the institution. Again context, and the interactions between context and individual agency, are stressed as important units of analysis in attempting to understand the development of self. The approach presented in Jensen's chapter is in the social-pedagogical tradition and traces its roots back to the hermeneutic philosophy of the likes of Dilthey and Natorp, which views humans as profoundly social and decline any understanding of individual outside the social context. The case studies analysed within this theoretical framework rely on an interpersonal concept of *fellowship*, which is expanded by the author to cover the notion of a social-pedagogical fellowship. In this specific setting, adolescents are viewed as co-responsible for judging which competences to develop, while they attempt to gain full acceptance from the social worker during the collaborative process of establishing common goals within the social-pedagogical fellowship. This process is meant to motivate the adolescent to engage in positive activities balanced with the expectations of the society and through the establishment of a relational contract. The asymmetry between a comprehending-interpreting approach, where the adolescent's perspective is followed, and a normative-evaluating approach, which compares the competencies of the adolescent with the general norms of the culture, is addressed as a potential threat to the successful establishment of a fruitful social-pedagogical fellowship. The approach acknowledges the existence of conflicts between adolescents and society, and rather than focusing on eliminating these conflicts Jensen argues that the social-pedagogical goal is to learn to handle ongoing dilemmas of conflicting knowledge-forms. The development of the adolescents' self while growing up in residential care is described as a movement from a position of a legitimate peripheral participant as in 'situated learning' (Lave & Wenger, 1991) to a position of a fully-fledged participant where the forming of the social-pedagogical fellowship is of central concern and importance, and this crucially depends on a comprehending-interpreting approach. Furthermore, it is argued that the adolescents' knowledge-forms need to be interpreted as meaningful actions within their individual history.

Formal schooling has historically been seen as a fundamental setting for socialisation, transmission and recreation of social values and plays a role in the constitution of the modern subject (Olsen, 1994). This is the focus of attention in chapter seven, by Manuel de la Mata, Andrés Santamaría Santigosa, Tia Hansen, Lucia Ruiz Ramos and Maria Ruiz Cancino. Following Bruner (1990), the authors propose that autobiographical memory can be conceived as a self-making discursive narrative, in which the individual's life is reconstructed and mediated through semiotic tools (Santamaría & Martínez, 2005). Narratives about early memories provided by Mexican adults with three different levels of educational background are compared and found to reflect a decrease in social content and an increase in individual content as the educational level of the participant increases. The notion of self as agent and the employment of mental verbs in narratives about self is more prominent for participants' with higher levels of education. Contrastingly, action verbs characterise the narratives of participants with less education. The study illustrates that schooling experiences within a culture are associated with forms of autobiographical remembering that mirror cultures of independence, suggesting that formal schooling can be perceived as a socio-cultural practice (Scribner & Cole, 1981) or activity setting (Wertsch, 1985) which promotes the construction of an independent self-construal.

The topic of chapter eight is memories of childhood and images of parents in adults. These mental entities are salient examples of how people use cultural concepts to organise their social worlds and to constitute themselves and others in meaningful ways. Personal images also give us the possibility to reflect on the 'inner' readiness to accept or reject different cultural discourses, and allow new gender relations to emerge within specific cultures. Focusing specifically on men's discourse of the psychological self, gender researchers Monica Rudberg and Harriet Bjerrum Nielsen have investigated the construction of ideas and practices of gender equality in a modern Norwegian context. Using examples from an ongoing study of men in three generations (interviewed in 1991-92, with a follow-up ten years later), the authors discuss the different cultural 'genres' that seem to be at work in the way the men memorise their childhood in relation to their presentation of self as well as their concepts of gender and equality. In order to grasp possible connections between such cultural discourses and more specific psychobiographies, Rudberg and Nielsen look closely at the chains of grandfather-father-son. This generational perspective is new in research on memory and self construction, and is important because memories of childhood are not only involved in the identity construction of any given individual here and now, but are also memorable constructions which are transmitted in different ways (accepted or rejected) and forms (families, relational, emotional) to later generations. In particular their study illustrates how narrative styles and patterns of psychological identification, and in particular parental identification, can be seen as dynamic and intertwined processes in the (co-)construction of new gender. The developmental pattern of the older generation is reflected in a narrative style where practical work and traditions are given more attention than the inner emotional world, whereas the middle generation expresses an inner but also more conflictual cultural world, and the younger generation's narratives waver between inner and outer life as well as between styles of relatedness and distance.

The final contribution of the present volume, by Peter Berliner, Line Natascha Larsen and Elena de Casas Soberón, draws upon yet another approach for capturing 'self in culture in mind', namely a social action learning approach inspired by community psychology and action research. The chapter documents the unfolding of a new self construal within a group of young Greenlandic mothers living in a society with a history of violence, suicides, drug abuse, and child neglect. Through a community mobilisation programme, young mothers-to-be are invited to engage in capacity-building activities and encouraged to take charge of their own situation as well as the developmental possibilities of their new-born child. The study rests upon an activity theory based on understanding of how identities are shaped in social interaction in particular contexts with political, economic and livelihood aspects as forces and mediators. Taking this point of departure, the authors of chapter nine analyse and describe changes in the group in terms of the mothers' development of a semi-structured civil society promoting social responsibility, social support through respect for motherhood as a social activity, and a sense of community. This developmental process, though far from completed, is seen as a 'breaking of the silence' and sees the individual mothers develop from mainly being part of a kinship system to becoming part of a civil society organisation. Mediated by active participation in the programme, the mothers learn to augment a discourse of rights against unwanted interference and abusive behaviour that previously was culturally accepted and perceived as a natural process. The changes identified in the group of mothers were observable in their understanding of social support as mediated through horizontal practices of social interaction rather than dependent on traditional vertical structures.

Converging evidence from different approaches

All chapters concern the same basic issue of how human beings see ourselves, and how the culture in which we live manifests itself in the way that we see ourself and others. Furthermore, they all focus on specific processes by which the macro-levels of culture and history are reflected at the intrasubjective level and mediated by intersubjective and practical actions; and they all see the person's own agency as crucial for the findings of research (although this is reflected in very

DEVELOPMENT OF SELF IN CULTURE

Chapter	Approach	To	Examines	Design/comparison	Special indicators
2	General conceptual / historical overview	The phenomena self, culture, and their interrelations	Basic interactional processes that are a prerequisites of developing a self	Core concepts and findings Biology and culture	Apes vs chrildren, child development Language, activity
3	Keller's contextual approach to cultural models	The role of culture and gender for parental goals and practices	Bicultural families (West African-German couples in Germany)	Cultural background vs gender Interviews, content analysis	Child rearing practices Which parental goals are given priority (card sorting method)
4	Socio-historical approach with concepts from information processing and constructivism	Development of self-referring complex emotions	Children age 3-5 Danish, Spanish, and Zapotec	Quasi-experimental by culture and age Compares responses to picture story	Attribution of the emotions envy and schadenfreude to protagonists
5	Discursive practice approach	Relationship between upbringing context and later self	Dinner conversations, identity strategies German	Longitudinal Compares types of dinner conversation in infancy to later identity strategy	Typology of utterances around dinner table Typology of identity strategy in youth

SELF CONSTRUCTED IN CULTURE

Chapter	Approach	To	Examines	Design/comparison	Special indicators
6	Socio-cultural practice approach	Assisted self development of youth in trouble	Residents and staff in a residential institution	Field study. Shadowing method	Interpretative, using concepts of fellowship formation and knowledge forms
7	Sevilla activity setting approach	Relationship between formal schooling and self construal	Mexicans with three different levels of schooling	Quasi-experimental by educational level. First memories, self-descriptions	Self/other and mental/action references. Narrative coding system
8	Psychodynamically inspired subjectivity construction approach	Gendered life story narratives	Norwegians from 3 generations (focus on men)	Semi-structured life story interviews. Generation, also noting background as urban / rural, and educational level	Interpretative. Style and emotions of narratives, signs of identification
9	Social action learning approach	Community psychology and development	Mothers in a village in Kalaallit Nunaat (Greenland)	Action research and interviews	Collective conceptualisations in the group, reports of feeling empowered

Table 1. Approaches and indicators

different ways throughout the chapters). Last but not least, each chapter suggests a particular approach and documents its empirical indicators of how the intertwined nature of the cultural and the individual level, with regard to issues of self and personal identity, are mediated by the everyday practices, material and discursive, that the person engages in. For an overview of approaches and indicators, see table 1.

Taken together, these contributions serve to document two major points, one substantial, and one methodological:
- Cultural and subcultural differences in everyday practices mediate cultural and subcultural differences in the person's development of self.
- Several theoretical frameworks, each with their associated methods, converge on establishing this finding – each with their specific indicators – despite some of them having historically been construed as orthogonal or even irreconcilable approaches.

Self in culture in mind in development

The current and first volume of the *Self in culture in mind* series, *Development of self in culture*, constitutes original theoretical and empirical contributions within the growing body of work interested in understanding how humans are able to construe self within culture and mind. From a methodological point of view, the book demonstrates the importance of appreciating that variation in methodologies is extremely crucial for understanding different types of self-construals as well as for understanding any developmental phenomenon. The use of cross-sectional, longitudinal and follow-up studies, quantitative as well as qualitative, to investigate the development of self and self-consciousness allow us to examine the unfolding of continuous development *in vivo*. This great advantage when investigating the ontogenesis of self can also be considered as an advance in the field of developmental psychology towards reaching a better understanding of how individuals come to gain understanding of self and other. The relatedness between the contributions to this specific volume can be seen to arise from the shared goal of understanding the emergence and expansion of self in mind within society, from a cultural and contextual approach. Several of the studies set out from the participants' subjective view and rely on qualitative and quantitative methods in tandem. The ability to combine methods in this fashion is yet another common theme uniting the contributions in this volume.

With this first volume we hope to expand the documentation of life-long development of self, as well as to illustrate the convergence of many approaches' findings about everyday practices as sites of culture-self-mediation, and to offer the reader a varied set of scientific issues and methodologies that can be used in future work.

References

About IACCP (2011). Retrieved December 20th from http://www.iaccp.org/drupal/node/1

About ISCAR (n.d.). Retrieved December 20th from http://www.iscar.org/da/about

Barth, F. (2002) An anthropology of knowledge. *Current Anthropology*, 43, 1-18.

Brockmeier, J., & Carbaugh, D. A. (Eds.) (2001). *Narrative and identity: Studies in autobiography, self and culture*. Amsterdam: John Benjamins Publishing Company.

Bruner, J. (1990). *Acts of meaning*. Harvard University Press.

Carpendale, J. I. M., & Lewis, C. (2004). Constructing an understanding of mind: The development of children's social understanding within social interaction. *Behavioral and Brain Sciences*, 27, 79-151.

Cole, M. (1998). *Cultural psychology. A once and future discipline*. Harvard University Press.

D'Andrade, R. (1984). Some propositions about the relations between culture and human cognition. In J. W. Stigler, R. A. Shweder, & G. Herdt (Eds.), *Cultural psychology. Essays on comparative human development* (pp. 65-129). New York: Cambridge University Press.

Göncü, A. (1999). *Children's engagement in the world: Sociocultural perspectives*. Cambridge University Press.

Greenfield, P. M., & Suzuki, L. (1998). Culture and human development: Implications for parenting, education, pediatrics, and mental health. In I. E. Sigel & K. A. Renninger (Eds.), *Handbook of child psychology. Vol. 4: Child psychology in practice* (5th ed., pp. 1059-1109). New York, NY: Wiley.

Harkness, S., Super, C. M., & van Tijen, N. (2000). Individualism and the 'Western mind' reconsidered: American and Dutch parents' ethnotheories of the child. *New Directions for Child and Adolescent Development, 87*, 23-39.

Harkness, S., & Super, C. (1996). *Parents' cultural belief systems: their origins, expressions, and consequences*. New York, NY: Guilford Press.

Hofstede, G. (1980). *Culture's consequences*. Beverly Hills, CA: Sage.

Jensen de López, K. (2006). Culture, language and canonicality: Differences in the use of containers between Zapotec (Mexican indigenous) and Danish children. In A. Costall & O. Dreier (Eds.), *Doing things with things: The design and use of everyday objects* (pp. 87-109). London: Ashgate.

Kagitçibasi, C. (1997). Individualism and collectivism. In J. W. Berry, M. H. Segall, & C. Kagitçibasi (Eds.), *Handbook of cross-cultural psychology. Vol. 3, Social behavior and applications* (2nd ed., pp. 1-49). Boston: Allyn & Bacon.

Keller, H. (2007). *Cultures of infancy*. Mahwah, NJ: Erlbaum.

Keller, H., Voelker, S., & Yovsi, R. (2005). Conceptions of parenting in different cultural communities. The case of West African Nso and Northern German women. *Social Development, 14*, 158-180.

Knüppel, A., Steensgaard, R., & Jensen de López, K. (2007). Mental state talk by Danish preschool children. *Nordlyd, 34*, 110-130. Retrieved December 1st, 2011 from http://www.ub.uit.no/munin/nordlyd

Larson, R.W., Wiley, A. R., & Branscomb, K. R. (Eds.). (2006). *Family mealtime as a context of development and socialization New directions for child and adolescent development, no. 111*. San Fransisco, CA: Wiley Periodicals.

Lave, J., & Wenger, E. (1991) *Situated learning: Legitimate peripheral participation*. Cambridge: Cambridge University Press.

LeVine, R. A., Dixon, S., LeVine, S., Richman, A., Leiderman, P. H., Keefer, C. H., & Brazelton, T. B. (1994). *Child care and culture: Lessons from Africa*. New York, NY: Cambridge University Press.

Markus, H. R., & Kitayama, S. (1991). Culture and the self: Implications for cognition, emotion, and motivation. *Psychological Review, 98*, 224-253.

Mead, G. H. (1934). *Mind, self and society: From the standpoint of a social behaviorist*. Chicago: University of Chicago Press.

Nelson, K. (2003). Narrative and the emergence of a consciousness of self. In G. D. Fireman, T. E. McVay & O. J. Flanagan (Eds.), *Narrative and consciousness: Literature, psychology, and the brain* (pp. 17-36). Oxford: Oxford University Press.

Ochs, E., & Capps, L. (2001) *Living narrative: Creating lives in everyday storytelling*. Cambridge, MA: Harvard University Press.

Ochs, E., & Shohet, M. (2006). The cultural structuring of mealtime socialization. *New Directions for Child and Adolescent Development, 111*, 35-49.

Olson, D. (1994). *The world on paper*. Cambridge: Cambridge University Press.

Reddy, V. (2008). *How infants know minds*. Cambridge, MA: Harvard University Press.

Santamaría, A., & Martínez, M. A. (2005) La construcción del significado en el marco de una psicología cultural: el pensamiento narrativo [The construction of meaning in the context of cultural psychology: narrative thinking]. In M. Cubero & J. D. Ramírez (Eds.), *Vygotski en la psicología contemporánea* (pp. 167-190). Buenos Aires: Miño y Dávila.

Schütze, F. (1983). Biographieforschung und narratives Interview [Research on biographies and narrative interview]. *Neue Praxis: Zeitschrift für Sozialarbeit, Sozialpädagogik und Sozialpolitik, 3*, 283-293.

Scribner, S., & Cole, M. (1981). *The psychology of literacy*. Cambridge, MA: Harvard University Press.

Shotter, J. (1993). *Conversational realities: Constructing life through language*. London: Sage.

Singelis, T. M. (1994). The measurement of independent and interdependent self-construals. *Personality and Social Psychological Bulletin, 20*, 580-591.

Sinha, C., & Jensen de López, K. (2001): Language, culture and the embodiment of spatial cognition. *Cognitive Linguistics, 11*, 17-41.

Tomasello, M. (1999). *The cultural origins of human cognition*. Harvard University Press.

Tomasello, M., Kruger, A., & Ratner, H. (1993). Cultural learning. *Behavioral and Brain Sciences, 16*, 495.552.

Triandis, H. C. (1995). *Individualism and collectivism*. Boulder, CO: Westview Press.

Wertsch, J.V. (1985). *Vygotsky and the social formation of mind*. Cambridge, MA: Harvard University Press.

Jeremy I. M. Carpendale
Charlie Lewis

Self constructed in culture

2

"The self is not something that exists first and then enters into relationship with others, but it is, so to speak, an eddy in the social current and so still a part of the current" (Mead, 1934, p. 182).

"Man is an animal suspended in webs of significance he himself has spun. I take culture to be those webs…" (Geertz, 1973, p. 5)

"Culture makes humans as much as the reverse" (Griffiths & Stotz, 2000, p. 45).

The topics addressed in this book—self and culture and development—are at the nexus of interlinked webs of vastly complex processes. The extent and implications of these massive topics requires that we first map out the piece of the puzzle that we will grapple with in this chapter, and conversely, what we mention but do not pursue. We first very briefly situate our view of the self, then turn to consider views of the nature of culture before finally turning to our central topic of how humans are created in culture, while acknowledging that this is a system with reciprocal processes in which cultures create persons and persons create cultures. Humans evolve within this social-cultural niche and cultural systems develop through historical processes.

Thus we grapple with the questions Norbert Elias posed, namely:

> "'Which biological characteristics of man make history possible?' Or, to phrase it in sociologically more precise terms: 'which biological characteristics are prerequisites for the changeability, and particularly for the capacity for development, shown by human societies?'" (1970/1978, p. 107).

We, however, will focus on those underlying interpersonal processes that make it possible for humans to conceptualise themselves. This involves moving from being a self to come to conceptualise and thus to have a sense of self. We explore the issues that are central to the volume in order to suggest that a long tradition in psychology emphasises the embeddedness of individual identities within social processes. In order to provide a synthesis, some analysis is needed first.

Self

What is a self and how does it develop? We take it to be a coherent and enduring sense that humans have as individuals, separate from, but related to, others. Various forms of complexity of both interactions and self-understanding emerge throughout child development and, indeed, adulthood. From this starting point self understanding is constructed within social activity in particular socio-cultural contexts. It is necessarily embedded within the complexity of relationships during child development and shows variations across cultures, but also similarities as well as similarity in processes. We argue that children gradually come to conceptualise their activity in terms of their enduring and coherent individuality. That is, they first are a self and only later come to understand themselves as having a self (Campbell, Christopher & Bickhard, 2002). Conceptualizing the self requires taking the self as an object and thus requires taking others' perspectives on that self, an ability that emerges in the social process and becomes increasingly complex.

This process can be linked through further development to identity, which can be considered an enduring sense of oneself across differing aspects of one's experience, as well as providing continuity and coherence across time. The major issues here concern both content and structure (Erikson, 1968), and the ways in which such identities are constructed or adopted (Marcia, 1966): "Identity formation involves a synthesis of childhood skills, beliefs, and identifications into a more or less coherent, and unique whole that provides the young adult with a sense of continuity with the past and a direction for the future" (Marcia, Waterman, Matteson, Archer & Orlofsky, 1993, p. 3).

The nature of such identities may vary across cultures. That is, particular identities are only possible given particular local resources. This variation often extends to ways in which individuals make use of strategies to provide self-continuity over time. For example, young people from First Nations communities on the West coast of Canada tend to make use of narratives of varying levels of complexity to make connections across time resulting in a sense of personal persistence, whereas the majority of non-Native youth employ an essentialist strategy in which they derive self continuity through denying change and focusing instead on those underlying aspects of themselves that endure despite other changes (Chandler, Lalonde & Sokol, 2000). Although ways to provide a sense of self-continuity seem to vary across cultures, having some way of ensuring a feeling of continuity across time may be a requirement of functioning as a normal human (ibid.).

In this chapter, however, we focus on those more basic interactional processes that make a sense of self possible. That is, prior to the complexities of developing identities, it is the more rudimentary possibility for a conception of self that we consider here—a possibility that appears to be lacking in other animals. At least this may be a useful contrast, but evolution is about continuities as well as differences, so we must keep an open mind about whether or to what extent other species develop a sense of 'self', especially closely related ones, like enculturated apes.

Culture

Culture can be conceptualised in a variety of ways. One way is as a set of traditions that endure but also change and are passed on across generations. This is what Tomasello, Kruger and Ratner (1993) referred to as a 'ratchet effect' of culture in which ways of doing things are passed on to the following generations but change, and any improvements in technology and know-how can be passed on. That is, individuals do not always have to 're-invent the wheel' themselves. They can learn about wheels from their parents and perhaps also improve upon them with modifications or new applications that they can pass on to their offspring. For this process to work, individuals must be capable of learning about such improved traditions, and perhaps it may also require teaching cultural ways of doing things to others (ibid.). Although there are debates regarding whether other species such as chimpanzees and whales have cultures, the extent and variety of human cultures make these qualitatively different (e.g., Boesch, 2007; Rendell & Whitehead, 2001).

Cultures are incredibly varied, yet the complex forms that we usually identify with the word are all created by humans and they all create humans, all wonderfully varied. Although when thinking about communication across cultures we tend to focus on misunderstanding and breakdowns in communication, what should be more surprising is that communication is possible across cultures. It is because we share common human ways of acting that language can be built on these common patterns of interaction (Canfield, 1995).

Cultures come in many sizes; we even talk about 'subcultures'. Bruner (1987/2004, p. 700) considers a family to be a "miniature culture." Children, however, are influenced by culture only through engagement with others. Abstract notions have an effect only through actual interaction. And this is not a one-way street. The child's own characteristics affect forms of interaction in the family (e.g., Bell & Chapman, 1986).

The construction of selves in cultures

Humans are cultural creatures. The 'desert island baby', the idea of a child brought up with sufficient physical needs met but no social contact, is a myth for good reason, because becoming human only occurs within a social-cultural environment. Such a social environment is an expectable and required part of human development—genes alone are far from sufficient. Given this, it is possible to focus on the variations that arise due to cultural differences. There are several examples of how this works as in the area of children's cognitive and social-cognitive development. For example, recent research shows differences in the development of executive functions across cultures. In China (Sabbagh, Xu, Carlson, Moses & Lee, 2006) and Korea (Oh & Lewis, 2008) preschoolers show advanced performance on measures of self-control over their Western counterparts. While there could be a biological (i.e., genetic) explanation for such differences, the more likely possibility is that these Confucian societies place an emphasis on the role of self-control and appropriate behaviour in everyday conduct. Human cognition and selves are constructed in cultures and vary across cultures (e.g., Boesch, 2007) as well as within cultures, depending on various factors such as socio-economic circumstances (Carpendale & Lewis, 2004). These differences arise only because the child experiences different forms of interaction—abstract notions of culture have their effect in the trenches of actual interaction:

> "Human development is, not uniquely but certainly outstandingly, reliant on external scaffolding. This scaffolding is commonly referred to as culture. Part of the rationale of the traditional idea of human nature was to isolate features that do not depend on culture. These 'biological' features represent our true nature—the naked ape stripped of its cultural clothes. It seems to us that this traditional project is as misguided as seeking to investigate the true nature of an ant by removing the distorting influence of the nest! Human beings and their cultures have co-evolved as surely as ants and hives or dogs and packs. Human nature must inevitably be a product of a

developmental matrix which includes a great deal of cultural scaffolding" (Griffiths & Stotz, 2000, pp. 44-45).

It is important to consider what is required for human self-understanding to be possible at all. That is, what are the ingredients required for humans to be cultural creatures. It is the capacity to engage in and develop within interaction that we need to account for. There are many interacting levels of influences here. There is an increasing tendency to look for genetic and neurological factors, and these may well play a role. Consider autism, in which children experience typical interaction but are not able to profit from it, and fail to develop within such interaction to the same extent as typically developing children. But this is not necessarily due to a deficit in an evolved mental module, as claimed by some (e.g., Baron-Cohen, 1995). Instead it could be due to some small differences that affect how an infant can engage with others. For example, it could be that the individual with autism does not perceive the salience of nonverbal signals (Klin, Jones, Schultz & Volkmar, 2003) or has a problem with emotional reactivity (Shanker, 2004). This could result in different developmental trajectories.

Although there are clear cultural differences in how social interactions take place and in the construction of the self, we can also think about forms of interaction that may be universal due to being rooted in our embodied interaction with others, e.g., requesting, greeting and directing others' attention (Canfield, 1993, 1995). These acts may be accomplished in different ways across cultures but it seems that any form of human society would need at least these acts.

Culture provides a complex social environment in which child development occurs that is enduring but is not simply encoded in genes. We thus see it as a form of inheritance; it results in regularity in the life cycles of individuals. This is due to a bi-directional interaction of many levels of factors including those at the genetic level and the cultural level. If an aspect of the environment is consistently present it can be relied on in the developmental process. Such consistency can be identified at various levels – across a whole culture, within subcultures and, indeed, within families. Thus, there are multiple sources of inheritance including genes *and* culture (Gottlieb, 2007; Jablonka & Lamb, 2007). Recent research has shown that a particular gene may be expressed in one environment (e.g., 'sensitive parenting') in very positive terms (e.g. low aggression), while in a different environment (e.g. 'poor parenting') it may correlate with negative outcomes (e.g. high aggression) (Bakermans-Kronenburg & van IJzendoorn, 2007). Of course, even such subtle examples too simplistically split nature and nurture.

Culture is our human niche; it is the environment in which humans develop and have evolved. Culture creates humans and humans create and change cultures (e.g., Griffiths & Stotz, 2000). This is a system of individual and culture that co-evolves. We need an account of how our biological natures make culture possible (Elias, 1970/1978), and an account of how this system of behavioural practices is learned by children, transformed and passed on. We propose such an account next.

The relational approach to self: individualistic versus relational frameworks

Two contrasting perspectives form the foundations for families of theories which straddle fields of language, evolution, and the development of thinking (Overton, 2006). A common assumption is to start with the individual and explain thinking from this individualistic perspective. This view has ancient roots but is often linked with the especially clear articulation of this position from Descartes (Hacker, 1997). More recently this approach is exemplified by Chomsky and many approaches in cognitive science. From an individualistic perspective, the individual is taken as given, as the starting point. In Mead's (1934) analogy this is as if infants are like prisoners in isolated cells who can already think and must attempt to learn how to communicate with each other through some sort of code. Much contemporary developmental psychology takes an observer's third person perspective largely depicting the individual as an unfolding biological entity.

In contrast, from a relational perspective, relations are primary and a sense of self and other gradually develop (Jopling, 1993). That is, the mind and thinking are not taken as given but are explained as emerging through the social process. Taking others' perspective on the self allows for the emergence of the self and for the development of language and thinking. Scholars such as Mead, Piaget, and Wittgenstein provide classic examples of this way of thinking. More recently this perspective is in evidence in developmental psychology (Overton, e.g., 1994) and embodied approaches to cognitive science (Pfiefer & Bondard, 2007). We take such a relational perspective, in which a sense of oneself is only possible through taking others' perspectives, so it is only possible within social interaction (following Mead). From this starting point what needs to be explained is the social process and changes in this process as the communication develops.

Mead addressed the problem of "how the human mind and self arise in the process of conduct" (Morris, p. xv in Mead, 1934). In Mead's (1934, p. 178) words,

> "The self is not so much a substance as a process in which the conversation of gestures has been internalized within an organic form. This process ... is simply a phase of the whole social organization of which the individual is a part. The organization of the social act has been imported into the organism and becomes then the mind of the individual."

This approach is biological in the sense that the biological level makes social interaction possible. However the approach also requires the social level for further development: the 'mind-brain system' would not develop without social shaping. This system is not simply a bonus of living in a social environment. It is a key factor in development and evolution. The social nature of the environment is an expectable aspect of development for human infants—they require care. The biological cannot be separated from the social, as also recognized by Vygotsky:

> "From the very first days of the child's development his activities acquire a meaning of their own in a system of social behavior and, being directed towards a definite

purpose, are refracted through the prism of the child's environment. The path from object to child and from child to object passes through another person. This complex human structure is the product of a developmental process deeply rooted in the links between individual and social history" (Vygotsky, 1978, p. 30).

Phylogeny and ontogeny: infant social development within relations

"The evolution of infancy created a niche for the interactive emergence of specific human cognitive capacities" (Griffiths & Stotz, 2000, p. 45).

Evolution has resulted in a social/cultural niche in which human infants develop (Laland, Odling-Smee & Feldman, 2000). Human infants are born early relative to other similar species but with relatively developed senses (Gould, 1977; Portmann, 1944/1990). Portmann referred to this as secondary altriciality, a shortening of the gestation period resulting in human infants being born in a relatively helpless state. They must be cared for if they are to survive. But humans are still precocial in the sense that their eyes are open at birth. This ensures that early development takes place in a social environment (Bowlby, 1958; Bruner, 1972; Suttie, 1935) and, consequently, the brain is shaped within this context (Mareschal et al., 2007). This creates a social niche in which humans develop. Infants interact with others—their social world—in complex sequences of turn taking. This does not require innate knowledge; people react differently than the physical world (Bibok, Carpendale & Lewis, 2008).

This makes possible a form of communication that differs from those in other species. We learn both sides of the interaction; we anticipate and react to how others respond to our gestures. Would the social systems of social insects count as cultures? Ants and bees do not need to do this; they live embedded in a system based on one form's response to another's action, through pheromones. They become involved in complex coordination of conspecifics; the system makes individuals and these individuals make and maintain the system. The system pre-exists the individual; it has co-evolved with the species. Yet this system can only change through further biological, not social, evolution, which contrasts with the way human cultures change. These incredibly complex systems function without individual forms needing to develop expectations about how others will respond to their actions. This is not required for the coordination to function (Mead, 1934).

There is a difference in the nature of social interaction of human infants compared to closely related species such as chimpanzee young. We use the example of the development of requests as a prototypical example of the difference between our and related species. Chimpanzees do not appear to use pointing gestures when not in the wild, but they often begin pointing to make requests in captivity when cared for by human caretakers; i.e., an environment in which they experience the same interactional demands as human infants. These requests seem like a form of interaction that would be universal across human cultures though, of course, the form that they take could vary widely.

Consider other aspects of human embodiment that differ from chimpanzees and seem to result in forms of interaction in which a self could develop. Chimpanzee infants are able to hold on to their mother as she travels on all fours. Humans walk upright and can carry their infants in their arms. Although the way that humans carry their infants varies cross culturally and through historical time, it is likely that human infants' attitude toward aspects of the world—their interest, directedness, as indicated by leaning and reaching toward objects—will be evident for their parents, unlike the infant chimpanzee who must just hold on (Savage-Rumbaugh, Fields, Segerdahl & Rumbaugh, 2005). This creates a social context of development in which human infants' attitudes are evident to their caregivers. Although infants at this point are not intending to communicate, their actions do function to communicate information to their caregivers and their caregivers may respond. This response may then set up patterns of interaction in which human infants gradually come to develop expectations, like learning to expect to get picked up when they raise their arms. The development of a gesture like pointing in humans might appear to be insignificant or trivial, but developmental psychologists like Bates, Bruner and Tomasello have long argued that the implications for potential forms of cognition and self-understanding are profound, in that such gestures form the basis of language.

Self and language

> "A speck of behavior, a fleck of culture, and—viola!—a gesture" (Geertz, 1973, p. 6).

If taking the self as an object results in consciousness of self or self-awareness, and is only possible through taking the attitudes of others toward the self, how can this perspective taking take place? If we reject a Cartesian view of mind and body (that consciousness allows people to see themselves as an object), then an ability to take perspectives cannot be a magical process of mentally putting oneself in another's shoes. This does not require mental mindreading. Instead, others' attitudes are manifest in their bodily orientation to the world. From Mead's perspective the process is rooted in interaction and others' attitudes are manifest in their action orientation to aspects of the world. We develop this argument from our recent work (Carpendale & Lewis, 2004, 2006). Understanding self in relation to other occurs not through the magic of mindreading but rather through attitudes that are manifest in others' actions (Carpendale & Lewis, 2009).

Within this framework a 'self' becomes possible. The central skill requires taking others' perspectives on ourselves. Within interaction children acquire characteristic ways of being which they gradually conceptualize; i.e., they gain a sense of themselves, or self-awareness, through taking others' perspectives on themselves. This is not caused by a 'Eureka' moment, but is rather a slow incremental progression as the child abstracts more understanding from the way in which interactions work and their place within them. We see this achievement in humans but not most other species, although there could be debate about apes. So a sense of self is not an all or nothing matter. Consider the rouge (mirror) test, in which a mark is placed on a child's nose. The question is when the child sees herself in a mirror does she touch her nose, indicating an understanding that she is seeing herself in the mirror? Does this indicate a sense of self? Some chimpanzees pass this test whereas others fail, depending on the extent of their social experience; those living in isolation tend to fail, but even elephants and dolphins also appear to have some success (Boesch, 2007).

Mead was a 'social behaviourist' not a behaviourist in John Watson's sense of splitting physical movement from mental states. Watson's attitude toward consciousness and related phenomena was "off with their heads" (Mead, 1934, pp. 2-3); i.e., to reject their study. But in doing so he overlooked the central topics of psychology. Instead, Mead's approach is to root mind in behaviour. Behaviour for Mead is not merely physical movement divorced from attitudes. Rather, behaviour is conduct or human activity, and thus tied up with the person's attitudes toward aspects of the world. For Mead communication begins with natural reactions. In this he was inspired by Darwin's (1872/1998) view of emotions as expression.

The selves that are constructed could vary across cultures, but not this general process. This gives rise to two families of questions or lines of inquiry: studying the variations across cultures or, second, explicating the requirements for culture; the question posed by Elias at the start of the chapter. We feel that such questions are fundamental to the processes that give rise to variation in selves. But conceptualizing one's self in a truly reflexive sense requires language. Thus we have to explain the development of language. Views of language can be grouped into individualistic approaches based on a mechanistic view of meaning well known from Chomsky (e.g., 1988) and Pinker (1994), and contrasting approaches viewing language as based on shared activity (Carpendale & Racine, 2006; Cottrell, 1978; Mead, 1934; Tomasello, 2003; Turnbull, 2003; Wittgenstein, 1968). These latter accounts fit with the view of development we have outlined.

Conclusion

In this chapter we have discussed the underlying processes through which humans are able to conceptualise themselves, resulting in what we refer to as a 'self.' That is, to take the self as an object through adopting others' attitudes toward the self. It is only through interacting with others that the individual can take herself as an object as well as a subject, that is to react to herself in the ways that others do, and thus develop a conception of herself. These basic interpersonal processes then make the incredible complexities of culture and forms of selves possible. The processes through which selves develop are not biological givens, they do not begin within individuals, but rather emerge only in interaction. Thus our response to Elias' question is to outline some of those biological characteristics which set the social process going, and through which language, selves, and culture emerge

References

Bakermans-Kranenburg, M. J., & van IJzendoorn, M. H. (2007). Research review: Genetic vulnerability or differential susceptibility in child development: the case of attachment. *Journal of Child Psychology and Psychiatry, 48*, 1160–1173.

Baron-Cohen, S. (1995). *Mindblindness: An essay on autism and theory of mind*. Cambridge, MA: MIT Press.

Bell, R. Q., & Chapman, M. (1986). Child effects in studies using experimental or brief longitudinal approaches to socialization. *Developmental Psychology, 22*, 595-603.

Bibok, M. B., Carpendale, J. I. M., & Lewis, C. (2008). Social knowledge as social skill: An action based view of social understanding. In U. Müller, J. I. M. Carpendale, N. Budwig, & B. Sokol, (Eds.), *Social life and social knowledge: Toward a process account of development* (pp. 145-169). New York: Taylor Francis.

Boesch, C. (2007). What make us human (*Homo sapiens*)? The challenge of cognitive cross-species comparison. *Journal of Comparative Psychology, 121*, 227-240.

Bowlby, J. (1958). The nature of the child's tie to his mother. *International Journal of Psychoanalysis, 39*, 350-373.

Bruner, J. (1972). Nature and uses of immaturity. *American Psychologist, 27*, 687-708.

Bruner, J. (2004). Life as narrative. *Social Research, 71*, 691-710. (Original work published 1987).

Campbell, R. L., Christopher, J. C., & Bickhard, M. H. (2002). Self and values: An interactivist foundation for moral development. *Theory & Psychology, 12*, 795-823.

Canfield, J. V. (1993). The living language: Wittgenstein and the empirical study of communication. *Language Sciences, 15*, 165-193.

Canfield, J. V. (1995). The rudiments of language. *Language and Communication, 15*, 195-211.

Carpendale, J. I. M., & Lewis, C. (2004). Constructing an understanding of mind: The development of children's social understanding within social interaction. *Behavioral and Brain Sciences, 27*, 79-151.

Carpendale, J. I. M., & Lewis, C. (2006). *How children develop social understanding.* Oxford: Blackwell.

Carpendale, J. I. M., & Lewis, C. (2009). More smoke than mirror neurons? Letter to *Human Development,* retrieved November 2011 from http://www.online.karger.com/ProdukteDB/produkte.asp?aktion=PDFLetter&serial=0018716X&datei=HDE-Letters-to-Editor-03-11-2009

Carpendale, J. I. M., & Racine, T. P. (2006). Mead and meaning: Implications of views of meaning for developmental theories. In T. Haukioja (Ed.), *Papers on language theory* (pp. 1-19). University of Turku: Publications in General Linguistics.

Chandler, M. J., Lalonde, C. E., & Sokol, B. W. (2000). Continuities of selfhood in face of radical developmental and cultural change. In L. P. Nucci, G. B. Saxe, E. Turiel (Eds.), *Culture, thought, and development* (pp. 65-84). Mahwah, NJ: Erlbaum.

Chomsky, N. (1988). *Language and problems of knowledge.* Cambridge, MA: The MIT Press.

Cottrell, L. S. (1978). George Herbert Mead and Harry Stack Sullivan: An unfinished synthesis. *Psychiatry, 41*, 151-162.

Darwin, C. R. (1998). *The expression of emotion in man and animals.* London: HarperCollins Publishers. (Original work published 1872).

Elias, N. (1978). *What is sociology?* New York: Columbia Press. (Original work published 1970).

Erikson, E. H. (1968). *Identity: Youth and crisis.* New York: Norton.

Geertz, C. (1973). *The interpretation of cultures.* New York: Basic Books.

Gould, S. J. (1977). *Ever since Darwin.* Harmondsworth, Middlesex: Penguin Books.

Gottlieb, G., (2007). Probabilistic epigenesis. *Developmental Science, 10*, 1-11.

Griffiths, P. E., & Stotz, K. (2000). How the mind grows: A developmental perspective on the biology of cognition. *Synthese, 122*, 29-51.

Hacker, P. M. S. (1997). *Wittgenstein: On human nature.* London: Phoenix.

Jablonka, E., & Lamb, M. J. (2007). Précis of evolution in four dimensions. *Behavioral and Brain Sciences, 30*, 353-392.

Jopling, D. (1993). Cognitive science, other minds, and the philosophy of dialogue. In U. Neisser (Ed.), *The perceived self* (pp. 290-309). Cambridge, MA: MIT Press.

Klin, A., Jones, W., Schultz, R., & Volkmar, F. (2003). The enactive mind, or from actions to cognition: Lessons from autism. *Philosophical Transactions of the Royal Society, London B, 358*, 345-360.

Laland, K. N., Odling-Smee, J., & Feldman, M. W. (2000). Niche construction, biological evolution, and cultural change. *Behavioral and Brain Sciences, 23,* 131-175.

Marcia, J. E. (1966). Development and validation of ego-identity status. *Journal of Personality and Social Psychology, 3,* 551-558.

Marcia, J. E., Waterman, A. S., Matteson, D. R., Archer, S. L., & Orlofsky, J. L. (1993). *Ego identity: A handbook for psychosocial research.* New York: Springer-Verlag.

Mareschal, D., Johnson, M. H., Sirois, S., Spratling, M. W., Thomas, M. S. C., & Westermann, G. (2007). *Neuroconstructivism, Vol. 1: How the brain constructs cognition.* New York: Oxford University Press.

Mead, G. H. (1934). *Mind, self and society: From the standpoint of a social behaviorist.* Chicago: University of Chicago Press.

Oh, S., & Lewis, C. (2008). Korean preschoolers' advanced inhibitory control and its relation to other executive skills and mental state understanding. *Child Development, 70,* 80-99.

Overton, W. F. (1994). Contexts of meaning: The computational and the embodied mind. In W. F. Overton & D. S. Palermo (Eds.), *The nature and ontogenesis of meaning* (pp. 1-18). Hillsdale, NJ: Erlbaum.

Overton, W. F. (2006). Developmental psychology: Philosophy, concepts, methodology. In R. M. Lerner (Ed.), *Handbook of child psychology, vol. 1: Theoretical models of human development* (6th ed., pp. 18-88). Editors-in-chief: W. Damon & R. M. Lerner. Hoboken, NJ: John Wiley & Sons.

Pfiefer, R., & Bongard, J. (2007). *How the body shapes the way we think: A new view of intelligence.* Cambridge, MA: The MIT Press.

Pinker, S. (1994). *The language instinct.* New York: Harper Perennial.

Portmann, A. (1990). *A zoologist looks at humankind.* New York: Columbia University Press. (Original work published 1944).

Rendell, L., & Whitehead, H. (2001). Culture in whales and dolphins. *Behavioral and Brain Sciences, 24,* 309-382.

Sabbagh, M., Xu, F., Carlson, S. M., Moses, L. J., & Lee, K. (2006). The development of executive functioning and theory of mind: A comparison of Chinese and U. S. preschoolers. *Psychological Science, 17,* 74-81.

Savage-Rumbaugh, S., Fields, W. M., Segerdahl, P., & Rumbaugh, D. (2005). Culture prefigures cognition in *Pan/Homo* Bonobos. *Theoria, 20,* 311-328.

Shanker, S. G. (2004). Autism and the dynamic developmental model of emotions. *Philosophy, Psychiatry & Psychology, 11,* 219-233.

Suttie, I. D. (1935/1988). The origins of love and hate. London: Free Association Books.

Tomasello, M. (2003). *Constructing a language.* Harvard University Press.

Tomasello, M., Kruger, A. C., & Ratner, H. H. (1993). Cultural learning. *Behavioral and Brain Sciences, 16,* 495-552.

Turnbull, W. (2003). *Language in action: Psychological models of conversation.* Hove, UK: Psychology Press.

Vygotsky, L. S. (1978). *Mind in society: The development of higher psychological processes.* Cambridge, MA: Harvard University Press.

Wittgenstein, L. (1968). *Philosophical investigations.* Oxford: Blackwell.

Astrid Kleis

Child rearing in bicultural families
Socialisation goals and parental ethnotheories in West African-German families

The process of globalisation and mobility is increasingly bringing different cultural groups into contact with each other. In Germany, along with the growth of the foreign population due to migration, the number of bicultural couples and children being raised in families with different cultural influences has also risen. In every sixth marriage in Germany at least one partner originates from another country, in 1999 already 24% of all marriages in Berlin were bicultural, and every fifth child born in Germany has at least one parent with a cultural background other than German (Statistisches Bundesamt, 2002).

This chapter discusses challenges and possible benefits of child rearing in bicultural families based on an investigation of parental ethnotheories and socialisation goals in 40 West African-German families in Germany.

Any relationship is associated with conflicts and may mean a great personal challenge for both partners. However, in bicultural relationships, besides the usual man-woman polarity there is another – cultural – dimension exerting influence on the relationship. Each partner is bringing his or her cultural 'stamp', values and ideas about marriage, family and gender roles into the relationship. Therefore, bicultural partnerships have to deal with oppositional cultural values and both partners are often confronted with strong inner and outer demands. Usually, this situation further intensifies with the birth of a child. Parents in bicultural families have often been raised quite differently themselves and therefore hold different concepts of partnership or marriage, family life and child rearing with various conflicts likely to arise. However, the co-presence of cultural differences not only raises problems for bicultural couples but also holds many resources and yields the opportunity to develop special competencies. Thus, in the literature it is reported that children being raised in bicultural families are advantaged regarding the acquisition of cultural competencies, the development of social sensibility, and the capacity to deal with conflicts as well as in terms of self confidence and assertiveness (Khounani, 2000). In this way, different cultural views, attitudes and practices can contribute to an enrichment of family life as well as the personal development of its members. In an ideal case, parents and children learn to be tolerant and accept different views and attitudes, to change perspectives, and to understand each other (and themselves) better.

Although quantitatively the relevance of bicultural marriages and families has increased, family issues and the upbringing of children in this bicultural context are rarely empirically investigated. The present case study on bicultural families chose West African-German families to illuminate the question since, although they are a small group numerically, according to canonical theories they represent oppositional cultural concepts of independence and interdependence (Markus & Kitayama, 1991) or autonomy and relatedness (Kağitçibaşi, 1996, 2005), which are demonstrated to be reflected also in family life and child rearing (see Keller, 2007 for an overview). Apart from a few studies concentrating on the partnership level (see Baum, 1999), which take into account only the perspective of German women in African-German couples, this family constellation has not been subjected to psychological research before. Thus, special characteristics of West African-German families have not previously been described. Analyses of parental attitudes and behaviour in German and West African parents are necessary to answer questions such as: Do we find a clash of different socio-cultural orientations with possibly problematic consequences in such bicultural families – or rather a balanced combination of both autonomy and relatedness, as suggested by the model of Kağitçibaşi (1996, 2005)? Do parents in bicultural relationships with such extremely different socio-cultural backgrounds seem to adapt to each other? And if that is the case, what are the underlying factors for such an adaptation process? Furthermore, which influence do culture and gender have when explaining different outcomes?

West African-German families are not statistically registered as a distinct part of the German population. However, we know that the West African population in Germany has continuously increased since World War II, and whereas marriages between Germans and Africans were exceptional in the 60s and 70s, nowadays they are – at least in bigger cities – no longer rare. Since the majority of the West African population in Germany is made up of young men, the more frequent constellation is 'German wife – West African husband'.

The overall aim of my PhD-study was to disentangle the influence of culture and gender on parental ethnotheories with respect to the cultural models of autonomy and relatedness. Since German and West African families can be viewed as prototypical examples of the expression of autonomous and related conceptions of parenting, respectively, a deeper look at these families might provide further insight into the implementation of different sociocultural orientations in everyday family life and child rearing.

The present chapter focuses on the part of the study that concernsed bicultural families. Socialisation goals and parental ethnotheories of bicultural West African-German families are described and discussed in the following way. First, the conceptual model of parenting by Heidi Keller (2007) is introduced. The model is discussed within the theoretical framework of a contextual approach that defines cultural models according to their orientations towards autonomy and relatedness. Next, a case study of 40 bicultural West African-German families' parenting is summarised in terms of socialisation goal priorities, parental ethnotheories, and conflicts. The results are interpreted and discussed in relation to the research questions, and the chapter concludes with some reflections on usefulness of such findings and the need for further research.

Parental ethnotheories, cultural models and gender

It is widely acknowledged that parents build up expectations about child development as well as ideas and beliefs about effective child rearing according to their own childhood experiences. These expectations, ideas and beliefs constitute subjective theories of parenting and child development. Although individual differences with respect to parenting goals and practices exist in every culture (e.g., LeVine et al., 1994; Palacios & Moreno, 1996), members of the same cultural environments can be viewed as groups of individuals who co-construct a shared (cultural) reality in various domains of life (Harkness et al., 2000). Thereby members of the same cultural environment tend to share conceptions about proper infant care, child development and family life. These reflect a cultural view on how to become a competent member of the relevant community Thus, *parental ethnotheories* represent an organised set of parental expectations, ideas and beliefs that is influenced by cultural norms and values (also see chapter 4 on emotional socialisation, chapter 5 on discursive practices, and chapter 9 on changing community expectations).

According to Keller (2006, 2007), the concept of 'cultural model' refers to common scripts, ideologies, values and habits that are transmitted from generation to generation and serve as guidelines for individuals to live their lives in a specific cultural context, which can be oriented more towards autonomy or towards relatedness. Thus, cultural models have a normative character and define also parents' socialisation goals, e.g. '*help others*' or '*obey*' (relatedness oriented), or '*develop personal talents and interests*' or '*be assertive*' (autonomy oriented). This way socialisation strategies are adapted to specific eco-social contexts and reflect their demands (LeVine, 1977). At the same time they are building the framework for the definition of parental ethnotheories (Keller, 2003), that is, the theories parents have about child rearing and development. This means that parental ethnotheories indicate which measures parents have to take to achieve certain socialisation goals. Therefore, parental ethnotheories can be seen as mediators between general cultural meta models (cultural models) and concrete parental practices (Harkness et al., 2000).

The hierarchy of relations between cultural models and parenting behaviour is specified in a conceptual model of parenting developed by Keller (2007) (see figure 1). The model suggests an implicit cultural model about family, children and parenting that exists at the more abstract or general level, and gradually narrows down to more specific and consciously held ideas about particular aspects of child development and child care practices. In this view, socialisation goals are derived from certain cultural models and further specified in parental ethnotheories. These parental ethnotheories provide the framework for behavioural strategies that influence the development of the child.

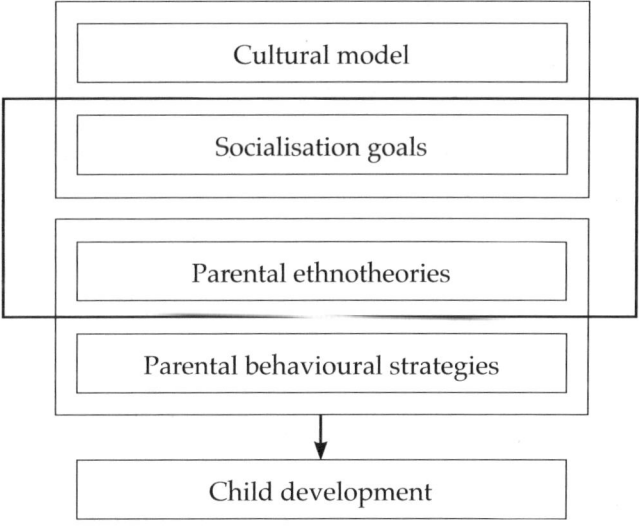

Figure 1. The conceptual model of parenting (Keller, 2007)

Cultural models of the self provide the essential framework for socialisation goals and parental ideas about what constitutes appropriate parenting behaviour (D'Andrade, 1984; Keller, Voelker & Yovsi, 2005; Super & Harkness, 1996). They can be seen as cultural filters regarding conceptions about appropriate child care which in turn are implemented in 'culturally appropriate' parental behaviour.

A large body of cross-cultural psychological research has given evidence for the cultural models of autonomy and relatedness (see Keller 2007 for an overview; also Hofstede, 1980; Kağitçibaşi, 2007; Markus & Kitayama, 1991). According to this contextual approach, cultural differences concerning ideas about parenting, socialisation goals and child care practices are defined as a representation of autonomy and relatedness (Keller, 2007). The emphasis on autonomy and/or relatedness, however, is assumed to vary depending on sociodemographic characteristics. In the literature, the *independent* value orientation with *autonomy* as the developmental organiser is mainly represented by highly educated families with older parents and few children in urban settings of Western industrialised societies (Greenfield, 1994; Harkness et al., 2000; Kağitçibaşi, 1997; LeVine, 1977; Markus & Kitayama, 1991; Triandis, 1995). According to Keller (2007), these families foster the independence and autonomy of their children from birth onwards. As primary socialisation goals they want their children to become self-confident and be able to make their own decisions not depending on anybody else. They should be able to spend time alone. Those conceptions are represented in parental ethnotheories where children are seen as comparatively equal partners with personal preferences and desires that must be taken into account.

Conversely, the *interdependent* value orientation with *relatedness* as the developmental organiser is represented by families from rural village contexts in traditional, mainly non-Western societies characterised by a lower formal education, early parenthood and high fertility. Those families would like to provide their children from birth with the feeling of relatedness with others. As primary socialisation goals children should show respect to their parents and elders, strive for harmony in life and avoid conflicts. They hold lifelong bonds with their family and the community they live in. These conceptions are also represented in their parental ethnotheories in which the adult family members know what is good and important for their children, while the children themselves are seen as novices who have to be trained and controlled and whose personal wishes and preferences are usually not solicited.

The concepts of independence and interdependence (Markus & Kitayama, 1991) as well as autonomy and relatedness (Kağitçibaşi, 1996; 2005) can be seen as prototypes of different cultural models. However, since autonomy and relatedness constitute two independent dimensions, models which combine enhancement of autonomy and relatedness are possible. Accordingly, Kağitçibaşi (1996, 2005) proposed a third cultural model, *autonomous relatedness*, which applies to urban educated people from traditionally interdependent societies. She describes the autonomous-related self as a healthy synthesis of the two basic human needs for autonomy and relatedness, which tends to arise in families characterised by economic independence but emotional interdependence that involves authoritative parenting (e.g., Keller al., 2004, which includes samples from Delhi, Beijing and San José / Costa Rica). This model seems to be particularly interesting when considering bicultural families. Can both cultural models be combined in a healthy way, or are clashes between the models of autonomy and relatedness prevalent in families characterised by the influences of two different cultures?

In addition, it has been shown that gender as well as culture plays a role for the expression of autonomy and relatedness. The literature suggests that many empirically demonstrated gender differences can be seen to reflect fundamental differences regarding independence and interdependence of the person. Specifically, there is evidence that men's self construals are more oriented towards independence and autonomy, whereas women's self construals are comparatively interdependent and relational (see Cross & Madson, 1997 for a review). For example, Rosenberg (1989) found that girls' socialisation encourages them toward the interdependent task of forming and maintaining close relationships to a greater extent than boys' socialisation. Girls were more likely to value characteristics related to interpersonal harmony and sensitivity towards specific others, whereas boys were more likely to value characteristics related to competitiveness and social dominance. Therefore, the present study seeks to disentangle the influence of culture and gender on parental ethnotheories by interviewing and comparing mothers and fathers in different cultural combinations.

Parental ethnotheories in West African-German families

Since German and West African families can be viewed as prototypical representatives of, respectively, autonomous and related conceptions of parenting, a deeper look at these families might provide further insight into the implementation of different cultural attitudes and practices in everyday family life and child rearing. Taking the *cultural models* approach, which model might apply to bicultural West African-German families? Do we find a clash between partners' different sociocultural orientations when it comes to parental conceptions and behaviour – or might these different attitudes and behavioural practices be enriching family life and the child rearing process by allowing for a combination of both autonomy and relatedness (cf. the model by Kağitçibaşi 1996, 2005)? Also, whose concepts or ideas about child rearing are more salient? Does the fact that mothers are still the ones most involved in child rearing processes lead to the mother's cultural model being more salient? Or, since the family lives in Germany, does the 'home field advantage' of the German parent lead to this parent's model being most salient? The questions could help us understand what influence culture and gender have upon the different outcomes.

By asking parents about their beliefs and attitudes regarding effective infant care and child development, a better understanding of their actual parenting practice (and its dependence on culture and gender) can be achieved. This in turn helps to deepen our understanding of how cultural norms and values are maintained and/or adapted in daily confrontation between extremely different sociocultural perspectives with respect to child rearing and family life.

The study presented below is one part of a PhD project investigating ideas about the parental relationship, family life, child rearing ideas and practices, and conflict patterns and strategies in five different mono- and bicultural samples (a German and a West African sample living in Germany, a West African sample in Conakry, Guinea and two Afro-German samples in Berlin, Germany, counterbalancing gender and cultural origin) were analysed. This chapter focuses on the two bicultural Afro-German samples and aims to answer the following research questions:

1. What do parental ethnotheories of bicultural Afro-German parents (holding two apparently very different cultural models) look like? Does one parent tend to adapt to the other's ethnotheory – and if so, is this a function of culture, gender or other influences? How do sociocultural orientations influence socialisation goals and childcare practices? Are differences in parental ethnotheories related to culture, gender or both?
2. What consequences do differences in parental ethnotheories have for family life? Are these differences (or the bicultural living situation in general) mainly seen as a source of conflict or of enrichment? How do parents in bicultural families deal with different conceptions about appropriate child rearing strategies (conflict patterns and coping strategies)? And do the parents themselves see these patterns as influenced mainly by cultural background, by gender, or by personal characteristics?

Participants

My PhD-study concerned five mono- and bicultural samples of 20 families each (N = 100 families = 200 participants).

This chapter presents analyses of the bicultural samples: 40 bicultural families living in Berlin, Germany. Of these, 20 families had a German mother and a West African father, while the other 20 families had a West African mother and a German father. All West African participants originate from a francophone country in West Africa (including the French-speaking part of Cameroon). See table 1.

	Cameroon	Guinea	Senegal	Ivory Coast	Burkina F.
West African					
- mothers	10	4	4	2	----
- fathers	10	6	2	----	2

Table 1. West African participants' countries of origin.

All families were living in Berlin and had at least one child aged 3 to 6 years. Table 2 provides socio-demographic information about the samples:

	n	Age	School	in Germany	Relationship
German mothers	20	33.7	12.8	---	6.7
West African fathers	20	31.6	14.1	9.2	6.7
West African mothers	20	31.3	11.6	9.9	7.4
German fathers	20	47.7	14.5	---	7.4

Table 2. Socio-demographic information of the sample by age, number of school years attended, years in Germany and duration of relationship.

Concerning socio-demographics, the most striking fact is that the German fathers are much older than all the other parents in the sample. The age difference between them and their West African wives is 16.4 years on average. When mentioning this age difference during the interviews, West African women informed us that in their country it would be very common for women to have a relationship with an older man. This kind of relationship seems to be preferred for reasons connected with maturity. On the other hand, German fathers mostly argued that they felt attracted by younger African women. Interestingly, in the second bicultural sample (German mothers and West African fathers), the age difference was only 2.1 years on average and here the mothers were the older of the two parents. Furthermore, in both samples men had slightly more years of schooling than women, regardless of culture, which reflected the fact that West African fathers mostly had come to Germany for study purposes. The West African parents of both samples had been in Germany for almost 10 years on average and the duration of their relationship with their German partners were so far about 7 years on average in both samples.

The families were recruited with the assistance of various African and Afro-German Associations and by snow-ball sampling. They were first contacted by phone and then visited at home.

Method

A card method developed at the 'Culture and Development Lab' at the University of Osnabrück was used to assess parents' socialisation goals in relation to the two central cultural dimensions of autonomy and relatedness. Mothers and fathers were separately asked to rank eight different socialisation goals written down on cards; four cards represented autonomous socialisation goals, e.g., *'develop personal talents and interests'* or *'learn to express own preferences'*, and the remaining four cards represented relatedness-oriented socialisation goals, e.g. *'learn to do what parents say'* or *'learn to share'*. These socialisation goals were generated qualitatively from interviews with parents and represent the topics mentioned most.

Additionally, problem-centred semi-structured interviews were conducted with mothers and fathers separately, to assess the parental ethnotheories concerning their conceptions about child rearing and family life as well as childcare practices and the activities they undertake with their children. Furthermore, they were asked about conflict issues and how they deal with conflicts regarding attitudes and child care practices. All 80 problem-centred semi-structured interviews (40 bicultural families divided into two groups with interviews conducted with mothers and fathers separately) were analysed with the method of Qualitative Content Analysis (Mayring, 2003). Categories were derived inductively from the material and gradually abstracted and aggregated in a three-step process of open, selective and theoretical coding. *Open coding*: categories in the terminology of the interview text were written next to the text. *Selective coding*: open categories within and between cases were condensed on a higher level of abstraction. *Theoretical coding:* selective categories were related to each other and to a main/core category, identifying themes at different levels (individual, relationship, child rearing, conflicts, etc.). The final categories were assembled into a coding manual. The coding of the interviews was supported by the software package Atlas-ti. As the last step, the data was summarised quantitatively.

Results
Socialisation goals

Figures 2 and 3 demonstrate the rank-ordering of socialisation goals by each of the four parental groups, highlighting the two highest (*'most important'*) and the two lowest (*'least important'*) ranked socialisation goals. The first half of the figures shows the results for those bicultural families with German mothers and West African fathers and the second half for those bicultural families with West African mothers and German fathers. The shaded socialisation goals in figure 2 are goals oriented towards autonomy, such as *'develop personal talents and interests'* and *'express own preferences'*. These socialisation goals are valued most by the German mothers and fathers; it also seems that German mothers are even more autonomy-oriented than the fathers in this respect.

German mothers	West African fathers	Rank	West African mothers	German fathers
Develop personal talents and interests (2.8)	Learn to do what parents say (3.7)	1	Learn to respect elderly persons (2.9)	Develop personal talents and interests (3.2)
Learn to express own preferences very clearly (3.3)	Learn to respect elderly persons (3.8)	2	Learn to share with others (3.4)	Learn to share with others (3.0)

Figure 2. Most highly ranked socialisation goals in West African-German families.

Furthermore, the white fields in figure 2 represent the orientation towards relatedness, expressed in socialisation goals such as *'do what parents say'*, *'respect elderly persons'* and *'share with others'*, which were especially highly ranked by the West African mothers and fathers, but partly (and unexpectedly) also by the German fathers. The numbers in brackets indicate the average ranking of the particular socialisation goal for the respective parental group.

In contrast, figure 3 shows those socialisation goals ranked lowest by both types of bicultural families. The shaded fields again represent those socialisation goals which are oriented towards autonomy, indicating that West African fathers and mothers do not value goals such as *'be assertive'* and *'be different from others'*, whereas the socialisa-

German mothers	West African fathers	Rank	West African mothers	German fathers
Learn to do what parents say (5.8)	Learn to be assertive (5.32)	7	Learn to be assertive (5.29)	Learn to respect elderly persons (5.3)
Learn that he or she is different from others in many respects (6.3)	Learn that he or she is different from others in many respects (5.95)	8	Learn that he or she is different from others in many respects (6.31)	Learn to do what parents say (5.61)

Figure 3. Lowest ranked socialisation goals in West African-German families.

tion goals oriented towards relatedness, like *respect* and *obedience* were the most important for West African fathers and to some extent, for mothers too). Furthermore, *'maintain social harmony'* was one of the lesser valued socialisation goals by German mothers and fathers.

The figures clearly indicate that there is not much consensus within the bicultural families regarding socialisation goals and values governing the upbringing of their offspring. The cultural background of the parent seems to account most strikingly for their parental attitudes.

Parental ethnotheories

Table 4 summarises categories derived from the most frequently mentioned answers of parents in the semi-structured interviews concerning family issues and child care.

Firstly, when asked who belongs to the family in their opinion, all German mothers and fathers answered that this would be only the nuclear family, whereas all West African fathers included the whole extended family, including their own parents, brothers and sisters and even cousins. Within the group of the West African mothers, most of them also answered that family to them means the whole extended family (80%) – only a small number included just the nuclear family (20%).

German mothers	West African fathers	West African mothers	German fathers
nuclear family (100%)	extended family (100%)	extended family (80%) nuclear family (20%)	nuclear family (100%)
family of origin < founded family (100%)	family of origin ≥ founded family (100%)	family of origin = founded family (100%)	family of origin < founded family (100%)
bicultural identity (80%) social competency (70%) assertiveness (50%)	respect (90%) African identity (70%) social competency (60%)	respect (90%) bicultural identity (80%)	independence (80%) self-responsibility (70%) assertiveness (60%) achievement (60%)
common activities, meals (100%) time for each other (80%) family unity (70%)	contact to other family members (100%) mutual support (80%)	family unity (70%) mutual support (60%)	family unity (100%) common activities, meals (80%)
mistake phys. punishment (80%) pressure children (70%)	mistake phys. punishment (80%) spoil children (70%)	mistake phys. punishment (80%) spoil children (70%)	mistake phys. punishment (90%) spoil children (70%)

Table 4. Values regarding family life and child rearing in bicultural families.
Categories derived from semi-structured interviews. < is used for "less important than", > is used for "more important than".

Secondly, whereas both German mothers and fathers gave less importance to their family of origin than to their newly founded family, again, West African fathers valued the family of origin at least as highly or more highly than their newly founded family. West African mothers valued their nuclear and extended family equally. This attitude may indicate that West African mothers married to German fathers are more adapted to the host culture (or to their partner) than West African fathers married to German mothers.

Furthermore, when asked to name some positive and some negative aspects of childcare practices in their family of origin, both West African mothers and fathers mentioned aspects oriented towards relatedness (e.g. strictness, respect and unity as positive aspects; no liberty and no free expression of opinion as negative aspects). Conversely, German mothers and fathers tended to mention autonomy-oriented aspects like promotion of interests, talents and independence. However, when asked what they feel is important within a family, all groups of parents mentioned relational aspects. Furthermore, when talking about conceptions of proper childcare and childcare practices, West African mothers and fathers alike said that they would ask for help and exchange information within their family of origin or friends, whereas the German mothers and fathers would rather read and look for help in the literature or on the internet. Men especially would not ask or talk about this topic with anybody but rather trust their intuition. When asked which aspects were the most important to them concerning childrearing or which values they would like their child to have, again, West African mothers and fathers mentioned relatedness-oriented aspects such as respect, social competencies, etc., whereas the German fathers mentioned more autonomy-oriented aspects such as independence, self-realisation, assertiveness, self-responsibility and achievement orientation. However, German mothers gave importance to both autonomy- and relatedness-oriented values such as, on the one hand, social competencies, and on the other, assertiveness. For example, one German mother said:

> "It is important to me that she [her daughter] will grow up to be a strong personality having self-confidence so

that she'll be able to assert herself – because that's important in life. But most importantly, I want her to be happy, enjoying life and be able to realise her dreams. What is rather unimportant in my opinion is her ability to be obedient or silent when other people talk… when adults talk… this whole issue of respect: To respect older people just because they are older than oneself. But this is very important to my husband."

Regarding child care conditions and activities, German mothers and fathers emphasised individual furtherance, striving for independence and having free space for creativeness and preferred exclusive activities with the child only – whereas West African parents, regardless of gender, once again highlighted the extended family and contact to other people from the African community whom they liked to visit with their child. When asked what would be mistakes in childcare, all parents in all groups mentioned physical punishment. Additionally, German parents mentioned that *putting pressure* on the children would be a mistake – whereas the West African parents mentioned that *spoiling* the children would be a mistake. Often, interviewed parents immediately pointed out the differences concerning attitudes and practices about childcare between themselves and their partner, even without being asked to do so. For example, a Guinean father said:

"I never understood why she [his wife] was talking so much to our child when she was still a baby. At that age she was still peeing in her pants and I'm sure she had no clue about what her mother was talking about."

And a Cameroonian mother said:

"Even when our daughter was still very small, he [her husband] said that she should have her own bed and her own bedroom – which was fine. But then, when I wanted to get up during the night to take her because she was crying, he told me to let her cry so she would get used to it. This seems really cruel to me. She is still a baby. She needs us and wants to be with us. Nobody likes to sleep alone and it's my duty as a mother to comfort her."

Additionally, when asked to evaluate positive and negative aspects in childcare when comparing Germany and West Africa, the aspects evaluated as positive as well as negative in Germany were autonomy-oriented (e.g. development of individual interests and freedom of personal choice as positive aspects – as well as too much freedom and a loss of guidance as negative aspects). Moreover, the aspects evaluated positively as well as negatively in the West African way of childrearing were rather oriented towards relatedness (togetherness with family and sharing as positive aspects, as well as unquestioning obedience and lack of freedom as negative aspects).

Conflict themes and strategies in bicultural families

Attitudes, beliefs and parental practices in these bicultural West African-German couples were experienced and described as rather different and problematic. Table 5 gives an overview of conflict themes and strategies pointed out by German and West African mothers and fathers.

Whereas general ideas about child rearing were described similarly in all cultural groups, the implementation of child rearing strategies were experienced as different and leading to conflicts. Differences in child rearing practices were especially salient regarding obedience and rules as well as the implementation of cultural traditions such as circumcisions. West African parents (fathers slightly more than mothers) gave more importance to punishment strategies than German parents – although physical punishment was avoided by all the parents – and also considered traditional practices like circumcision as very important or unquestionable. Such differences were often mentioned as leading to conflicts in these bicultural couples. Even strategies used in conflict situations were described as very different depending on the cultural background of the parent. Whereas parents of all cultural groups mentioned that they would talk and discuss cultural differences (and every group stated that they would give in more

German mothers	West African fathers	West African mothers	German fathers
general conflicts reliability (90%) organising daily life (80%)	***general conflicts*** organising daily life (70%) reliability (70%)	***general conflicts*** organising daily life (90%)	***general conflicts*** organising daily life (70%)
relationship diff. ideas relationship (80%) money (60%) paternal absence (50%) lack time together (50%)	***relationship*** paternal absence (70%) diff. ideas relationship (60%) power & control (50%) roles, task sharing (50%)	***relationship*** lack time together (70%)	***relationship*** diff. ideas relationship (80%)
child care German culture (60%) punishment, rules (50%) African culture (40%) television (40%) friends, visits (40%)	***child care*** punishment, rules (60%) nutrition, meals (40%) diff. ideas child care (40%) roles, task sharing (40%)	***child care*** punishment, rules (80%) circumcision (60%) friends, visits (50%)	***child care*** nutrition, meals (50%) television (50%) circumcision (40%) punishment, rules (30%)
strategies talk, discuss (100%) give in (70%) being aggressive (40%) different strategies (80%)	***strategies*** talk, discuss (90%) keep silent (60%) leave, talk later (60%) different strategies (60%)	***strategies*** talk, discuss (70%) give in (70%) tolerant, patient (70%) different strategies (70%)	***strategies*** talk, discuss (100%) dominant, assertive (70%)

Table 5. Conflict themes and strategies in bicultural families (% that mentions).

than their partners), West African fathers were described by their German partners (and often also by themselves) as rather staying silent or leaving the house when conflicts arose, while German women liked to discuss issues extensively. In many cases, this different conflict behaviour even increased the potential for further conflicts. When asked about the reasons for different attitudes, beliefs and practices regarding child care, in all cultural groups 'culture' was given as the first answer. West African mothers mentioned 'gender' second, while German mothers mentioned 'personality' as an important influence. The fathers in both cultural groups named only 'culture' as predominant reason for different outcomes.

Discussion

The aim of the present investigation was to disentangle the influence of culture and gender on socialisation goals and parental ethnotheories of bicultural West African-German families, given their differences with respect to the cultural models of autonomy and relatedness (Kağitçibaşi, 1996; 2005; Keller, 2007). Did bicultural West African-German families experience a clash or a synthesis of their theories, as according to Kağitçibaşi (1996), on child rearing?

In conclusion, regarding *socialisation goals*, German mothers were most autonomy-oriented, followed by the German fathers; West African mothers as well as fathers were mainly relatedness-oriented. Analysis of interviews showed that *parental ethnotheories* concerning family life and childcare, as well as child care practices seemed to be influenced by culture more than gender in these bicultural West African-German families. The expected gender difference according to the literature (Cross & Madson, 1997; Rosenberg, 1989) of women being more relatedness-oriented than men was only slightly replicated in this sample. Thus, the results are in line with the assumptions that cultural models of autonomy and relatedness are the main influence: German parents were more autonomy-oriented, West African parents more relatedness-oriented. Gender differences regarding the expressed models were not evident in the expected way, which suggests that the 'culture' factor has a stronger impact on the ethnotheoretical variation of up-bringing than does 'gender'. Overall, child rearing in bicultural West African-German families seems to indicate a high potential for *conflicts* since strategies are experienced as very different. Furthermore, strategies for solving these conflicts are also described as oppositional, which in turn leads to augmented difficulties for the couple and in the families.

However, the results above are from bicultural families only and warrant comparison with mono-cultural German and mono-cultural West African samples, too. Interviews with these groups have also been conducted, and further analysis and comparison of these different samples will deepen our insight regarding the interplay of gender and cultural context when it comes to socialisation goals and conceptions of child development and parenting practices in West African, German, and mixed families.

Furthermore, the present analysis of interviews only regarded the answers mentioned most frequently. Less frequent answers might provide some insight into which factors lead to certain outcomes.

This study may inform the counselling of West African-German couples and it increases our understanding of bicultural couples and families in general. Understanding the impact of different cultural models of partnership, family life and child rearing is an important tool for counsellors. It could also help kindergarten and school teachers in assisting children and parents' discovery and handling of different ways of dealing with problems or different attitudes between the family and the school.

Parents themselves need to develop a joint identity as a couple – and as parents – and have to agree on how the different cultures can be integrated in family life and child rearing, to create a new 'family culture'. Oppositional conflict strategies (that in the worst case lead to a reinforcement of the conflict) can, once taken into account, lead to more cautious and tolerant ways of getting along with each other. Considering and being conscious of those different perspectives combined with the willingness to seek a deeper understanding and tolerance from both cultural sides to reach a necessary balance may allow all family members to benefit from the advantages of a bi- or multicultural family life.

Acknowledgements

I thank the Friedrich-Naumann Foundation for Freedom for funding and my research assistant Malina Hobai for helping with the transcriptions and codings of the interviews.

References

Baum, R. (1999). *Die Liebe im Spannungsfeld von Solidarität und Abgrenzung – Zur Psychodynamik in deutsch-afrikanischen Liebesbeziehungen aus der Sicht deutscher Frauen.* [On the psychodynamics of German-African love relationships from the perspective of German Women]. Berlin: Forschungbericht.

Cross, S. E., & Madson, L. (1997). Models of the self: Self construals and gender. *Psychological Bulletin, 122*, 5-37.

D'Andrade, R. (1984). Some propositions about the relations between culture and human cognition. In J. W. Stigler, R. A. Shweder, & G. Herdt (Eds.), *Cultural psychology. Essays on comparative human development* (pp. 65-129). New York: Cambridge University Press.

Greenfield, P. M. (1994). Independence and interdependence as developmental scripts: Implications for theory, research, and practice. In P. M. Greenfield & R. R. Cocking (Eds.), *Cross-cultural roots of minority child development* (pp. 1-40). Hillsdale, NJ: Lawrence Erlbaum Associates.

Harkness, S., Super, C. M., & van Tijen, N. (2000). Individualism and the "Western mind" reconsidered: American and Dutch parents' ethnotheories of the child. *New Directions for Child and Adolescent Development series, 87*, 23-39.

Hofstede, G. (1980). *Culture's consequences.* Beverly Hills, CA: Sage.

Kağitçibaşi, C. (1996). The autonomous-relational self: a new synthesis. *European Psychologist, 1*, 180-186.

Kağitçibaşi, C. (1997). Individualism and collectivism. In J. W. Berry, M. H. Segall, & C. Kağitçibaşi (Eds.), *Handbook of cross-cultural psychology: Vol. 3. Social behavior and applications* (2nd ed., pp. 1-49). Boston: Allyn & Bacon.

Kağitçibaşi, C. (2005). Autonomy and relatedness in cultural context: Implications for self and family. *Journal of Cross-Cultural Psychology, 36*, 403-422.

Kağitçibaşi, C. (2007). *Family, self, and human development across countries. Theory and applications* (2nd ed.). Mahwah, NJ: Erlbaum.

Keller, H. (2003). Socialization for competence: Cultural models of infancy. *Human Development, 46*, 288-311.

Keller, H., Yovsi, R. D., Borke, J., Kärtner, J., Jensen, H., & Papaligoura, Z. (2004). Developmental consequences of early parenting experiences: Self-regulation and self-recognition in three cultural communities. *Child Development, 75*, 1745-1760.

Keller, H., Voelker, S., & Yovsi, R. (2005). Conceptions of parenting in different cultural communities. The case of West African Nso and Northern German women. *Social Development, 14*, 158-180.

Keller, H., Lamm, B., Abels, M., Yovsi, R., Borke, J., Jensen, H., Papaligoura, Z., Holub, C., Lo, W., Tomiyama, A. J., Su, Y., Wang, Y., & Chaudhary, N. (2006). Cultural models, socialization goals, and parenting ethnotheories: A multicultural analysis. *Journal of Cross-Cultural Psychology, 37*, 155-172.

Keller, H. (2007). *Cultures of infancy*. Mahwah, NJ: Erlbaum.

Khounani, P. M. (2000). Binationale Familien in Deutschland und die Erziehung der Kinder. Eine Vergleichsuntersuchung zur familiären Erziehungssituation in mono- und bikulturellen Familien im Hinblick auf multikulturelle Handlungsfähigkeit. [Binational families in Germany and the education of their children. A comparative investigation of mono- and bicultural families]. Frankfurt am Main: Peter Lang GmbH.

LeVine, R. A. (1977). Child rearing as cultural adaptation. In P. H. Leiderman, S. R. Tulkin, & A. Rosenfeld (Eds.), *Culture and infancy: Variables in the human experience* (pp. 15-27). New York: Academic.

LeVine, R. A., Dixon, S., Levine, S., Richman, A., Leiderman, P. H., Keefer, C. H., & Brazelton, T. B. (1994). *Child care and culture: Lessons from Africa*. Cambridge: Cambridge University Press.

Markus, H. R., & Kitayama, S. (1991). Culture and the self: Implications for cognition, emotion, and motivation. *Psychological Review, 98*, 224-253.

Mayring, P. (2003). *Qualitative Inhaltsanalyse. Grundlagen und Techniken* [Qualitative content analysis] (8th ed.). Weinheim: Beltz Verlag.

Palacios, J. G., & Moreno, M. C. (1996). Parents' and adolescents' ideas on children. Origins and transmission of intracultural variability. In S. Harkness, & C. M. Super (Eds.), *Parents' cultural belief systems: Their origins, expressions, and consequences* (pp. 215-253). New York: Guilford Press.

Rosenberg, M. (1989). The self-concept: Social product and social force. In M. Rosenberg & R. H. Turner (Eds.) *Social psychology: Sociological perspectives* (pp. 593-624). New York: Basic Books.

Statistisches Bundeamt (2002). Mikrozensus 2002. Retrieved from http://www.destatis.de/presse/deutsch/pk/2002/mikrozensus2001b.htm.

Super, C. M., & Harkness, S. (1996). The cultural structuring of child development. In J. W. Berry, P. R. Dasen & T. S. Saraswathi, (Eds.). *Handbook of cross-cultural psychology, Vol. 2: Basic processes and human development* (2nd ed., pp. 1-39). Boston: Allyn & Bacon.

Triandis, H. C. (1995). *Individualism and collectivism*. Boulde, CO: West View Press.

Laura Quintanilla
Kristine Jensen de López

Perceiving self through envy
A multi-culture comparison of preschool children

Developmental psychology has a long tradition of studying children's development of basic emotions, such as happiness, sadness, anger or fear, while more complex and self-conscious emotions such as jealousy and envy have received less attention. Children's development of envy has largely been neglected (Mascolo & Fisher, 2007; Miceli & Castelfranchi, 2007). The objective of this chapter is to provide insight into how young children from different cultures come to understand the complex emotion of envy.

Our study is nested within a socio-historical approach which integrates central concepts and interpretations from developmental psychology, psychology of information processing, and constructivist theories concerning children's understanding of their social environment. We use a multi-methods approach, allowing us to integrate quantitative and qualitative methods (ethnography, quasi-eksperiments and interviews) in order to reach a better understanding of the concept of envy in development. This is not an eclectic methodology, but one that arises from the deep conviction that confining research to one unique way of analyzing reality may bias our understanding of the phenomenon under study.

Specifically, we integrate anthropological and sociological views of *understanding envy* while emphasising the importance of socio-cultural practices. In doing this, we point out some of the cognitive and affective aspects underlying children's development of the understanding of envy in relation to their construal of self.

Developmental psychologists have argued that, in the course of the child's development, different aspects of *emotional understanding* can be grouped into three hierarchically organised components. Sequentially, the first component consists of identifying emotional expressions and understanding that external factors cause emotions (Harris, 1989). The second component of emotional understanding includes taking into account that emotions can result from individual beliefs and desires; this depends on the child's understanding of mental states and emerges at the age of 4 years (Harris, 1989; Wellman, Cross & Watson, 2001). The third component includes mixed emotions, moral emotions and mental control of emotion and emerges at the age of 8 to 9 years. This hierarchical model clearly echoes Piaget's universal approach to emotional development while focusing less on development's socio-cultural dimension. In this chapter we expand on previous research on emotional development by considering socio-cultural aspects that may influence children's development, and in particular by exploring the developmental trajectory of a less widely investigated self-conscious emotion, namely the emotion of envy.

The particular socio-moral emotions that co-develop with the toddler's emergence of self include shame, guilt and anger (Mascolo & Fisher, 2007) and these emotions are known to regulate the child's prosocial behaviour (sharing, reciprocity norms, norms of responsibility, etc.). In accordance with this functional view, we argue that the child's experiences with different emotions while engaging in social interactions with other people, and in particular parents' styles of child-raising practices, foster the child's development of self-conscious emotions. In this sense the daily social interaction of the child plays a central role in organising the child's experience, awareness and actions. For example, self-conscious emotions such as guilt and shame involve the child's evaluation of the self and offer the child the possibility of experiencing self-reflection in comparison to social standards. On the other hand, experiencing the emotion of shame may cause the child to devalue herself in the eyes of others, while experiencing the emotion of guilt may cause the child to evaluate her own acts as wrong under a set of specific social norms. These particular experiences forge the social skills of children and lead them to engage in prosocial behaviours. Developmental psychologists from socio-cultural traditions argue that, in order for a child to display appropriate prosocial behaviour, she needs to understand emotions with reference to her existing knowledge of the societal and cultural expectations underlying these emotions (Denham et al., 2003; Mosier & Rogoff, 2003; Sy, DeMeis & Sheinfield, 2003). Previous studies have shown that the emotions of shame, guilt and anger emerge by the age of two years (Barrett, 2005; Lewis, Alessandri & Sullivan, 1992; Shore, 1994; Zhan-Waxler & Kochanska, 1990).

Feelings of empathy and the development of self-conscious emotions are similarly considered to play an important role in the child's development of self-construal. However, Hoffman (2007) argues that it is important to distinguish different types of empathy. According to Hoffman, what may seem like empathy at the behavioural level, as seen in infants' and toddlers' prosocial reaction to the distress of another child, could be a mere response to the toddler's own distress in the sense that the underlying motivation behind her reaction is actually to free herself from her own distress by alleviating the distress of the other child. This is because the exposure to another child being distressed causes unpleasantness for the child itself. Consequentially, the child's act of empathy towards the other might be seen as a purely egoistic act, with the intention of improving her own emotional state. In this sense the child's experience of distress is disguised as an empathetic action, whereas in the case of true empathy the child feels true distress about another child's suffering. Obviously, this intricate differentiation is challenging as even the most generous act most often holds some kind of hidden benefit (to self).

In one scenario of envy, as we will see later, the child feels distressed about the fact that a second child possesses an object which she herself highly values and desires. Hence, empathy twisted with the desire to obtain the object possessed by the other contributes to the unfolding of the sensation of envy.

Experiencing envy

The experience of envy has been defined as emulation or as the feeling of spite and resentment at seeing the success of another person, and refers to the desire to obtain what someone else has and the consequent suffering (Miceli & Castelfranchi, 2007; Silver & Sabini, 1978; Smith & Kim, 2007). Envy is characterised by a certain pattern of behaviours engendered by the loss of one's own prestige compared with someone else's success, and in addition envy involves a moral component and the evaluation of the self (Dogan & Vecchio, 2001; Vecchio, 2005). Apart from the aspect of morality, additional socio-cognitive and interpersonal aspects contribute to the complexity of envy. Envy is an emotion that is generated within a social context involving at a minimum two individuals and an object (which can also be a personal quality or an abstract idea). Clearly, envy is unfolded within a triadic relationship where basic cognitive and affective processes are at stake. The experience of envy involves comparing oneself to specific characteristics or properties of another person. Hence, to attribute a person with the emotion of envy we first need to analyse the antecedents and consequences of a specific situation. The initial cause of envy could be the inequality of ownership observed through social comparison which may lead to low self-esteem and feelings of inferiority and injustice (Parrot, 1991; Smith & Kim, 2007); for example, recognising that your neighbour has a car that is newer and nicer than your own car. Consequently, low self-esteem can provoke one to direct feelings of ill-will or vengeance towards the envied person (Miceli & Castelfranchi, 2007). The feeling of ill-will may allow the envier to restore her own self-esteem through experiencing the sensation of pleasure (Powell, Smith & Shurtz, 2008). This achieved state of emotion is even expressed lexically in some Indo-European languages, for example in the German word *Schadenfreude* and the Danish word *skadefryd*. Whereas current scholars separate schadenfreude from envy (see Silver & Sabini, 1978; Smith, 2008), historically philosophers such as Aristotle, Spinoza and Gracián considered the emotion of schadenfreude to form a central part of the emotion of envy (Powell, Smith & Shurtz, 2008).

The envied object

The complexity of envy is not only constituted by social interactions and emotions as described in the above section. In general terms, envy is constituted by three elements: two people and one object. What then makes a specific object become enviable? In accordance with the socio-cultural approach the answer should be sought within the social and historical context of the object. First of all, and common to all societies, values concerning possessions or personal qualities are the products of social conventions and agreement among members of the society. Hence, the specific value of an object is mediated through social agreement and consequently a particular object may very well have a different value in different contexts and different cultures. For example, in ancient rural Mesoamerican and European societies children were considered the object of envy because they were perceived as future workers and therefore a potential source of wealth for the family, while this conception no longer holds in modern industrialised societies (Foster, 1987). In addition, having ownership of an object transfers a certain value to the owner and this may either increase or decrease the person's self-esteem.

Expressing envy is thus most appropriately conceptualised as a dynamic process, where two different people - the envier and the envied – engage in an unequal relationship centred on a third constituent, the object. Additionally, the person who holds the unfavourable position is expected to hide her pain or suffering. This complex constellation is concurrently seen as a challenge for the study of envy and for understanding children's development of mental abilities and self-consciousness in conjunction with their development of emotional attribution.

Most importantly, understanding contexts of envy requires the ability to recognise the unsatisfied desires of the envier when comparing the possessions of the protagonists within a triadic relationship. It also requires the ability to attribute suffering, frustration, or negative emotions to the envier. In other words, understanding envy rests upon a set of complex mental abilities. These abilities emerge early in infancy and rest upon the child's experiences in interpersonal social settings involving joint attention.

The development of self-conscious emotions

Given the above considerations, we expect that children will be capable of understanding the self-conscious emotion envy from the age of three years. At this age children have been shown to understand others' minds (Astington, Harris & Olson, 1988; Carpendale & Lewis, 2004; Flavell, 2004; Perner, 1991; Wimmer & Perner, 1983). This implies that 3-year-olds should be able to understand that someone feels bad if she does not obtain what she desires, a similar situation to what we have described as envy. Around this age period, children should also be able to understand that someone can feel happy while witnessing the misfortune of another person, similar to what we have described as schadenfreude. This is different from Harris' (1989) proposed hierarchical organisation of components of emotions, addressed above, in which complex emotions such as envy are not expected to emerge until the age of eight years. Harris proposes that children's understanding of emotions forms part of their wider cognitive development and anticipates that children, despite growing up in markedly different cultural settings, will display a similar pattern of development. In general terms we are sympathetic to this universal view but find Harris' approach limited in that it disregards the socio-cultural components that mediate the development of emotional understanding, particularly when investigating complex emotions.

In the following section we set out to disentangle on the one hand the relationship between consciousness and emotion and on the other hand the relationship between emotions and culture in development. Basic emotions are thought to be universal and appear early in development, while complex or secondary emotions are to a higher degree culture-specific and rely on the child's development of self-consciousness (Dragui-Lorenz, Reddy & Costal, 2001; Lewis, 1993). Complex emotions such as envy, guilt and shame are human emotions that require a certain level of self-consciousness. Furthermore, we consider that emotional understanding and self-consciousness are intertwined. Some developmental psychologists consider self-consciousness to be a prerequisite for the child's experience of complex emotions like embarrassment (Lewis, Sullivan, Stanger & Weiss, 1989). Early studies of self-recognition and embarrassment showed that infants who were able to touch their nose when looking into a mirror (self-recognition) were able to express embarrassment as well. However, these classical studies are all based on correlational data and are not conclusive enough to support the statement that self-recognition or self-consciousness is a precondition for the emergence of complex emotions. In fact, an equally valid interpretation of the results could be that embarrassment is a condition fostering self-awareness.

In a similar vein, Dragui-Lorenz et al. (2001) discuss this methodological issue in an extended review on non-basic emotions. Based on studies of infancy, they claim that certain types of emotions could foster the development of children's self-awareness. In Reddy's (2005) recent study she investigated the experiencing of 'showing off' in infancy and found that this appeared at an early age and before the child's expression of self-recognition, despite being considered as a complex emotion. According to Reddy, the relation between self-consciousness and emotion is bi-directional rather than uni-directional (a view also expressed by chapter two of this volume). That is, certain emotions could serve as a facilitating experience in fostering self-consciousness, and at the same time self-consciousness could become a useful tool in learning how to discriminate and understand complex and subtle emotions. Last but not least, these experiences are unfolded within interpersonal relations, which may follow different patterns within specific cultures and languages. In addition, we need to acknowledge the possibility that one can experience different levels of emotional consciousness. For instance, one could identify an emotional expression in others; experience an emotion without having recognised it; experience an emotion while at the same time recognising it or additionally expressing an emotion; or be able to control an emotional expression and even use it to benefit oneself. What is common for all these manifestations of emotional consciousness is that they rely on our personal relationships, which are embedded within the environment in which we practice and develop our socio-emotional competences and our social cognition (Carpendale & Lewis, 2004; Tracy and Robins, 2007).

Emotion mediated through culture

Let us first turn our attention to some of the existing studies that have addressed emotional development cross-culturally. In general it has been affirmed that basic emotions are universal and biologically based, while complex emotions are suggested to be influenced by culture and acquired during the child's engagement in the process of socialisation. Russell (1991) notes that intercultural studies about emotion mainly report differences in terms of the frequencies, causes, and consequences of emotions.

Studies about emotional reactions in children from different cultures support this tendency. Cole, Brushi & Tamang (2002) compared children's emotional attributions in situations involving either a basic emotion (anger) or a complex emotion (shame) across three different cultures, showing variations between Braham-Nepal, Tamang-Nepal and American participants. The results showed culture-specific patterns of emotional attributions for both complex and basic emotions. In several situations American children endorsed more anger than the Tamang children, while the Tamang children endorsed more shame than the American and Brahman children. Furthermore, Tamang and American children communicated that they felt shame more frequently than Brahman children did. Cole et al. (ibid.) explain the behaviour of the Brahman children as being highly influenced by their experience of living in a caste system, which requires a high level of self-control and consciousness of the self in relation to others. Tamang children, following a Buddhist philosophy, tend to report feeling 'okay' and did not report anger but only shame. Finally, in the American society, anger is tolerated as an expression of self-assertion, while shame is considered a negative emotion that is harmful for the individual's self-esteem.

Thus, these patterns of emotional attribution are the outcome of important aspects of socialisation, which contribute to the child's development of self-construal. Participation in a specific culture offers the child a particular system of beliefs about what is adequate or appropriate to do or to feel in a specific situation. Also, cultural practices involve the proper management of the rules to display emotions. Consequently, the emergence of self-construal within the child is dependent on and mediated by the cultural beliefs and practices surrounding the child (Dennis, Cole, Zhan-Waxler & Mizuta, 2002; Keller, 2007).

Despite evidence suggesting that some cultures foster specific feelings more frequently than other cultures, we expect that envy is universal. In the following section we review some anthropological studies that suggest this.

Envy in different cultures

Anthropologists and sociologists suggest that envy is a universal emotion (Foster, 1972; Schoeck, 1966). However, we argue that since cultural beliefs and human practices differ significantly across cultures, the particular coping strategies children learn in order to solve conflicts caused by envy might differ across cultures. Foster (1972) has provided a detailed description of how humans employ different cultural practices, as well as different types of symbolic behaviour, in order to cope with their fear regarding the consequences of envy as a prevalent emotion. Frequently cited symbolic behaviour, which supports the claim that Mesoamerican[1] cultures view envy as a threat is the notion of the evil eye. The *evil eye* expresses the subjectively perceived threat to one's material possessions, which leads one either to hide one's material goods or to share them widely with others in order to avoid the other person feeling envious. According to Foster, Mesoamerican people hold the view that resources are limited in the world so the way to obtain goods is by taking them from another person. Consequentially, an envied person is a potential candidate for being stripped of something. Hence, being envied means being threatened. In Mesoamerican and Zapotec cultures, people strive to free themselves from the threat associated with being envied through participation in magical cures that are believed to remove envy caused by the *evil eye* (Whitecotton, 1985).

In contrast, in Western societies someone who is envied enjoys the pleasure of being recognised by others. Western people do not avoid showing off their new acquisitions but in fact feel proud about their acquired status, and it is even common to celebrate the purchase of a new car, a new house, a raise, etc. with friends and close family.

Although Western people do not feel threatened by the envier, they do follow social rules in order to avoid lowering the self-esteem of the other person or to reduce the admiration expressed about the highly valued object. Depreciating the value of the admired object is one way to avoid potential threat to the self-esteem of the other person. For example, when wearing a brand new dress, the complimented person may response to a received compliment by saying: "oh! I bought it on sale and it was really cheap". This expression of modesty does not, however, indicate that the envied person has given up their pride about the possession. Being envied illustrates that the person's possessions are highly rated in that particular society. Sharing goods or distributing them fairly is looked upon as a highly valued practice with clear norms of how to distribute goods existing within the society. These social rules are implemented by Western parents, who express a high level of concern that their young children learn to share their possessions with their nearest friends or siblings. Although these cultural norms for the distribution of goods are not always explicitly directed towards coping with the consequences of envy or with avoiding envy they could play a functional role when managing envy situations (Mui, 1995; Ramírez Barrios, Díaz Ochoa & Schneider, 2006).

Nevertheless, the situation of the envier is considered similar in all cultures. The envier is considered to suffer because of her longing to reach the position of the envied. This unsatisfied desire, the sense of helplessness and inferiority leads the envier to feel ill will, and to feel pleasure at another's misfortune, i.e., schadenfreude.

Television advertisements are known to use envy as a way to motivate people to buy material goods. In one particular commercial for cars the plot is as follows: someone notices there is a new car on the street and he guesses that his neighbour is the owner. So, he admires the car, and when he sees that his neighbour is indeed the owner he expresses ill will by spreading birdseeds around the car. As a consequence, masses of birds approach the site to eat the seeds, and they dirty the new car. The commercial concludes by showing the protagonist laughing through the window of his house at the misfortune of his neighbour whose car is now covered in bird excrement. This hostile reaction of the envier is motivated by the fact that the new car caused the car owner's prestige to increase; therefore the envier, in order to restore his self-esteem, sets out to 'damage' the new possession, thereby assuring a decrease in the elevated prestige of the envied person. The rationale behind this commercial seems to be "this possession makes you highly rated, which causes your prestige in the eyes of others to increase, as evinced by the envy this possession causes".

Contrary to this unconscious Western mechanism driven by envy, local newspapers in Oaxaca, Mexico commonly advertise *curanderos* (witch doctors) who offer their service to remove the envy directed to one. Removing envy in this sense includes a self-defence and egocentric component. And Mesoamerican envied people happily pay *curanderos* to get rid of the envy of them by others.

To sum up, what we view as similar between people in Mesoamerican and Western cultures is that envy seems to play a central role in relationships to other people. We anticipate that the child's development of the ability to attribute envy emerges in conjunction with the development of self-construal and self-esteem. Across cultures, envy is mediated by possessions or personal qualities, which form part of cultural and social values. Having said this, we consider that the meanings of envy differ across cultures and arise from people's world conception about the particular cultural practices regarding access to goods. Children are enmeshed within these practices through the process of socialisation. This brings us to question the degree to which the developmental trajectory for self-conscious emotions is universal.

Children's understanding of envy across different cultures

Research on children's understanding of emotion has rarely focused on children from non-industrialised countries who might follow a different developmental trajectory than children reared in industrialised countries. The objective of our research is firstly to explore the development of the child's understanding of envy among non-Western (Zapotec) and Western (Spanish and Danish) preschool children, and secondly to explore the types of strategies children suggest for resolving conflicts arising from envy situations. We anticipate that children from different cultures may respond differently in terms of the strategies of solution they offer for resolving conflicts arising in situations of envy. Furthermore, we expect children's strategies of solution to reflect their cultural practices and values regarding the complex emotion of envy.

In the present study a total of 172 three- to five-year-old children (90 Danish[2], 45 Spanish and 37 Zapotec) from Brovst, Northern Jutland, Denmark; El Carpio de Tajo, Toledo, Spain; and Ocotlán de Morelos, Oaxaca, Mexico participated in the study. The children were individually interviewed in their respective day care institutions. The interview concerned four stories, which convey the emotion of envy. In this chapter we present analyses and results for two of the stories, the Backpack Story and the Camera Story.

The Backpack Story. The plot of the Backpack story is that one girl (Sara) possesses a nice, big, new backpack, while a second girl (Teresa) has a small, old backpack but expresses her desire to have a new backpack as well as her inability to obtain it. In the story the unequal allocation of goods is first highlighted to the child followed by two emotion questions: how does Sara feel, and how does Teresa feel? If the child responds that Sara feels good and Teresa feels bad we consider her answer to reflect her ability to understand envy. In the second scene Sara's backpack has now been torn. We ask the child the same two questions about the feelings of the two protagonists emphasising the fact that Sara's backpack has been torn. If the child attributes a positive emotion to the envier (Teresa), we consider that she is able to attribute schadenfreude. Conversely, if the child attributes a negative feeling to the envier we consider this the attribution of empathy.

The Camera Story. The camera story is similarly about two girls (Maria and Klara) who are playing together in the playground. Maria picks up a piece of rubbish and pretends it is a camera. Klara then expresses that she also wants to play with the object. Maria drops the 'camera' and starts to look around the playground for other toys that she could play with. Klara immediately picks up the pretend camera and starts to play with it pretending it's a camera. Maria then returns to play with the pretend camera, but now sees that Klara has taken possession of the attractive object. In each scene a character is depicted as either possessing or not possessing the target object (the pretend camera). Relying on our previous analysis of envy (antecedents of envy situations), we expected children to be able to link a positive emotion to the possession of a desired object, and a negative emotion to the lack of possession. This involved the following target questions: 1) How does Maria feel? 2) How does Klara feel? The expected responses to both questions were *good* if the child had the camera, and *bad* if she did not have it.

The final question posed to the child is an open question aimed at gaining information about the child's suggestions for solving the conflict arising because Klara has obtained the pretend camera, which Maria originally identified as a valued object. The prompt question was: *What will Maria do to feel happy again*?

The backpack and the camera story were both introduced using a set of photographs and the child was requested to assist the interviewer in completing the stories.

Results
Attribution of envy

We first present the results for the backpack story. Due to incomplete answers we discharged 22 children from the analysis. We analysed the children's responses to the two questions of how Teresa felt, and present the results in table 1. When Teresa (the envier) was in an unfavour-

How does Teresa feel?	**After torn backpack**		
Before torn backpack	GOOD	BAD	Total
BAD	76	51	**127**
GOOD	18	5	23
Total	**94**	56	150

Table 1. Frequencies of emotional attributions to Teresa, before and after Sara's backpack is torn.
Numbers indicate N for this combination of answers; bold N indicate total number of children whose answers reflect the understanding of envy and schadenfreude, respectively.

able position; that is when her backpack was less worth than Sara's new backpack most children (127/150) attributed her a negative emotion; however once Sara's backpack was torn (and now suggesting that Teresa's backback is the most valuable) a large proportion of the children (94/150) attributed a positive emotion to Teresa. This difference was significant ($\chi^2_{\text{McNemar}, 1\, gl,} = 60.5$, $p = .001$). A total of 85% of the children demonstrated the ability to attribute envy; that is, they considered Teresa to be sad in the first sequence. 63% of the children additionally demonstrated the ability to attribute the notion of schadenfreude; that is, they considered Teresa to be happy in the second sequence.

In table 2 we present descriptive results for the children's attribution of envy and schadenfreude for the age and culture groups (nine groups in total).

A high proportion of Spanish and Danish children attributed the emotion of envy to Teresa from the age of three years, and this increased with age (from 81%/71% of the children to 90%/100% of the

Emotion Question	Age	Emotion	Cultural Group			N
			Spanish	Zapotec	Danish	
How does Teresa feel when Sara's backback is new? (envy)	3	BAD	81%	40%	71%	29
	4	BAD	100%	79%	90%	50
	5	BAD	90%	100%	100%	48
						127
How does Teresa feel when Sara's backpack is torn? (schadenfreude)	3	GOOD	81%	50%	70%	30
	4	GOOD	67%	63%	69%	38
	5	GOOD	52%	71%	45%	26
						94

Table 2. Frequencies of responses to both questions in the backpack story; Envy and Schadenfreude by age and cultural groups.

children). However, for these two cultural groups the proportion of children that attributed the emotion of schadenfreude decreased with age (from 81%/70% to 52%/45% of the children). Zapotec children showed a different developmental path reflected in the proportion of children that attributed the two types of emotions. The emotion of envy was attributed by less than half of the children at age three, while at the age of five the Zapotec children showed a ceiling effect, similar to the children in the Western cultures. For schadenfreude, the Zapotec children produced an increase in the proportion of children attributing this emotion to Teresa with age. This is opposite the pattern of the two Western groups. We carried out a logistic regression analysis to examine whether the culture and age were predictive factors for the perceived differences in envy and schadenfreude attribution. The results indicate that for the envy question age is the only predictive factor explaining the differences, (Wald (2) = 12.2, $p < .05$). It is particularly the group of three year olds that contributed to these differences (B (1) = 2.45, $p < .05$). For the responses to the schadenfreude question neither of the two factors, culture (Wald (2) =1.3, $p > .05$) or age (Wald (2) = 3.7, p > .05) are significant. In all three cultures the children gave a similar proportion of responses reflecting their recognition that the envier felt good when the backpack was torn. It is important to point out that the group of five-year-old Zapotec children was small (N = 7) so the results should be enterpretated with caution.

Strategies for dealing with envy

For the camera story, we conducted an analysis of the children's strategies expressed for resolving the envy situation. In this analysis we identified a total of four different response categories, which were employed by the children in response to the final question, e.g. in the camera story, "What will Maria do to feel happy again?" The categories were: 1) *Irrelevant:* the child either did not respond to the question or the given response was irrelevant (e.g. "I like the big backpack"), 2) *Maria regains the camera:* the child suggests that Maria should ask politely to have the object and wait until the other child offers her the object, 3) *Maria shares the camera:* the child suggests a social rule such as sharing; and 4) *Look for other object*: the child suggests that Maria

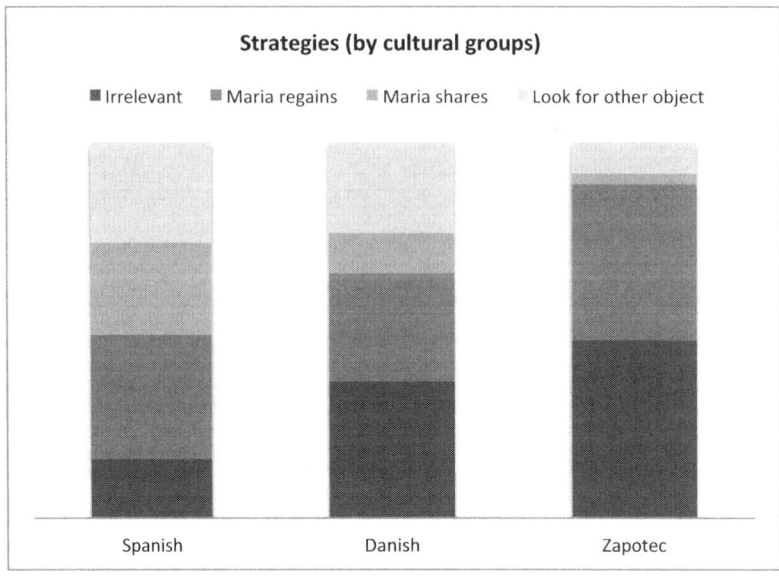

Figure 1. Proportion of solution strategies to Maria's emotional state, by cultural group.

should use a sophisticated mental strategy in order to get the camera back (e.g. searching for another object to play with in order to distract Klara's attention from the camera). Figure 1 shows the distribution of percentage of responses to the camera story for each of the four response categories across the three cultural groups.

Each cultural group showed a different pattern of responses to the target question. Close to 50% of the Zapotec children did not offer a concrete strategy for a solution (strategy 2 to 4). Between 30 and 40 percent of the children within each culture group suggested the second resolution "the character regains the object" as a means for making the protagonist feel happy again. The resolution "sharing the object" was suggested by respectively 11% and 24% of the Western groups, but only by 3% of the Zapotec children. Similarly, whereas 24 to 26 percent of the Western children suggested the solution involving "look for other object/distracting the other" this was only suggested by 8% of the Zapotec children.

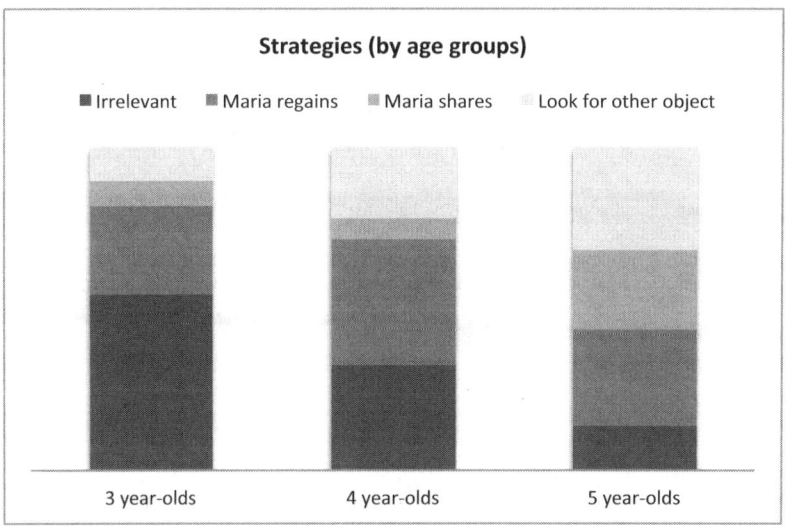

Figure 2. Proportion of the four resolution strategies, by age group.

In addition, we encountered different overall response patterns about resolving the envy situation within each of the age groups. Figure 2 illustrates that more than 50 percent of 3-year-old children responded within the category irrelevant and this response preference diminished with age.

Conversely, the response type "look for other object/distracting the other" increased with age. In all age groups the percentage of responses referring to Maria regaining the object was between 30 to 40 percent. Five year-olds specifically opted for the resolution "sharing the camera" and for this age group we observed that the three culture groups obtained similar percentages.

Discussion

In general terms, the results indicate that three- to five-year-old children understand basic situations involving envy, as we did not find any difference for age or for cultural group. The children endorsed a negative feeling for the envier when she was in a disadvantaged position and pleasure in the scenario where the envied object suffered damage. We therefore suggest that children from the age of three years understand situations of envy independently of whether they live in a Western or a non-Western society. This result supports the argument proposed by Foster (1987) and Schoeck (1966) about the universal presence of envy.

Comprehending envy seems to be an important developmental achievement for the emergence of self-construal through interpersonal practices. When experiencing envy the child is exposed to its own negative feelings caused by social comparison and evaluation of the self. Preschool children seem to be capable of evaluating their selves through reference to their ownership of specific objects and to be able to take into account that a specific object is perceived to be of high value by significant others. Clearly, this demands a minimum level of mental understanding of the notions of *I*, *me* and *others*, most importantly because the child needs to weigh whether the desires of the protagonist are fulfilled or not. This process of mere evaluation seems to be present in the three cultures that we have studied here, as children in all three groups were able to attribute envy and schadenfreude. The ability to evaluate the self contributes to the child's ability to engage in prosocial behaviour. As Foster (1972) and Schoeck (1966) suggest, it is plausible that envy is a universal emotion; at least, there is empirical evidence that mental understanding underlying the comprehension of envy is universal (Callaghan et al., 2007; Quintanilla & Sarriá, 2003).

Contrasting with these universal findings, the results from our analysis of the children's solutions to the conflict presented in the camera story suggest that children focus on different strategies for solving conflicts reflecting their specific age or developmental trajectory as well as their specific cultural background. What is salient about these strategies in terms of development is that young children utilise fewer strategies related to self-control – such as distracting the envied – and more strategies related to external control and rules of distribution (e.g. sharing and retaining the object) than do older children. As they become older, children tend to utilise an overall more diverse set of strategies.

It is worth noting that the pattern of responses expressed by the Zapotec children comprises a higher percentage of "Irrelevant" and "Maria regains the camera" responses, compared to the Spanish and Danish children who expressed a relatively high proportion of prosocial and mentalist strategies. We interpret this cultural difference as mediated by the specific modes of socialisation that are unfolded within different cultural settings. As seen in previous anthropological observations of early patterns of socialisation in Zapotec societies (Jensen de López, 2004; Quintanilla, 1999), the canonical pattern of child-caretaker conversation is uni-directional rather than bi-directional. Hence, Zapotec children are not 'trained' or socialised by their significant others to explicitly express mentalistic solutions to emotional conflicts and the dialogue is clearly unequal. Demuth, Keller, Gudi and Otto address similar cultural differences in their contribution in chapter 5 of this volume.

While it is common practice for Western caretakers to intervene when children argue about objects, and to scaffold children explicitly on how to establish rules during playtime, such as uttering: "you need to share things", "you shouldn't pick that up, it's not yours" etc., Zapotec caretakers do not practice this activity. It is uncommon for Zapotec caretakers to intervene verbally on their children's play activities. They simply monitor the playing activities carried out by the children or at the most comment on the outcome of the child's interaction with another child in terms of moral issues. Expressing explicit guidelines or rules for social interactions with peers is less frequent in Mesoamerican communities than in Western communities. Danish caregivers, in the opposite extreme, follow clear and overt democratic practices of socialisation when interacting verbally with young children. They frequently invite the child to engage in detailed discussions of how to reach a solution, taking into account what the specific motives of the protagonists could be. This intervention might promote a high degree of self-consciousness within the child and enhance explicit knowledge about social rules.

We do not suggest that self-consciousness is more developed in Western children compared to non-Western children, nor vice versa. What we do suggest is that culture forms the means by which social regulation and self construal is expressed in action. In sum: social interaction during child-rearing practices should be seen as a source of information that allows the child to acquire strategies for coping with emotions such as envy, and at the same time is the niche where the *We* becomes self-conscious.

Notes

1 The notion of evil eye has elsewhere been reported to be a general characteristic of rural communities (Schoeck, 1966).
2 We would like to thank the Danish psychology students at Aalborg University for their contribution to the data collection. This chapter was partially supported by the Spanish Ministry of Science through grant # I + D 2008 02174 awarded to the first author.

References

Astington, J. W., Harris, P. L., & Olson, D. R. (Eds.) (1988). *Developing theories of mind*. Cambridge: Cambridge University Press.

Barrett, L. F. (2005). Feeling is perceiving: Core affect and conceptualization in the experience of emotion. In L. F. Barret, P. M. Niedenthal, & P. Winkielman (Eds.), *Emotions: Conscious and unconscious* (pp. 255-284). New York: Guilford.

Carpendale, J. E., & Lewis, C. (2004). Constructing an understanding of mind: The development of children's understanding of mind within social interaction. *Behavioral and Brain Sciences, 27*, 79-150.

Callaghan, T., Rochat, P., Lillard, A., Claux, M. L., Odden, H. Itakura, S. Tapanya, S., & Singh, S. (2007). Synchrony in the onset of mental-state reasoning. *Psychological Science, 5*, 378-384.

Cole, P., Bruschi, C., & Tamang, P. L. (2002). Cultural differences in children's emotional reactions to difficult situations. *Child Development, 73*, 983-996.

Denham, S. A., Blair, K. A., DeMulder, E. L., Sawyer, K., Auerbach-Major, S., & Queenan, P. (2003). Preschool emotional competence: Pathway to social competence? *Child Development, 74*, 238-256.

Dennis, T. A., Cole, P. M., Zahn-Waxler, C., & Mizuta, I. (2002). Self in context: Autonomy and relatedness in Japanese and U.S. mother-preschooler dyads. *Child Development, 6*, 1803-1817.

Dogan, K., & Vecchio, R. P. (2001). Managing envy and jealousy in the workplace. *Compensation and Benefits Review, 33*, 57-64.

Dragui-Lorenz, R., Reddy, V., & Costall, A. (2001). Rethinking the development of 'non-basic' emotions: A critical review of existing theories. *Developmental Review, 21*, 263-304.

Flavell, J. H. (2004). Theory-of-mind development: Retrospect and prospect. *Merrill-Palmer Quarterly, 50*, 274-290.

Foster, G. (1972). The anatomy of envy: A study in symbolic behavior. *Current Anthropology, 13*, 165-186.

Foster, G. (1987). *Tzintzuntzan: Los campesinos mexicanoso en un mundo cambiante*. México: Fondo de Cultura Económica.

Harris, P. L. (1989). *Children and emotion: The development of psychological understanding*. Cambridge, MA, US: Blackwell.

Hoffman, M. L. (2007). The origins of empathic morality in toddlerhood. In C. Brownell & C. B. Kopp (Eds.), *Socioemotional development in the toddler years* (pp. 132-145). London: Guilford.

Jensen de López, K. (2004). Bcuaa quiaa – I stepped HEAD it! The acquisition of Zapotec bodypart locatives. In B. Pfeiler (Ed.), *Learning indigenous languages: Child language acquisition in Mesoamerica* (pp. 155-182). Hannover: Verlag für Ethnologie.

Keller, H. (2007). *Cultures of infancy*. Mahwah, New Jersey: Lawrence Erlbaum Associates.

Lewis, M. (1993). Self-conscious emotions: Embarrassment, pride, shame and guilt. In M. Lewis & J. M. Haviland (Eds.), *Handbook of emotions* (pp. 563-594). New York: Guilford.

Lewis, M., Alessandri, S. M., & Sullivan, M. W. (1992). Differences in shame and pride as a function of children's gender and task difficulty. *Child Development, 63*, 630-638.

Lewis, M., Sullivan, M. W., Stanger, C., & Weiss, M. (1989). Self development and self-conscious emotions. *Child Development, 60*, 146-156.

Mascolo, M. F., & Fisher, K. W. (2007). The codevelopment of self and sociomoral emotion during toddler years. In C. A. Brownell & C. B. Kopp (Eds.), *Socioemotional Development in toddler years* (pp. 66-99). London: Guilford.

Miceli, M., & Castelfranchi, C. (2007). The envious mind. *Cognition and emotion, 21*, 449-479.

Mosier, C. E., & Rogoff, B. (2003). Privileged treatment of toddlers: Cultural aspects of individual choice and responsibility. *Developmental Psychology, 39*, 1047-1060.

Mui, V.-L. (1995). The economics of envy. *Journal of Economic Behavior & Organization, 26*, 311-336.

Parrot, W. G. (1991). The emotional experiencies of envy and jealousy. In P. Salovey (Ed.), *The psychology of jealousy and envy* (pp. 3-30). London: Guilford Press.

Perner, J. (1991). *Understanding the representational mind*. Cambridge: MIT Press.

Powell, C. A., Smith, R. H., & Shurtz, D. R. (2008). Schadenfreude caused by an envied person's pain. In R. H. Smith (Ed.), *Envy: Theory and research* (pp. 148-164). Oxford: Oxford University Press.

Quintanilla, L. (1999). *La universalidad de la teoría de la mente y otras capacidades mentalistas: Un estudio evolutivo transcultural de niños zapotecos, españoles y regiomontanos.* UNED, Madrid: Unpublished Doctoral thesis.

Quintanilla, L., & Sarriá, E. (2003). Realismo, animismo y teoría de la mente: Características culturales y universales del conocimiento mental. *Estudios de Psicología, 24,* 315-345.

Ramírez Barrios, E., Díaz Ochoa, J. G., & Schneider, J. J. (2006). How fair is an equitable distribution? *Physica A: Statistical Mechanics and its Applications, 374,* 369-379.

Reddy, V. (2005). Feeling shy and showing-off: Self-conscious emotions must regulate self-awareness. In J. Nadel & D. Muir (Eds.), *Emotional development* (pp. 183-204). Oxford: Oxford University Press.

Russell, J. A. (1991). Culture and the categorization of emotions. *Psychological Bulletin, 110,* 426-450.

Schoeck, H. (1966/1970). *Envy: A theory of social behavior.* New York: Harcourt Brace and World.

Shore, N. (1994). *Affect regulation and origin of the self.* Hillsdale: Lawrence Erlbaum.

Silver, M., & Sabini, J. (1978). The social construction of envy. *Journal for the Theory of Social Behaviour, 8,* 313-312.

Smith, R. H. (2008). *Envy.* Oxford: Oxford University Press.

Smith, R. H., & Kim, S. H. (2007). Comprehending envy. *Psychological Bulletin, 133,* 46-64.

Sy, S. R., DeMeis, D. K., & Scheinfield, R. E. (2003). Pre-school children's understanding of the emotional consequences for failures to act prosocially. *British Journal of Developmental Psychology, 21,* 259-272.

Tracy, J. L., & Robins, R. W. (2007). The self in self-conscious emotions: A cognitive appraisal approach. In J. L. Tracy, R. W. Robins & J. P. Tangney (Eds.), *The self-conscious emotions: Theory and research* (pp. 3-20). New York: Guilford.

Vecchio, R. P. (2005). Explorations in employee envy: Feeling envious and feeling envied. *Cognition and Emotion, 19,* 69-81.

Wellman, H. M., Cross, D., & Watson, J. (2001). Meta-analysis of theory-of-mind development: The truth about false belief. *Child Development, 72,* 655-684.

Wimmer, H., & Perner, J. (1983). Beliefs about beliefs: Representation and constraining function of wrong beliefs in young children's understanding of deception. *Cognition, 13,* 103-128.

Whitecotton, J. W. (1985). *Los zapotecos. Príncipes, sacerdotes y campesinos*. México: Fondo de Cultura Económica.

Zhan-Waxler, C., & Kochanska, G. (1990). The origins of guilt. In R. A. Thompson, & R. A. Dientsbier (Eds.), *The 36th annual Nebraska symposium on motivation: Vol 36. Socioemotional development* (pp. 183-257). Lincoln: University of Nebraska Press.

Carolin Demuth
Heidi Keller
Helene Gudi
Hiltrud Otto

Developmental precursors of autonomy and relatedness

Discursive practices in childhood and autobiographical self-constructions in young adulthood

5

The focus of this chapter is on the relationship between child development and socio-cultural context from a discursive practice approach. It addresses the central and constructive role played by language in the forming and structuring of self and identity. Specifically, it aims at investigating how communicative practices in early family conversations can be considered as reflecting cultural models that will also become evident in the narrative self in adulthood. Our intention is to identify developmental precursors of identity formation with regard to the dimensions of autonomy and relatedness. In doing this, we hope to contribute to the understanding of the dialogical relationship between culture and self.

We will first give a theoretical outline of the interplay between self, narrative, and culture from a developmental perspective, followed by some empirical evidence from a longitudinal study to support our claim. We will conclude with a discussion of the presented data in light of the dynamic nature of culture and self over the lifespan.

The narrative nature of the self

The central role of narrativity for human psychological functioning has been widely acknowledged within the past two decades and is gaining increasing importance in the field of psychology (McAdams, 2008). As humans, we interpret events around us in terms of connections and relationships in order to make sense of our experiences and to create meaning. This allows us to achieve a sense of structure and order in the course of everyday activities and to get on in everyday life. The primary medium through which we do this is language, more specifically narrative (Carr, 1986). Narrative enables us to imbue life events with a temporal and logical order, to tie events together in a seamless explanatory framework. It is the connections or relationships among events that constitute the meaning and coherence of our experience. This is true for mundane everyday conversation (Ochs & Capps, 2001) but also, and particularly, for autobiographical narratives. Autobiographical narratives, moreover, serve to constitute identity and a sense of self by the construction and internalisation of self-defining stories (Brockmeier & Carbaugh, 2001; Bruner, 1990; McAdams, 2008). It is through autobiographical narratives that an individual brings separate 'stories' together, takes them all as 'mine', and establishes connections among them (Carr, 1986). This is the way we make sense of our lives, and provide reasons for our acts, as well as the causes of experiences (Sarbin, 1986). The constitution of the self in terms of unity, coherence and consistency across time is achieved by situating oneself in the past, present, and future through autobiographical narratives (Straub, Zielke & Werbik, 2005). One can say that it is through autobiographical narratives or 'life stories' that we become conscious of ourselves: the 'I' becomes objectified as the 'me' (Mead, 1934). The 'me' is then a narrative construction of my past experiences.

Autobiographical narratives are never a mere recapitulation of events in chronological order; they imply a selection of events that are told and the interpretation of the connections or relationships of these events with others. Based on Ricoeur's notion of 'plot', for instance, Mishler (2006) argues that meaningful connectedness among episodes is actively constructed by the narrator for a specific purpose. It is the ending of a story that primarily determines how a story is plotted or constructed. In other words: by looking backwards from the present, life stories are constructed in a way that allows the narrator to make sense of who he is today after what has happened to him in the past (Mishler, 2006, p. 36). The events that are chosen to be told in a life story are selected in the light of the *overall* narrative. As such, life stories serve a specific purpose and are a means by which identities are socially constructed (e.g., Crossley, 2000). Autobiographical narrations therefore have been closely linked to the self in terms of 'narrative identity' and can be conceived of as constituting the self (Bruner, 1990; Brockmeier & Carbaugh, 2001).

Language, from this viewpoint, cannot be conceived as merely referential, e.g., as a representation of some inner attitude or cognition. Rather, language is considered as a social practice by which we perform an action and constitute social reality. Similarly, the self is not conceived of in essentialist terms as an 'entity' inside people's minds; rather, a conceptualisation of the self is promoted "which sees it as inextricably dependent on the language and linguistic practices that we use in our everyday lives to make sense of ourselves and other people" (Crossley, 2000, p. 9). Self-stories are hence not only forms of representation but also socio-cultural practices. They are constructed in social interactions with others to achieve social and interpersonal objectives. When people tell of their personal experience the point of the story is not so much to recount the event but to show how the narrator has made that event into something in his or her life (Miller, Fung & Koven, 2007). Narrative identity from this ontological perspective, then, is an interactional achievement and hence located not inside a person but between persons. While there are versions of the self that are constantly reconstructed across contexts, there are also aspects of the narratively constructed self that are of a more stable nature and that may be told again and again throughout the person's life. These two aspects do not need to be considered in opposition to each other; rather, the self-constructions achieved in everyday interactions over the lifespan can be considered as a *process* by which we come to see the self as stable (Quigley, 2001). Moreover, this does not mean that narrative identity is merely a 'psychological construction'; there is sufficient empirical evidence that the brain's neurobiological mechanisms can alter as a result of different social environments and discursive practices (Harré & Gillet, 1994, quoted in Quigley, 2001).

The socio-cultural embeddedness of narratives

Narrativity serves to create meaning. Narratives are, however, not produced by isolated individuals; rather, they are formulated through cultural meaning systems that are transmitted and mediated across generations. "How a narrator selects and assembles experiences and events so they contribute collectively to the intended point of the story – the 'why' it is being told, in just this way in just this setting" (Mishler, 2006, p. 37) crucially depends on the cultural norms and values of what a 'good' story of one's life should look like. We are surrounded in our everyday life by broader cultural narratives and narrative genres of how to tell a life story. As individuals construct their life stories they draw on the stories they have heard before and hence create their stories in a dialogical relation to such cultural genres. This is in line with Bahktin's understanding of how (cultural) ideologies shape the use of language: in constructing a meaning of the world, an individual always draws upon the languages, the words of others to which he or she has been exposed. Language thus is never neutral but "tastes of the context and contexts in which it has lived its socially charged life" (Bakhtin, 1981, p. 293). These contexts are subject to socio-historical change as are cultural knowledge and language practices. Ideas, expressed in language, are hence always located outcomes of social and historical processes. This in turn has consequences for narrative self-construction. Slunecko and Hengl (2007) bring this to a point by stating that symbol systems such as language preexist the individual who grows into them and is transformed by them into a member, a reflection, and an embodiment of that culture. Hence, language 'owns' us; it structures thinking and feeling; it even provides us with formats of subjectivity. We are in this sense always the results of processes, which lie above and beyond us, since we, as individuals, do not choose our cultural and linguistic formats and imprints (ibid., p. 47).

The point we want to stress here is that autobiographical narratives are not only individual constructions but inextricably social, cultural, and historical. They are tools to construct the self and as such the self that is constituted through narrative is intimately linked with the social and cultural lives of the communities studied.

Narrative identity as a result of individualisation in Western societies

Some authors argue that constructing identity through autobiographical narratives is itself a cultural phenomenon typical of modern Western societies. They argue that macro-structural changes within the past decades have a crucial impact on the self-identity and agency of individual subjects. Drawing on Charles Taylor's book *Sources of the Self: The Making of Modern Identity* (Taylor, 1989), for example, Crossley (2000) argues that in earlier times, people lived in 'unchallengeable frameworks' of meaning which made 'imperious demands' on them. What was considered to be 'good' was pretty much set in stone and taken for granted. The decline of fixed traditions, and the loss of power of societal institutions, in particular religious institutions, through an increasing secularisation, has led to a worldview in which what is considered to be good has to be defined by the individuals themselves. This has led to the 'disembedding' of the society's ways of life so that identities can no longer be defined to the same extent by social group membership. As a consequence, modern individuals are forced to produce, stage, and compose their biographies themselves and to find coherence of the self through actively constructing autobiographies (Beck & Beck-Gernsheim, 1994; Giddens, 1990). According to Taylor, this has led to an 'inward' turn with regard to defining one's identity and to a modern Western notion of self that is constituted by self-reflexivity and self-control (agency): individuals are now forced to 'explore' and 'search' for the self in order to find their identity, and this is primarily achieved through autobiographical memory. The contemporary internalised concept of the self is defined by unity, coherence and consistency over time which is achieved through the construction of autobiographical narratives. In a similar vein, Bruner and Weisser (1991) have argued that more self-conscious, more agentic self-accounting within Western societies accompanies the turn to narrative and autobiographical narration for identity construction. Narrative identity can thus be said to be a state of consciousness and self-awareness which has emerged as a result of modernisation (see chapters 7 and 8, this volume, for findings that support this claim).

Autonomy and relatedness as panhuman cultural dimensions of the self

The emphasis on agency or autonomy prevailing in Western middle-class societies thus needs to be seen as a socio-historical development. At the same time, we want to stress here that autonomy is not to be understood as an exclusive alternative to relatedness but as standing in a dialogical relationship to it. In line with Kagitçibasi's (2005) family change model, we conceive of autonomy and relatedness as two panhuman needs (see Kleis, this volume, for a similar approach). The emphasis of the one over the other is to be understood as a consequence of the socio-cultural requirements of a specific society. This implies not only socio-historical changes due to urbanisation and economic development but, along with these, changes to the prevailing socialisation practices and the function of the family. An emphasis on relatedness over autonomy is considered to be functional in rural agrarian societies with low levels of affluence but is also seen in urban low socio-economic status (SES) contexts, where intergenerational interdependence is necessary for family livelihood (Kagitçibasi, 2005, p. 410). With urban lifestyles and increasing affluence, material interdependence between generations decreases, because elderly parents need no longer depend on the economic support of their adult offspring. Particularly with greater affluence, higher levels of education, and alternative sources of old-age support in Western middle-class societies, dependence on adult offspring turns out to be unnecessary and even unacceptable; thus, children are brought up to be independent and self-sufficient. The autonomy of the growing child is not seen as a threat to the family livelihood over the family life cycle but is highly valued (Kagitçibasi, 2005, p. 411). Families in formerly traditional societies experiencing the influence of modernisation do not materially depend on their children any more; nevertheless, psychological interdependence as closely-knit selves continues, because it is ingrained in the culture of relatedness and is not incompatible with changing lifestyles. According to this model, what emerges in these societal contexts is the 'autonomous-related self'. In a similar vein, Keller (2007) argues from an eco-cultural perspective that caregiver practices and beliefs are embedded in larger cultural models of autonomy and relatedness which will ultimately lead to distinct developmental pathways of the self.

The dimensions of autonomy and relatedness (or 'agency' and 'communion' as originally labelled by Bakan,1966) have also been identified as two general contrasting tendencies in life stories by a number of researchers (e.g., McAdams, Hoffman, Mansfield & Day, 1996). Life stories vary for instance with regard to the importance given to achievement, self-enhancement, and self-determination (qualities that closely correspond to the need for autonomy) as well as with regard to the importance given to intimacy, connectedness and prioritising the well-being of the community over one's own interests (qualities that closely correspond to the need for relatedness). (See also Rudberg & Nielsen's notion of 'sociological' versus 'psychological' genres of narratives as expression of socio-historic change over three generations in chapter 8.)

In a similar vein, various studies have provided evidence of culture-specific emphasis on autonomy and relatedness in adults' autobiographical memory as an expression of culture-specific self-construals (Conway, Wang, Hanyu & Haque, 2005; de la Mata et al., this volume; Demuth, Abels & Keller, 2007). There is also evidence that autobiographical life stories follow a cultural script (Habermas, 2007). In a study comparing earliest childhood memories among Euro-American and native Chinese college students, Wang (2001) found elaborated, specific, emotionally charged and self-focused memories in the Euro-American middle-class sample, whereas in the Chinese sample the remembered narratives were brief, general, emotionally unexpressive, and relation-centred. She relates these differences to the culture-specific forms of self-construals. Some researchers relate this cultural specifity to discursive practices that people participate in during the course of their socialisation. Wang and Spillane (2003), for instance, found that Euro-American and East Asian families show different patterns and tendencies when conversing with their children about the shared past, reflecting different orientations that focus on either autonomy or relatedness. They further argue that such differences, in turn, appear to have long-term consequences for the development of autobiographical memory.

Developmental precursors of adult narrative identity

If we want to understand the developmental aspects of cultural forms of self, expressed in (autobiographical) narratives, it is of course of primary interest to look at participation in routine discursive practices during childhood. If the self is to be considered as the result of narrative construction, and if this narrative construction is the result of accumulated experience of discursive interactions and co-constructions of social reality, then we need to look at the communicative practices prevailing in everyday family life during childhood.

The family can be considered the site of 'proximal processes' (Bronfenbrenner & Morris, 1998) through which the self develops in interaction with the socio-cultural environment (see also Bruner, 1990). It is primarily through repeated narrative practices within the family that children gradually learn and integrate intersubjective experience about themselves, the parent, and their interrelatedness as well as about the social environment and the role they play in this environment (Miller et al., 2007). By narratively co-constructing mundane everyday interactions, caregivers provide the child with a framework for making sense of their experience; they also provide the child with linguistic resources for constructing social meaning and thus lay the pathway for later narrative self-construction. Since caregivers' communicative practices are themselves embedded in broader cultural models, they function as mediators of culturally appropriate ways of narrative self-construction.

A number of cultural developmental psychologists and psychological anthropologists have shown how cultural knowledge is mediated through caregiver-child communication. It can be demonstrated, for example, how children gain access to a cultural understanding of norms and transgressions (Pontecorvo, Fasulo & Sterponi, 2001) and of one's role as a participant in interactions (Fatigante, Fasulo & Pontecorvo, 1998), as well as to a culturally appropriate sense of self and identity (Forrester, 2002; Miller et al.,2007) based on parents' discursive strategies. Chinese Taipei mothers have been found to use narrative patterns that index a high asymmetry between parents and children (Miller, Sandel, Liang & Fung, 2001) whereas Euro-American middle-class mothers use narrative patterns that foster the child's self-esteem (Miller, et al., 2001), independence and autonomy (Fasulo, Loyd, & Padiglione, 2007; Sirota, 2006), as well as close intimacy (Sirota, 2006). In contrast, Italian parents in Rome use discursive strategies that emphasise interdependence among family members (Fasulo et al., 2007). Schröder et al. (in press) provide evidence that cultural models of autonomy and relatedness find their expression in maternal talk about shared past events with their young children as well as in the communicative participation of these children.

Chen and colleagues (2005, quoted in Miller et al., 2007), by following up on the development of a Taiwanese boy, show how cultural models are discursively mediated by caregivers in early childhood and how they reappear in the child's communicative patterns some years later. These findings support the suggestion that narrative practices within the family in early childhood may be seen as precursors of the child's narrative identity later on in life. The development of narrative self in adulthood can thus be traced in two ways: at first, mainly through the language to which we are exposed in childhood, and later, through our own linguistic choices in narrating autobiographical experiences (Quigley, 2001, p. 148). Our claim here is that both narrative practices within the family of origin and autobiographical narratives later on in life are heavily informed by the prevailing cultural models of self and self in relation to others.

Mealtime conversations as 'cultural sites of socialisation'

A particularly fruitful approach to the study of parent-child communicative practices within Western societies has been the study of family mealtimes (e.g., Blum-Kulka, 1997; Ochs & Shohet, 2006). While regular shared family mealtimes might not exist in all societies and across all historic time, they can be said to be a regular and highly valued practice in today's European and North American middle-class families. Larson, Branscomb and Wiley (2006), for instance, argue that the idea of mealtimes as special occasions for family togetherness in the United States developed starting in the mid-nineteenth century as a consequence of urbanisation and industrialisation and as a symbol of achieving middle-class status. While there are certainly differences in length, specific activities, and the meanings and coordination of activities during mealtimes across families and subcultural groups, mealtimes can be said to constitute recurring meaning-laden activities, or 'practices', in modern European and North American middle-class contexts. In most Western middle-class contexts of the 20th century, mealtimes constitute a significant and regular part of family life. A recent large-scale interview study in Germany (Deutsch, 2008) shows that, in light of the challenges modern families have to face today, the performance of family life ('being family') through regular activities and rituals such as family dinner becomes increasingly important. They are social events that follow certain organisational principles and will be enacted with more or less the same participants (Blum-Kulka, 1997). Family mealtimes in these cultural contexts therefore have an element of replicability and allow comparison across families. They are not only an arena for sociability and enjoying family togetherness but are made up of dense social activity in which children are engaged in cultural practices and learn the meaning of these practices (Larson et al., 2006). They constitute regular mundane caregiver-child interactions and therefore provide special opportunities for young people's socialisation into family and broader cultural values. Cultural understandings of how to conceive of oneself and self in relation to others become especially evident in the way family interactions are enacted and reaffirmed. Ochs and Shohet (2006, p. 42) state:

> "Who participates in which kinds of communicative practices during mealtimes is linked to historically rooted ideologies and practices. In addressing children's socialization into mealtime communication, it is important to consider both norms of appropriate mealtime commu-

nication and the social positioning of children in mealtime communication."

Moreover, the presence of multiple family members as a 'reference group' may further contribute to children's perception that their family's mealtime practices represent normative reality (Ochs & Shohet, 2006). Family mealtimes can therefore be considered as "pregnant arenas for the production of sociality, morality, and local understandings of the world" (ibid, p. 35) and a site for the socialisation of children into their roles as competent members of society.

The cultural organisation of family mealtimes is discussed by a number of studies. Ochs and Taylor (1995), for example, show how children acquire an understanding of gender identity and gender hierarchy through family narrative interactions at mealtimes. Middle-class parents in the U.S. have been found to construct mealtimes in terms of the nutritional aspects and socialise children into eating 'healthily' by providing rewards (dessert) (Ochs, Pontecorvo, & Fasulo, 1996), and to structure mealtimes and overtly express conflict (Martini, 1996). Mealtimes of Japanese American families, in contrast, have been found to be less structured and more relaxed, and to involve less overt conflict than in the Anglo families (Martini, 1996). These differences were explained by contrasting cultural emphasis on family harmony versus individual expression. Vietnamese village families were found to socialise their children into displaying respect by chastising them for lapses in their comportment such as failing to sit still and be attentive (Rydsrom, 2003, quoted in Ochs & Shohet, 2006). Italian parents in Rome were found to emphasise food as pleasure in conversing with children and to use talk about food to link family members across generations, including family members no longer alive (Ochs et al., 1996). Children's participation in family meals as ratified participants has been been found to be typical of Western white middle-class families (Blum-Kulka, 1997) and can be related to the cultural convention of treating children as quasi-equal partners.

An interesting aspect of family mealtimes is their function with regard to the dimensions of autonomy and relatedness. On the one hand, conversations during mealtimes belong to the genre of mundane talk that is not explicitly directed towards a specific goal other than sociability. As Blum-Kulka (1997) states, "the focus of such conversation seems to be on the *building of rapport* rather than on the transmission of information" (p. 36, our emphasis). On the other hand, they bring together persons who stand in socially asymmetric power relations: the parents whose responsibility is to guide and teach the child, and the child in the position of the novice. It is thus largely in the control of the parents how much *autonomy* is accorded to the child. Within this particular configuration of power and social relatedness, parents need to balance what they consider to be a child's appropriate need for autonomy with what they consider a parent's responsibility for actively structuring the interaction. Family mealtimes therefore provide an excellent avenue for studying the cultural mediation of autonomy and relatedness.

In Western middle-class families subscribing to a socialisation model of autonomy, parents might feel uncomfortable in exerting direct control with their children and therefore use mitigating devices such as politeness strategies. Schieffelin and Ochs (1998) have argued, for instance, that Western middle-class mothers of young infants use self-lowering (e.g., simplified speech) as well as child-raising strategies (e.g., acting as if the child were more competent than his behaviour would indicate) to reduce the competence differential perceived between the adult and the child. Similarly, Blum-Kulka (1997) argues that while speech acts of control are common in any caregiver-child interaction based on the asymmetrical power relationship, the degree of politeness in the discourse of parental control is directly linked to the broader cultural models of child socialisation and the relative weight given to independence versus involvement.

Israeli parents have, for instance, been found to use more direct speech acts of control around the dinner table and follow a model of interdependence and involvement, compared to Jewish American parents who use more speech acts of control which reflect their concern with the child's autonomy and independence as prime values of socialisation (Blum-Kulka, 1997).

Similarly, Estonian and Latvian middle-class mothers have been found to show a more controlling conversational style towards young children during mealtimes than Swedish and Finnish (Tulviste, 2004) as well as U.S. middle-class mothers (Junefelt & Tulviste, 1997, 1998). Compared to Estonian (Junefelt & Tulviste, 1997, 1998) and Chinese immigrant parents (Wang, Wiley & Chiu, 2008), U.S. mothers used more praise during dinner interactions. Chinese-immigrant parents used praise strategies adhering to parental expectations which promote an interdependent self, whereas Euro-American parents used praise strategies adhering to child-initiated behaviours supporting the development of an independent self.

The existing evidence thus suggests that children's participation in shared meals is an important means of mediating cultural understandings of the self and self in relation to others. It can be expected that cultural self-understandings with regard to autonomy and relatedness may also become evident in narrative self-constructions later on in life. Although the literature on child socialisation is replete with arguments that communicative practices are the main tool to mediate cultural norms and values, empirical literature on the long-term developmental influences of narrative practices on self formation is scarce and hence has failed to convincingly support this theoretical contention.

What is more, the majority of prior research on autonomy and relatedness is based on cross-cultural study designs. Little attention has been given to the fact that autonomy and relatedness are dimensions of variation in any given socio-cultural group (but see Keller, Demuth & Yovsi, 2008; Raeff, 2006). In the following, we address this issue by discussing findings from a longitudinal study that was conducted in South Germany.

Autonomy and relatedness in early family communicative practices and autobiographical narratives later on in adulthood

The data on which our analysis is based stems from a larger longitudinal study which was originally conducted from 1977 to 1986 with a group of middle-class families in the city of Mainz and surroundings, from the time of the birth of their first child up to when the target child was 9 years of age. Part of the original study was the analysis of family dinner interactions when the target children were 3 years old. The participants were re-contacted in 2004/2005 at the age of 27/28. Our aim was to identify possible developmental precursors in the construction of the individual personal life stories that may account for the relative emphasis on autonomy and relatedness during the course of development. For this purpose, we conducted biographical narrative interviews with the now-adult participants, and also reanalysed the early family dinner interactions of the same participants. As a third step, we related the discursive patterns of the family interactions with narrative self-constructions in young adulthood.

Dinner conversations in early childhhood

The dinner conversations were recorded between 1980 and 1981. A total of 30 families participated in the study. At the time of the assessment of dinner interactions, all families consisted of father, mother and the target child. Some families also included a younger sibling or a grandparent. A fieldworker videotaped each family in their homes during dinner times. The fieldworker was present during the video recordings but interacted only minimally with the participants once the videotaping began. The interactions were transcribed verbatim.

In examining the dinner conversations, we focused on specific dimensions of parental communication that can be connected to the concepts of autonomy and relatedness. A coding scheme (see table 1) was developed based on an initial phase of inductive coding as well as on a variety of codes used in previous studies (Blum-Kulka, 1990; Keller, 2007).

The coding scheme comprised the categories 'Directness of control', 'Evaluations', 'Child's compliance', 'Autobiographical structuring', and 'Individual vs. Socio-centeredness' with a number of subcodes assigned to each category (see table 1). The logic of the coding scheme is that parents predominantly following the model of autonomy would use more indirect strategies of control, such as negotiations, decisive utterances and mitigated commands in order not to threaten the child's self-esteem, whereas parents predominantly following the model of relatedness would use more direct control strategies. In a similar vein, parents predominantly following the model of

Category	Code	Description
Directness of control	Unmitigated command	Direct command in an imperative form
	Mitigated command	Direct command using mitigating devices such as politeness markers (e.g. "please") or terms of endearment (e.g. "honey")
	Decisive utterance	Command formulated as decision (e.g. "you can eat this now")
	Negotiation	Negotiating the child's preference or formulating a requirement that the child needs to fulfill first
Evaluations	Praise	Positive appraisal of the child
	Critique	Negative appraisal of the child
Child's compliance	Compliance	Child complies with parent's command
	Non-compliance	Child does not comply with parent's command
Autobiographical structuring	Past events	Talking about past events that occured either earlier in the day or some time in the past
	Future events	Talking about any future events
Individual vs. socio-centeredness	Inner states and experiences	Talking about the child's personal traits, talents, feelings, thoughts, preferences or intentions
	Social rules	Talking about social conventions

Table 1. Coding scheme for dinner conversations in early childhood.

autonomy might praise the child more often and focus more on the child's inner states and experiences, thus focusing on the individuality of the child, whereas parents predominantly following the model of relatedness might criticise the child more often and refer to social rules, thus emphasising proper conduct and heteronomy. Finally, parents predominantly following the model of autonomy might have a stronger tendency to structure the child's experience in a biographical way by referring to past and future events (Demuth, 2008), while parents predominantly following the model of relatedness might focus their talk more on the here and now. The coding scheme was applied to all transcripts of the dinner conversations. Codes were assigned per occurrence and were not mutually exclusive.

A factor analysis revealed the following cluster of discursive strategies[1]:

Factor 1 *Autobiographical structuring* (25.4%) (comprising the codes "past events" and "future events")
Factor 2 *Egalitarian strategy* (21.9%) (comprising the codes "negotiation", "non-compliance", and "praise")
Factor 3 *Hierarchical strategy* (16.9%) (comprising the codes "mitigated command", "critique", and negatively "compliance")

In light of the small number of participants, the results of course need to be considered with care. However, there is no way of going back in time to increase this number. In any case, we think that the analysis of these data remains useful and that the findings carry relevance for the present study.

Biographical-narrative interviews in young adulthood

Twenty-four of the now-adult children could be recontacted and agreed to participate in an interview study on their lives. Participants were visited at home at a time that was convenient for them. After explaining the aim and the procedure of the study, the participants were asked to tell their personal life story from their individual perspective. The interview form was based on a combination of the 'narrative-biographical interview' (Schütze, 1983) and the 'problem-centred interview' (Witzel, 2000). The interview started with the prompt *"I would now like to ask you to tell me the story of your life. Please feel free to simply tell what happened in your life up to this day. You may feel free to take as much time as you like, and to tell as many details as you like. For me everything that you find important is interesting"*. When the end of the story was marked by a coda, a second, semi-structured part of the interview followed based on guidelines. The participants were asked to narrate further details on specific aspects relevant to the study which had not or had only partly been covered by the life stories (e.g. importance of their family, role of friends, colleagues and relatives, importance of self-enhancement and personal career). The interviews lasted between 1-3 hours and were tape recorded and transcribed. The interview data was then analysed based on Grounded Theory methodology (Strauss & Corbin, 1990) and the following typology of developmental pathways constructed from this analysis (see figure 1)

Space does not allow us to present the findings in detail here (the reader is referred to Demuth, Keller, Gudi, & Otto, in prep.). The main features of the three (five) developmental pathways that we were able to identify can be summarised as follows (and see figure 1).

1. Participants who constructed their life stories in a way that emphasises close and stable relationships, and who gave priority to social relationships over their professional career, followed one of the following two patterns:

1a. Their lifestyle can be seen as a *continuation* of the lifestyle of their parents of origin whom the participants experienced as very supportive throughout childhood and adulthood. The parents provide a role model of a satisfactory life embedded in closely-knit social relationships and traditional structures. There is strong cohesion of the local community; family members take responsibility for each other and the younger family members support the older ones. There have been few ruptures in the lives of the participants and hence little need to change things in life. What shines through the life accounts of the participants of this type is a preference for continuity and conformity over risk. We refer to this type of developmental pathway as 'functional relatedness'. As one participant formulates:

> "That really is, I think, what is really important for me. I am so to speak deeply rooted. I cannot imagine at all to – that's why we also built a house here […] – I cannot imagine at all to move away from here, if possible to the town in XY or something like that. No way! Wild horses couldn't drag me there. No way! See, I have the firefighters here, I have built a house here now, I have all my friends here. Well, some of them live in the surroundings but that's OK, well, by and large they all live nearby. Well I would by no means want to leave from here, right." (03:748-752)

1b. Their life style can be seen as in *opposition* to the life style of their parents whom the participants experienced as not supportive throughout childhood and adulthood. Participants in this group also construct their life stories centrally around relationships and report a strong emphasis on relatedness. However, they had not taken over these values from the family of origin; rather the strong orientation towards giving priority to relations over personal interests, especially founding one's own family, was rooted in the reported failure of the family of origin to fulfill their emotional needs in childhood. They experienced their childhood as being 'left on their own', and as 'not getting sufficient attention from their parents'. Other friends, their partner and their own children serve as a substitute family. We refer to this developmental pathway as 'dysfunctional relatedness'. As one participant reports:

> "The ideal family, that is really what, uhm, what I would like to have and what I try now to have at least with my own family, what I maybe did not have in my family with my parents, I mean, to build that now in the family and, uhm, well, I mean, I would say that is really, at the mo-

ment – the children and my husband are what, what is important to me. To have your own time or your own interests and time for you is what so many people say [...] That's not what I miss – to go to the movies or take a bath or something, but to have time with (name of husband), to have time to talk for twenty minutes with him on the sofa or to lie in bed in the evening without having someone else there. And that, THAT is what I miss." (19:142)

2. Participants who constructed their life stories in a way that emphasised both close and stable relationships as well as self-realisation and autonomy, especially in their professional career (see also Rudberg & Nielsen's findings referred to as 'relational individualism', this volume), followed a different pattern: they described their family of origin as a rich source of both emotional and material provision. The family is mostly characterised by stable relationships and strong cohesion; close family relationships were actively fostered. At the same time, the parents actively encouraged autonomy already early in childhood such as free choice and personal responsibility for one's decisions. They also provided a role model of autonomy and relatedness through their own lifestyle. Life trajectories could be handled relatively well because there are other people serving as a 'social buffer'. Participants report that they, to a large extent, identify with the way their parents combined relatedness and autonomy. We refer to this developmental pathway as 'autonomous-relatedness':

> "Well, in my family [...] simply the way people live together in the family, I mean for example, we have certain family traditions which I continue to practise in my marriage. [...] And I think this is indeed something that has had a strong influence on me. For instance, that we always had lunch together, uhm, since my father's office was in the basement and he came up for lunch every day [...] and because my granny still lived with us [...] and that of course makes a great difference, when the grand-

DEVELOPMENT OF SELF IN CULTURE

Family of origin	Ruptures / transitions	Life strategy

The developmental pathway of 'functional relatedness'

Ressource function: family experienced as supportive **Family Values**: social connectedness, local rootedness, cultivation of traditions **Exemplified Lifestyle**: actively fostering close and stable relationships	Largely no ruptures, stableflow of life: transitions (e.g., change of school) **buffered** by continuity of important close relationships	**Identification** with parental values **Priority of family and social relationships** over (professional) self-realisation **Security-orientation, stable social networks**

The developmental pathway of 'dysfunctional relatedness'

Ressource function: family not experienced as supportive **Family Values**: rigid social expectations **Exemplified Lifestyle**: unstable relationships	Ruptures/transitions (e.g., change of school, parents' divorce) without „**social buffer**"	**Opposition** to parental values **Priority of family and social relationships** over (professional) self-realisation **Substitute** for emotional deficits

The developmental pathway of 'autonomous relatedness'

Ressource function: family experienced as supportive **Family Values**: social connectedness, autonomy and self-determination **Exemplified Lifestyle**: actively fostering relationships, professional self-realisation	Ruptures/transitions (e.g., change of school, parents' divorce) **buffered** by supportive close relationships, self-initiated changes in life	**Identification** with parental values compatibility of **family and social relationships** on the one hand, and (professional) **self-actualisation** on the other hand; self-enhancement on the basis of **stable social networks**

The developmental pathway of 'compensatory autonomy'

Ressource function: family only partially experienced as supportive

Family Values: autonomy and self-determination

Exemplified Lifestyle: partly relational conflicts

Ruptures/transitions (e.g., change of school, parents' divorce) lead to conceiving oneself as different from peers, self-initiated changes in life

Striving for autonomy as **compensation**

Priority to (professional) **self-actualisation** over relationships, but increasingly realizing the importance of relationships

The developmental pathway of 'ambivalent automony'

Ressource function: family not experienced as supportive

Family Values: responsibility for parents (inverted roles), autonomy and self-determination

Exemplified Lifestyle: relational conflicts, professional self-realisation

Ruptures/transitions (e.g., change of school, parents' divorce) have largely to be dealt with on ones own, **no social buffer**, self-initiated changes in life

Opposition to parental lifestyle

Ambivalence between striving for autonomy on the one hand and responsibility for the family on the other hand

Figure 1. Typology of developmental pathways derived from interviews with now-adult participants.

mother lives in the house, and the parents are basically always around, and I think that there were certain values that got conveyed through that. And in situations, like when I moved to (name of city), I was in a way unsecure, but somehow on the other hand not so completely, not COMPLETELY lost". (02:75)

3. Participants who constructed their life stories around topics of self-realisation and autonomy did in a way consider relationships as relevant. A clear priority was given, however, to independence. They differed insofar as the *female* participants of this group showed a high ambivalence between wanting to live a very autonomous life on the one hand, and being hindered by feeling a strong responsibility for their family on the other; whereas the *male* participants have lived a very autonomous lifestyle but experience a certain ambivalence in that they have reached a point in life where they realise that relationships might be more important than they had thought previously. The two subgroups can be described as follows:

3a. Participants report that their own needs in childhood and adolescence were not met by their parents/family. What is more, very early in life they had to take over the role of an adult and be responsible for their family. Participants report that autonomy was already encouraged in childhood, e.g., by granting the child room to develop their own interests; they were, however, also strongly forced to become very independent and autonomous from early on due to the specific family situation. In adulthood, they explicitly distance themselves from their parents' lifestyle because they do not want to make the same mistakes themselves. Their strong desire for independence and freedom can be considered a counter-reaction to a co-dependent relationship to their parents. Yet they still feel compelled to take care of and be responsible for their family of origin, which is expressed in an ambivalence between striving for autonomy and being there for the family. We refer to this developmental pathway as 'ambivalent autonomy':

> "I uhm on the one hand very much love to be free, on the other hand, I am also very strongly bound to this region, uhm, also to my mother. This is a very difficult relationship. In a way very good, we often go on vacation together. But there is always this disease [referring to the mother's alcoholism], which is in the back of my mind. Uhum, that is somewhat ambivalent. On the one hand I would love to travel all the time and move to different places, but something is always hindering me." (39:161-165)

3b. Other participants who construct their life stories around topics of self-enhancement and autonomy can be said to have developed a striving for professional achievement which has priority over relationships. The participants emphasise neither the lack of emotional support of the family nor a strong cohesion within the family, although it becomes clear that their needs were not fully met during childhood. Independence and self-reliance were fostered from early on. What the participants of this group have in common is an experience of 'being different' or 'inferior' to peers which led them to strive for excellence. Their strong desire for a professional career which has priority over relationships can hence be considered as compensation for early childhood experiences. We refer to this developmental pathway as 'compensatory autonomy':

> "What kind of values are important to me? Well, professional success in any case, but more because of a striving for security and respect. THAT is important to me." (08:341)

Relating developmental pathways to early family communicative practices

Since we were interested in possible developmental precursors in early socialisation strategies for the self expressed in narrative accounts later on in adulthood, a third step was to relate the findings from the analysis of the dinner conversations to the typology derived from the

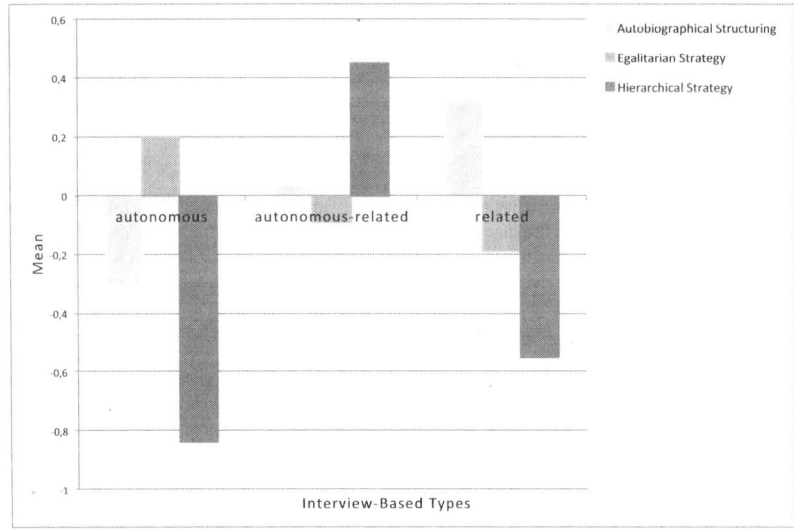

Figure 2. Dinner conversation factor scores across the three groups.

interview analysis. For this purpose, the distribution of factor scores was calculated for the three main types identified in the interviews (see figure 2; subtypes were not considered separately here).

Parental egalitarian strategies during dinner conversations were above average in the later 'autonomous' group of 27/28 years old participants and below average in the later 'related' group. Hierarchical strategies were above average in the later 'autonomous-related' group and below average in the two other groups. Autobiographical structuring was least prominent in the later 'autonomous' group, and most salient in the later 'related' group. This pattern becomes even clearer when we compare only the occurrences of reference to past events (as opposed to the occurrences of either past or future events). Figure 3 shows the distribution of means across the three groups.

While this finding is striking at first glance, when looking at the *content* of what was said we found that most comments referred to 'shared past events'. The focus was hence more on the joint social activity than on the individual experience of the child, which is in line with our argumentation.

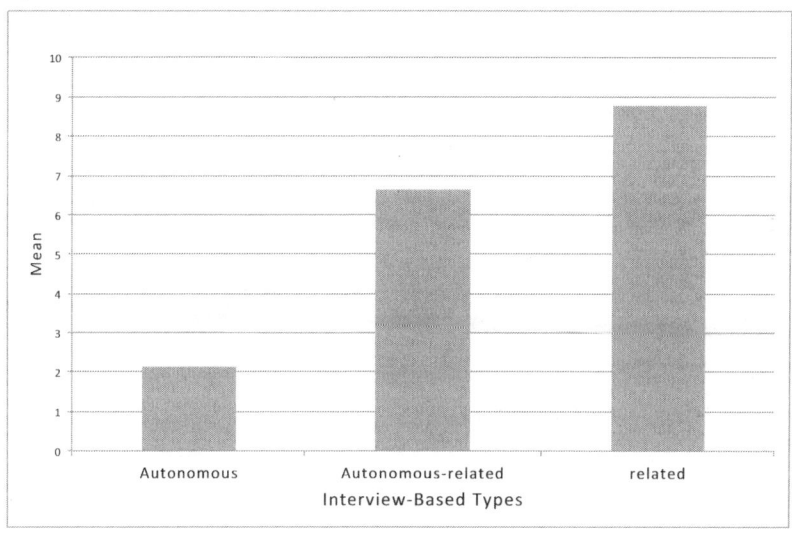

Figure 3. Dinner conversation about past events across the three groups.

Overall, the findings suggest that the children of our study who grew up in family environments which grant a great deal of autonomy to the child, as expressed by social practices such as negotiation of interests, praise, and allowing for non-compliance, were likely to incorporate a cultural model of autonomy in the expression of their later life narratives. Children in our study who grew up in family environments whose discursive practices focused on shared experiences were more likely to construct life narratives that go along with a cultural model of relatedness. Those children of our study whose family interactions were more hierarchically structured, as expressed by commands and critique whereby commands were mitigated by politeness strategies and terms of endearment, were likely to produce life narratives in adulthood characterised by a blending of autonomy and relatedness.

While these findings should of course not be understood in terms of a simple one-to-one relation between specific discursive strategies during dinner conversations and later developmental outcomes, they point to a broader interconnectedness of the cultural orientations of autonomy and relatedness expressed by parents' discursive practices and the later narrative constructions of their children.

This leads us to a more general point that we want to stress here: the present analysis of the dinner interactions was based on content analysis and focused primarily on the parents' talk. In order to do justice more fully to the complexity of social interactions and to gain a deeper understanding of the cultural meaning that is co-constructed in the flow of the interaction, a more fine-grained and sequential microanalysis following conversation analytical procedures would be necessary. Such an analysis could provide us with a better understanding of the value systems that are mediated in parent-child interactions. Nevertheless, the evidence reported above shows clear systematic variations of socialisation strategies that can be related to the different types of developmental pathways derived from the interview analysis.

Conclusion

This chapter has considered the relationship between cultural models reflected in early family dinner interactions and those reflected in biographical narratives of the children of these families later on in young adulthood. It has aimed at identifying developmental precursors of identity formation with regard to the dimensions of autonomy and relatedness. While we were able to find systematic variations in the way the young adults described their way of having become the person they are today, especially with regard to whether the family of origin was experienced as a source of support and to whether and how trajectories and ruptures were experienced, the relationship between early communicative practices within the family and self-constructions in the adult life narratives was less clear. Discursive practices in family interactions certainly point to broader cultural ideologies that go beyond the here and now situation, and the study of these discursive practices provides us with valuable insights into how cultural worlds are constructed in everyday interactions. However, we need to consider the dynamic nature of culture (Valsiner, 2000). Following an open systemic approach, and conceiving of culture as a process of mutual constitution of the person and the social world and a constant process of semiotic mediation, a person is not conceived of as a passive recipient of cultural values but as an active participant who can 'distance' him- or herself from the concrete activity setting through reflecting upon the context of which he or she is a part. He or she does so by considering the context of the past, imagining the context of the future and taking the perspective of other persons (Valsiner, 2000, p. 51). Thus cultural values are analysed and reorganised into personally novel forms before they are internalised. This occurs in the process of adapting to novel circumstances of life, which becomes necessary with the ongoing changes in society and is a lifelong process. The study of early socialisation practices hence allows us to gain valuable insights into a certain part of the lives of the individuals we study that took place at a certain time in history. We need to be careful, however, not to draw premature conclusions about the expected continuation of their developmental pathways. Nevertheless, we hope we have been able to demonstrate that the study of narrative practices is a fruitful avenue for studying the dialogical relationship between culture and the development of self and identity.

Acknowledgements

The dinner conversation study was part of a larger longitudinal study over a period of 9 years from 1977-1986 and was funded by the German Research Foundation (DFG). The interview study was partly funded by the University of Osnabrueck.

Notes

1 Four of the twelve codes showed high cross loadings. These codes were excluded and a new factor analysis computed.

References

Bakan, D. (1966). *The duality of human existence: Isolation and communication in western man.* Chicago: Rand McNally.

Bakhtin, M. M. (1981). *The dialogic imagination: Four essays by M. M. Bakhtin* (translated by C. Emerson & M. Holquist, edited by M. Holquist). Austin: University of Texas Press.

Beck, U., & Beck-Gernsheim, E. (Eds.). (1994). *Riskante Freiheiten. Zur Individualisierung der Lebensformen in der Moderne*. [Hazardous freedom: On the individualization of life forms in modernity]. Frankfurt: Suhrkamp.

Blum-Kulka, S. (1990). You don't touch lettuce with your fingers: Parental politeness in family discourse. *Journal of Pragmatics, 14*, 259-288.

Blum-Kulka, S. (1997). *Dinner talk: Cultural patterns of sociability and socialization in family discourse*. Mahwah, NJ: Erlbaum.

Brockmeier, J., & Carbaugh, D. (Eds.) (2001). *Narrative and identity: Studies in autobiography, self and culture*. Amsterdam: John Benjamins Publishing Company.

Bronfenbrenner, U., & Morris, P. A. (1998). The ecology of developmental processes. In W. Damon (Series Ed.) & R. M. Lerner (Vol. Ed.), *Handbook of child psychology: Vol. 1. Theoretical models of human development* (5th ed. , pp. 993-1028). New York: Wiley.

Bruner, J. (1990). *Acts of meaning*. Cambridge MA: Harvard University Press.

Bruner, J., & Weisser, S. (1991). The invention of self: Autobiography and its forms. In D. R. Olson, & N. Torrance (Eds.), *Literacy and orality* (pp. 129-148). Cambridge: Cambridge University Press.

Budwig, N. (1995). *A developmental-functionalist approach to child language*. Hillsdale, NJ: Erlbaum.

Carr, R. (1986). *Time, narrative and history*. Bloomington: Indiana University Press.

Conway, M. A., Wang, Q., Hanyu, K., & Haque, S. (2005). A cross-cultural investigation of autobiographical memory. *Journal of Cross-Cultural Psychology, 36*, 739-749.

Crossley, M. L. (2000) *Introducing narrative psychology. Self, trauma and the construction of meaning*. Buckingham: Open University Press.

Demuth, C. (2008). *Talking to infants: how culture is instantiated in early mother-infant interactions. The case of Cameroonian farming Nso and North German middle-class families*. Dissertation, University of Osnabrück.

Demuth, C., Abels, M., & Keller, H. (2007). Autobiographical remembering and cultural memory in a socio-historical perspective. In G. Zheng, K. Leung & J. Adair (Eds.), *Perspectives and progress in contemporary cross-cultural psychology* (pp. 319-331). Beijing: China Light Industry Press.

Demuth, C., Keller, H., Gudi, H., & Otto, H. (in prep.). Developmental precursors of autonomy and relatedness over the life span: a reconstruction from autobiographical narratives.

Deutsch, K. H., (2008). *Kinderweltenstudie „Familien im Umbruch"* [Children's world study "Families in transition"]. Retrieved December 2011 from http://www.ip-deutschland.de/ipd/forschung_und_service/forschung/zielgruppen/familien_im_umbruch_.cfm

Fasulo, A., Loyd, H., & Padiglione, V. (2007). Children's socialization into cleaning practices: A cross-cultural perspective. *Discourse & Society, 18*(1), 11-33.

Fatigante, M., Fasulo, A., & Pontecorvo, C. (1998). Life with the alien: Role casting and face-saving techniques in family conversations with young children. *Issues in Applied Linguistics, 9*(2), 97-121.

Forrester, M. A. (2002). Appropriating cultural conceptions of childhood: Participation in conversation. *Childhood: A Global Journal of Child Research, 9,* 255-276.

Giddens, A. (1990). *The consequences of modernity.* Cambridge: Polity Press.

Habermas, T. (2007). How to tell a life: The development of the cultural concept of biography. *Journal of Cognition and Development, 8,* 1-31.

Junefelt, K., & Tulviste, T. (1997). Regulation and praise in American, Estonian, and Swedish mother-child interaction. *Mind, Culture, and Activity: An International Journal,* 4(1), 24-33.

Junefelt, K., & Tulviste, T. (1998). American, Estonian and Swedish mothers' regulation of their children's discourse construction. In M. de Lyra & J. Valsiner (Eds.), *Construction of psychological processes in interpersonal communication: Vol. 4. Child development within culturally structured environments* (pp. 137–154). Stamford, CT: Ablex.

Kagitçibasi, Ç. (2005). Autonomy and relatedness in cultural context: Implications for self and family. *Journal of Cross-Cultural Psychology, 36,* 403-422.

Keller, H. (2007). *Cultures of infancy.* Mahwah, NJ: Erlbaum.

Keller, H., Demuth, C., & Yovsi, R. D. (2008). The multi-voicedness of independence and interdependence: the case of Cameroonian Nso. *Culture & Psychology, 14,* 115-144.

Larson, R. W., Branscomb, K. R., & Wiley, A. R. (2006). Forms and functions of family mealtimes: multidisciplinary perspectives. *New Directions for Child and Adolescent Development, 111,* 1-15.

Martini, M. (1996). "What's new?" at the dinner table: Family dynamics during mealtimes in two cultural groups in Hawaii. *Early Development and Parenting, 5,* 23-34.

McAdams, D. P. (2008). Personal narratives and the life story. In L. A. Pervin (Ed.), *Handbook of personality psychology: Theory and research* (3rd ed., pp. 242–262). NY: Guilford Press.

McAdams, D.P., Hoffman, B. J., Mansfield, E. D., & Day, R. (1996). Themes of agency and communion in significant autobiographical scenes. *Journal of Personality, 64,* 339-377.

Mead, G. H. (1934). *Mind, self, and society: From the perspective of a social behaviorist.* Chicago: University of Chicago Press.

Miller, P. J., Fung, H., & Koven, M. (2007). Narrative reverberations. How participation in narrative practices co-creates persons and cultures. In S. Kitayama & D. Cohen (Eds.), *Handbook of Cultural Psychology* (pp. 595-614). New York: Guilford Press.

Miller, P. J., Sandel, T. L., Liang, C.-H., & Fung, H. (2001). Narrating transgressions in Longwood: the discourses, meanings, and paradoxes of an American socializing practice. *Ethos, 29,* 159-186.

Mishler, E. (2006). Narrative and identity: The double arrow of time. In A. De Fina, D. Schiffrin & M. Bamberg (Eds.), *Discourse and identity* (pp. 30-47). Cambridge: Cambridge University Press.

Ochs, E., & Capps, L. (2001). *Living narrative: Creating lives in everyday storytelling.* Cambridge, MA: Harvard University Press.

Ochs, E., Pontecorvo, C., & Fasulo, A. (1996). Socializing taste. *Ethnos, 60*(3), 7-46.

Ochs, E., & Shohet, M. (2006). The cultural structuring of mealtime socialization. *New Directions for Child and Adolescent Development, 111,* 35-49.

Ochs, E., & Taylor, C. (1995). "Father knows best" dynamic in dinnertime narratives. In K. Hall and M. Bucholtz (Eds.), *Gender articulated: Language and the socially constructed self* (pp. 97-120). New York: Routledge.

Pontecorvo, C., Fasulo, A., & Sterponi, L. (2001). Mutual apprentices: The making of parenthood and childhood in family dinner conversations. *Human Development, 44,* 340-361.

Quigley, J. (2001). *The grammar of autobiography: A developmental account.* Mahwah, NJ: Lawrence Erlbaum Associates.

Raeff, C. (2006). *Always separate, always connected: Independence and interdependence in cultural contexts of development.* Mahwah, NJ: Lawrence Erlbaum.

Sarbin, T. R. (1986). *Narrative psychology: The storied nature of human conduct.* Westport, CT: Praeger Publishers/Greenwood Publishing Group.

Schieffelin, B. B., & Ochs, E. (1998). A cultural perspective on the transition from prelinguistic to linguistic communication. In M. Woodhead, D. Faulkner & K. Littleton (Eds.), *Cultural worlds of early childhood* (pp. 48-63). Oxford: Routledge.

Schröder, L., Keller, H., Kärtner, J., Kleis, A., Abels, M., Yovsi, R. D., Chaudhary, N., Jensen, H., & Papaligoura, Z. (in press). Early reminiscing in cultural context: Cultural models, maternal reminiscing styles, and children's memories. *Journal of Cognition and Development.*

Schütze, F. (1983). Biographieforschung und narratives Interview [Research on biographies and narrative interview]. *Neue Praxis: Zeitschrift für Sozialarbeit, Sozialpäda-*

gogik und Sozialpolitik [New praxis: journal for social work, social pedagogy, and social politics], 3, 283-293.

Sirota, K. G. (2006). Habits of the heart: Children's bedtime routines as relational work. *Text & Talk, 26,* 493-514.

Slunecko, T., & Hengl, S. (2007). Language, cognition, subjectivity: A dynamic constitution. In J. Valsiner & A. Rosa (Eds.), *The Cambridge handbook of sociocultural psychology.* (pp. 40-61). New York, NY, US: Cambridge University Press.

Straub, J., Zielke, B., & Werbik, H. (2005). Autonomy, narrative identity and their critics: A reply to some provocations of postmodern accounts in psychology. In W. Greve, C. Rothermund, & D. Wentura (Eds.), *The adaptive self, personal continuity and intentional self-development* (pp. 323–350). Cambridge, MA: Hogrefe & Huber.

Strauss, A. L., & Corbin, J. (1990). *Basics of qualitative research: Grounded theory procedures and techniques.* London: Sage.

Taylor, C. (1989). *Sources of the self: The making of the modern identity.* Cambridge, MA: Harvard University Press.

Tulviste, T. (2004). Socio-cultural variation in mothers' control over children's behavior. *Ethos, 32,* 34-50.

Valsiner, J. (2000). *Culture and human development: An introduction.* London: Sage.

Wang, Q. (2001). Culture effects on adults' earliest childhood recollection and self-description: Implications for the relation between memory and the self. *Journal of Personality and Social Psychology, 81,* 220-233.

Wang, Q., & Spillane, E. L. (2003). Developing autobiographical memory in the cultural contexts of parent-child reminiscing. In S. P. Shohov (Ed.), *Topics in cognitive psychology* (pp. 101-116). New York: Nova Science Publishers.

Wang, Y., Wiley, A. R., & Chiu, C. Y. (2008). Independence-supportive praise versus interdependence promoting praise in Chinese immigrant parent-toddler dinner interactions. *International Journal of Behavioral Development, 32,* 13-20.

Witzel, A. (2000). The problem-centered interview [27 paragraphs]. *Forum Qualitative Sozialforschung / Forum: Qualitative Social Research.* Retrieved April 2008 from http://www.qualitative-research.net/fqs-texte/1-00/1-00witzel-e.htm, .

Mogens Jensen

Development of self in an institutional context

6

This chapter sketches a frame for understanding core aspects of the pedagogical treatment undertaken in residential care, where the aim is changes in the personalities or selves of the children and adolescents placed there. This frame is inspired by socio-cultural theory (Wertsch, 1998), cultural psychology (Cole, 1996) and theories on situated learning (Lave, 1988; Tanggaard, 2004). A focal element is the formation of a so-called 'social-pedagogical fellowship' between the adolescent and the social worker; a fellowship that demands a common understanding of the problems at hand. I discuss different perspectives on these problems in order to develop more specific concepts for improving the pedagogical treatment. Both the adolescent and the social worker have to act in forming situations and in doing so they manoeuvre between different understandings and interests. This aspect is analysed using the concept of 'knowledge-forms' (Barth, 2002), thereby illustrating some levels in pedagogical treatment, and possible ways out of some dilemmas. Finally I consider the relation of this to the continuing processes in both the pedagogical treatment and the lives of the adolescents in residential care.

The chapter rests on my PhD study (Jensen, 2010), which investigated psychological processes in the pedagogical treatment of adolescents in residential care. The institution from which the examples are taken is situated in Denmark and houses eight adolescents with behavioural and personal problems which cannot be taken care of within their own families. This includes criminal acts, severe behavioural problems in school and at home, violent relations within their family etc. The institution is staffed by 14 social workers with at least one always in attendance, and more in afternoons and evenings. One or two of the social workers at the home are designated as 'primary social workers' for each adolescent; these are also in charge of contact with parents, writing annual reports to the municipality etc. During the daytime the adolescents go to a school, which is run by the institution but situated in another part of town, and when they grow older internship, education and work is organised.

In the theoretical traditions of socio-cultural theory (Wertsch, 1998), cultural psychology (Cole, 1996) and situated learning (Lave, 1988; Tanggaard, 2004), development is seen as inevitably connected to context. These traditions stress the importance of context in the development of the individual and the self. For this reason I focus on the interaction between the context and the actions of the individual, embarking upon what is called a discussion of agency. As neither of these two aspects in themselves can be seen as the determining aspect, for practical and pedagogical purposes it is interesting to understand this interaction in order to be able to intervene in the development of the individual.

Sometimes development under special conditions – that is, in a non-normal context or influenced by dysfunctions such as infantile autism – will make certain aspects of development more evident and thereby enhance our understanding of development in general. On the other hand, a general theory of development ought also to be able to support professionals working with children and adolescents, though not necessarily by prescribing the actions that professionals should take. This is a tricky question in itself, as discussed by Jensen (2010). In this chapter I will develop some concepts that could be useful for understanding aspects of the pedagogical treatment and thus for improving it.

Adolescents placed in residential care for a few years or more develop in a special context. The reason for the placement is often either that the adolescent's family has been assessed as an inappropriate context for development, or that the adolescent has been assessed as dysfunctional from a social point of view. An adolescent placed in residential care is often split between their loyalty to the parents and their loyalty to the social workers, and in opposition to 'the system', which removed him from home. As a result the cooperation between adolescent and adults, which is more or less established automatically in a biological family, needs some conscious effort to develop in a positive form within the context of residential care. This demonstrates some of the dynamic processes involved in forming these personal bonds.

The pedagogical task in residential care

The following characterisation of the pedagogical treatment of adolescents in residential care follows a so-called social-pedagogical tradition tracing its roots back to hermeneutic philosophy in the 19th century and to names such as Dilthey and Natorp (Mathiesen, 1999). Within this tradition, humans are seen as profoundly social, and it makes no sense to consider them outside their social context. This perspective is also applied to pedagogical treatment, and the social worker and the adolescent are regarded as forming a so called fellowship (Rothuizen, 2001), which I call the *social-pedagogical fellowship*. This fellowship has a common project, which is the life and development of the adolescent, and the two should contribute to the fellowship and the common goal: a good life in accordance with the wishes of the adolescent balanced with the expectations of society. This of course includes the development of the adolescent's self construal and in relation to competencies as well as desires and values. The social worker and the adolescent are not equal partners and have different competencies. The social worker has a greater understanding of the future demands that will be placed on the adolescent, and also a greater understanding of personal development. As a practical competency, the social worker is good at making social interactions and fellowships with others function even if the other participants in these interactions are less competent in doing so. On the other hand, the adolescent has a detailed knowledge of his own history, his way of coping with life in the past and his interests and wishes for the future. As humans are social by nature, the adolescent will engage in social relations with others, but in accordance with their own experience of social relations and therefore in what they judge to be the best way to achieve personal goals in the present situation. As to which competencies to develop, the adolescent in fact has a power of veto as the developmental processes are sensitive to the adolescent's acceptance. If the social worker and the adolescent agree on developments, the process will be easier than if the adolescent opposes, as will be illustrated later.

This social-pedagogical fellowship has to be established and maintained by the joint contributions of both its participants. Hundeide (2004) uses the concept of 'contract' to capture the content of a relation between two persons. Where 'relation' in psychology is often associated with emotions and positive values, a contract can equally be a relation in which both participants agree on not liking each other and fighting every time they meet. Hundeide sees these contracts as dynamical in the sense of being negotiated in every interaction, resulting in adjustment and/or confirmation of the contract. Applying this approach to the social-pedagogical fellowship, each situation is seen as maintaining or reconstituting the fellowship, and a central concern of the pedagogical work is to adjust the fellowship in a way which seems attractive to the adolescent. Pedagogical work also includes more traditional aspects of upbringing or socialising – in fact, the reason for placing the adolescent in residential care is often that the adolescent has been assessed as not acting in accordance with acceptable norms of society or as pursuing interests which are seen as unsuitable for his further development. Therefore the action of the social worker in each situation has to balance considerations of the maintenance of the fellowship and the upbringing of the adolescent. The fellowship unifies interests, which can be contradictory and which potentially can destroy the fellowship, but which also provide a dynamic to the development. One could say that the challenge of the social worker is to change his participation in this fellowship in a way that establishes dynamic development while at the same time maintaining the fellowship.

A defining aspect of social-pedagogical treatment is that it takes place in the same context in which its outcome will be relevant, whereas many types of teaching and treatment take place in contexts separate from the context where the achieved competencies could be used (the problem of transfer; cf. Macaulay, 2000; Tennant, 1999). Here the social worker and the adolescent are jointly engaged in handling the life of the adolescent as it is taking place, each of them contributing with his special competencies. The challenge to the social worker is to handle each situation in a way that provides the adolescent with the best opportunities to develop those competencies and aspects of self that are most important for the rest of his life – whatever that might bring.

This is relevant to many aspects of self-development, but in this chapter I will focus on two of these: (a) The focus and priority of the adolescent concerning developmental goals, and (b) The choices the adolescent faces when forming contracts with others and how the context, seen as different groups or subcultures with distinct demands, influences these choices.

Priorities when choosing goals for development

When a fellowship between a adolescent and a social worker is established and maintained, their different competencies (as described above) can result in them having different priorities at given moments.

Case example of different perspectives: As part of my PhD research I spent 5 days at a residential care home for adolescents. During my visit I carried out interviews with a young 15 year old girl named Maria. She had been at the home for six months, and was 'shadowed' for one day a week. I concluded each visit with an interview in the afternoon. Maria was a lively girl who openly commented on everything and everybody at the place. Both she and her mother were quick-tempered, and Maria was highly impulsive in her actions. She was opinionated about her surroundings and often a little unbalanced. She was enthusiastic in school and ambitious to pass her exams, and she was popular among the other adolescent residents.

On the first two visits, Maria discussed her boyfriend, who lived outside the home, but the relation appeared rather loose.

On the fourth visit, Maria said that the social workers were due to discuss the topic of 'sweethearts' during their weekly meeting that day. Maria wanted to be sweethearts with a boy also resident at the home, but the social workers opposed it. Their experience was that such relationships were short-lived, and created great problems when they ended as the rejected partner could get very angry – on one such occasion, a boy hit a girl, causing her to lose a couple of teeth. Unfortunately the social workers did not reach that point on their agenda, and indeed could not even promise to reach it at the following week's meeting.

The following week I observed a regular meeting between Maria and her two primary social workers. Most of the meeting was given over to the relation between Maria and her mother, as they tended to quarrel when Maria was at home at weekends. On the preceding weekend, a quarrel began only half an hour after Maria arrived home, so she left and stayed with her friends for the rest of the weekend including overnight. The social workers emphasised the necessity of finding a way of cooperation between Maria and her mother, but this seemed of no interest to Maria. Although Maria listened to the social workers, it appeared unlikely that the conversation would have any influence on the relationship between her and her mother.

After the meeting Maria complained to me, that the social workers had still not come to any decision about 'sweethearts', and she intended to wait no longer - she and the boy would be sweethearts anyway.

Many other events happened during the course of observation, but the above report is summarised for the purpose of the following analysis.

When I consider the above observations from the perspective of social-pedagogical treatment it leads me to focus on the fellowship between Maria and her primary social workers. Maria is asking for permission from the social workers before relating to a boyfriend. It is quite evident from other observations, that when it is her mother that does not allow her to do things, she is more likely to do them in order to provoke her mother, but apparently she wants to cooperate with the social workers. During the meeting with her primary social workers she remains in attendance and continues to participate, albeit to the minimal extent possible without being seen as obstructing. This shows that she is actively engaged in maintaining the social-pedagogical fellowship with the social workers.

Unfortunately the social workers failed to prioritise the discussion of 'sweethearts', which was very important for Maria. Instead they focused on the relation between Maria and her mother, which at that time was not important for Maria. Only half a year ago she moved from her home to residential care and the conflicts with her mother were apparently still too fresh in her mind.

My model of perspectives (figure 1) is based on these perspectives.

Perspectives		The adolescent's	
		In focus	Out of focus
The social worker's	In focus	Common perspective	Professional perspective
	Out of focus	Adolescent' perspective	External perspective

Figure 1. Model of perspectives.

The *common perspective* comprises the topics which social workers and the adolescent share, or to put it in other words, it is the common project of the fellowship. Here the pedagogical work has the best prospects as it will not meet opposition from any of the partners of the fellowship. In Maria's case, a good example of this is her enthusiastic work at school in order to pass her exam.

The *adolescent's perspective* comprises the topics which Maria considers a high priority and the social workers do not - clearly the 'sweetheart-problem' is an example in this case. Maybe the social workers are right in their judgement of the endurance of the relation - nevertheless the negotiations forming the social-pedagogical fellowship includes the topic and to Maria it is important. Following Hundeide (2002, 2004) and his concept of contract as the negotiation of the common project of the fellowship, Maria will experience the lack of discussion of the possibility of a boyfriend as a signal that the fellowship cannot include her interests in this case. This could weaken the fellowship, because why should she involve herself in a fellowship that fails to take her interests into account? Given the costs inherent in ignoring Maria's interests, it could be important for the social workers to consider whether this issue is sufficiently important to them to justify the tax on Maria's goodwill, a goodwill that Maria's actions show exists.

The *professional perspective* should include some of the considerations which the social workers have due to their enhanced experience and knowledge about the future conditions of the life of the adolescent. Here the relation between Maria and her mother is a good example: sooner or later it will be beneficial for her to develop a way of handling or at least understanding this relation. However, these future benefits do not necessarily justify the decision to work on this issue at present. If social workers insist upon pedagogical treatment on topics which reside only in the professional perspective, they should at least aware that it may tax heavily on the goodwill established in the fellowship, and consequently they must balance the importance of the topic with the need to maintain the fellowship. On the other hand, social workers should of course have a professional perspective, and part of their work should be to move topics from the professional perspective to the common perspective. Nevertheless, it may sometimes be better to wait until a topic is part of the common perspective before working on it.

The *external perspective* is a kind of blind spot for both parties. It is called external because it typically involves topics which external observers discover more easily. In the following second case I present an example of such a topic.

The model of perspectives could be seen as a extension of Vygotsky's (1978) concept of the Zone of Proximal Development (ZPD), where the professional perspective is outside the ZPD and the common perspective is inside, the last two perspectives being extensions of the ZPD.

The hermeneutical tradition discusses the 'horizons of understanding' of individuals, with each participant perceiving a phenomenon or a situation within his own horizon of understanding. A mutual understanding demands a rapprochement and ultimately a merging of these horizons. To put it in another way, an understanding between Maria and her social workers can only be achieved when they approach a common perspective, and in this case the social workers will presumably be more competent to approach Maria's perspective than vice versa.

The most effective work in social-pedagogical treatment depends on balancing the different perspectives on the development of the adolescents while maintaining the social-pedagogical fellowship. This implies the necessity of what Hundeide (2004) calls a comprehending-interpreting approach, where it is vitally important to engage with the adolescent by acknowledging his perspective. This is demonstrated clearly with reference to the question of sweethearts, which is a topic of great motivation, versus the question of the relation between Maria and her mother. The alternative approach, according to Hundeide, is a normative-evaluating approach which focuses on comparing the behaviour and competencies of the adolescent with the norms for adolescents in general. Here there is a great risk of establishing an opposition between an adolescent and the social workers instead of the fellowship within which they could cooperate on the common project. A comparison could also confirm the self-perception of the adolescent as a person not good enough focusing on shortcomings. The comparison with norms is of little value in the planning and execution of pedagogical treatment, because of the diversity of constitutions of the adolescent (Fischer et al., 1997; Sroufe, 1997) – including personal and behavioural problems – which must be taken into account in striving for optimal development. A normative-evaluative approach could, however, be of value as support for the social workers when they elaborate their professional perspective.

When you see the adolescent as an active agent in his own life, rather than as an object for treatment, this demands that the adolescent's goals, motivations and ways of perceiving and understanding are taken into account.

Systems of meaning among which to manoeuvre

A person's self is not an established entity but a phenomenon which has to be constantly maintained. In another connection Neisser (1976) describes a perceptual circle, where concepts are used in perceiving the world, but in every instance the concept is also adjusted using the present experience. Similarly, the self is maintained by acting in the present context, drawing on experiences, interpreting the situation, judging one's own interests and navigating between possibilities, and the situation again leads to an adjustment of the self. This adjustment will partly be based on the reactions of other persons in the situation, and the interpretation of their reactions and way of acting towards the person.

Here the adjustment of self is seen as a dynamic process just like 'contracts' mentioned above. It could be argued that there is no stable self or there are several selves depending on contexts, but I prefer to refer to a 'dynamic' concept of the self. The sense of stability of a self is obtained by inertia in the continuing adjustments of the self. The older individuals get and the more contexts of different kinds they have experienced, the smaller the adjustments will get, because numerous experiences are included in the self-conception, and one single new experience is rarely enough to counterbalance these and change the self-conception.

As humans are socially oriented, relations to other people are important in the navigation through a specific situation. They will act to take care of their interests, which among other things includes that they keep or enhance their social position in groups. As social groups include values, meanings and norms of behaviour, they will act in accordance with the values, meanings and norms of the groups they want to be part of or in which they want to enhance their social position. Different groups differ in their values, meanings and norms, and a person has to manoeuvre in situations in which the motivations of different groups diverge.

Stokholm (2006a) has done anthropological fieldwork at two institutions for children in residential care. She uses the concept of knowledge-forms from Barth (2002), where knowledge-forms are characterised by three aspects:

1 "a corpus of substantive assertions and ideas about aspects of the world"
2 "it must be instantiated and communicated .... in the form of words, concrete symbols, pointing gestures, actions"
3 "it will be distributed, communicated, employed and transmitted within a series of instituted social relations" (ibid., p. 3)

An analysis based on this concept includes the possibility of several knowledge-forms influencing the life of an individual and setting up dilemmas when different knowledge-forms conflict in a single setting.

To Barth, 'knowledge-forms' are less encompassing than the concept of 'culture', because culture includes the actual reflections and actions performed by individuals (ibid., p.1). Culture sometimes also has a more structuralistic association, where it defines roles, values, actions etc. and more or less determines the individuals. Knowledge-forms are meant to focus on "a corpus of substantive assertions and ideas" which are "instantiated and communicated" in different forms (ibid., p. 3), but they leave the individual with the task of deciding how to act in the present situation - whether to live up to certain ideas or how to handle particular assertions within this specific context. Knowledge-forms represent Barth's attempt to handle the classical discussion of structure versus agency.

As we grow up, we learn about the knowledge-forms we meet. They guide us not only in acting but also in perceiving and understanding the context we live in - what is seen as important and valued and what is not (see also chapter 3 and 4 of this volume). We cannot perceive without the influence of these forms, but they do not determine our life. They are used for constructing potential interpretations of the situation, and the individual then has to choose how to act in relation to the present situation. Different knowledge-forms can lead to contradicting interpretations, and we can deliberately search for new interpretations, so we are not determined by them. Each time we apply a knowledge-form it might be rejected, adjusted or confirmed according to the present situation. The more experience we achieve using different knowledge-forms, the more instances of confirmation we accumulate, and the more convincing the evidence would have to be in order to compel us to drop certain knowledge-forms. This accounts for the relative stability of adult ways of understanding compared to children.

Barth (2002, p. 3) stresses that knowledge-forms are "instantiated or communicated" in some media and it is only then that we can study them, but this can be in form of "words, concrete symbols, pointing gestures, actions". This still leaves us with the task of interpreting the observations, and here he stresses the values of focusing on the processes by which the knowledge-form is developed. An important point in the concept of knowledge-forms is the focus on the way they are passed on to new participants and the changes they undertake in time. It adds a dynamic aspect in which knowledge-forms are considered more procedural rather than being seen as entities – or could be considered dynamic structures which are constantly reconstituted by people acting in their everyday lives.

In her study of children in residential care Stokholm (2005, 2006a) describes a knowledge-form called 'change and re-socialisation', which is connected to the social workers and the task they are performing. The children are aware that they need support from the social workers to learn how to behave in a more appropriate way and that this is the reason they are there, so they want to cooperate – or to use the concepts from above, they want to form a social-pedagogical fellowship. This knowledge-form describes roles for both children and social workers, where social workers are the ones who determine what the children have to learn in order to leave the institution, and they have the 'power of definition' (Bae, 1996) for positive/negative behaviour, values etc. The children are by definition the ones who are dysfunctional.

Here I argue that the transmission of the knowledge-form will be most obvious when new children arrive at the home and the social workers help them to settle down, but it could also be exposed clearly when new social workers are introduced to the ways of working at the institution. It might in part be verbalised in the pedagogical program for the home, although there might be differences between the official pedagogical attitude and the reality (see for example Højlund, 2006), where the relevant concept of knowledge-form is based in the reality.

Stokholm (2006a) in addition describes another knowledge-form called 'children's relations', which is connected to the endeavours undertaken by the children at the institutions in relation to the other children. As social workers are only at the place during their working hours, the other children constitute a more stable social group to relate to, and it is of great importance to all the children to establish a place relatively high in this hierarchy. Stokholm describes different actions used by the children in order to advance in the social hierarchy: they can become close friends with children higher in the hierarchy, they can provoke the social workers (but not too much or in a 'wrong' way), they can share their candy (but not too much, because it will be seen as trying to buy friends) etc. Other actions have a negative influence on their social position: sneaking to social workers, not keeping secrets, failing to share candy, etc. This knowledge-form is transmitted to new children who arrive by interactions within the group of children, but it also changes depending on the attitude of the children at the top of the hierarchy (ibid., p. 168).

Each of these knowledge-forms includes values, possibilities of acting, social hierarchies etc., and leaves room for each child to find his or her own way of coping with residence at the institution. Sometimes, however, these knowledge-forms may conflict with one another. Stokholm (2005, p. 9) gives an example where children start an alarm at the home by entering the kitchen in the evening, when they are not allowed to go there. The social workers interrogate other children in order to find out who did it. Here the children are clearly placed in a dilemma between the two described knowledge-forms: 'change and resocialisation' which obliges them to help clear up matters where rules are violated, and 'children's relations' which forbids them to sneak.

The dynamics of knowledge-forms in development

The concept of knowledge forms can also be used to interpret challenges of subcultural norms.

Case example af social subculture: A young man of 17 has been living in a residential home for 2 years. He was admitted because of a series of crimes such as shoplifting and burglary. He is very interested in sports, and has been a valued member of the local soccer club team. He is very competitive in many aspects of his everyday life and is eager to win at almost any cost. This has been a recurring subject of discussion between him and the social workers at the place, as they see him as lacking social competencies and showing too little empathy.

He is now going to choose an education, and his own suggestion is a career as a computer salesman, because he wants to earn a lot of money in a short time and have a smart car in order to impress the girls - which he is very good at already. The social workers see this as an example of his immature development.

He gets a short education in commerce and leaves the home. He starts work as a salesman, where he does very well.

Four years later he revisits the home. He has now stopped work as a salesman and started training as a social worker, because he wishes to work with adolescents as they do at the home. The social workers find him more mature than when he left four years earlier.

Three years later he graduates, but he only gets short periods of work at adolescents' residential care homes. He regularly receives feedback that he is too rigid and rule-focused and does not show the necessary flexibility for the job. He wants to work at the home at which he once lived, and keeps applying for the positions advertised there. They appoint him for half a year, but reach the same conclusion as other places, still finding him too competitive for the job. When he is working with the adolescents at the place, the other social workers see him as caring and accepting in a deliberately overt way. It seems as though he cannot perform this role in an 'authentic and relaxed' way - rather he is eager to be a 'good social worker' in his usual competitive way.

If we apply the concept of knowledge-forms mentioned above, it is part of the 'change and re-socialisation' knowledge-form that the adolescents will change their norms of interaction and adopt at least partially the norms of the social workers. Often adolescents placed in residential care experience this social context as very accepting and caring compared to their previous experience. Because the social workers are very good at making their interactions and the social-pedagogical fellowship function even when the adolescents are not capable of taking their part, the adolescents experience more satisfactory interactions than they would otherwise. This can lead to them adopting the social norms and attitudes of the pedagogical milieu and seeing this as the ideal of their own life, thereby fulfilling the aim of the placement and acting in accordance with the 'change and re-socialisation' knowledge-form. However, one aspect of this knowledge-form emphasises caring for others who function less well, even when this involves subjugating the individual's own interests. This can conflict with subcultures and professions in society which are more competitive - salesmen being one potential example.

Another knowledge-form could be 'competition', where you are supposed to do the best you can in order to win. This applies more naturally to the role of salesman. In this form, you respect the others as equal participants who are able to take care of their own interests, and indeed treating them differently is seen as devaluing them in a patronising manner. Not doing your best will ruin the game. When a game is running you compete and are allowed to use tricks within the rules, but when the game is over, you remain friends irrespective of the result. You might even have the right to be proud of winning and to exult about it.

The young man in the example could be seen as split between these two sets of norms: the competitive attitude towards interaction and the pedagogical attitude with its emphasis on caring for the weaker party. Adopting the norms of the pedagogical milieu could thus hinder the adolescent in finding a place and profession in society, if he retains the 'competition' knowledge-form, and is uncertain when to apply which knowledge-forms.

Barth stresses the importance of knowledge-forms concerning agency, which leave room for the agent to perceive and interpret, choose and act in a situation instead of determining these actions. To apply this approach we have to insist on the dynamic quality of knowledge-forms - they are maintained by individual agents acting in ways which reject, adjust or confirm them, but as several agents may be acting in a context and all applying to the same knowledge-form in their own way; one agent alone cannot decide to change it. Nevertheless, the agent has the opportunity to act in different ways. Knowledge-forms guide the perception of situations, prioritising interests and the choice of action, but they do not determine that choice.

The kitchen-alarm example of Stokholm (2005, op. cit.) concerns an episode in which the children are placed in an acute dilemma and in opposition to the social workers. Following the characterisation of pedagogical treatment earlier, I would say that the task of the social workers is twofold: the children should accept common norms and act to maintain them, but at the same time they should learn to handle dilemmas such as the one mentioned, because their future life will involve such dilemmas. It is not a question of ranking norms or even knowledge-forms in a hierarchy, but rather to learn how to handle the problem of conflicting knowledge-forms.

In the last example, the knowledge-forms guiding pedagogical treatment are so entrenched in the thinking of the pedagogical milieu that they might result in the adolescent being guided in a direction that makes his life more complicated than it otherwise might have been. The 'change and re-socialisation' knowledge-form specifies norms which are well suited to pedagogical treatment, but might be disadvantageous in other professions. Here a clear-cut 'competition' knowledge-form might be better for doing a good job. If however you want to work as a social worker, and you have a strong tendency to compete as your default knowledge-form, you will end up acting in a very controlled way, which is in conflict with the pedagogical work. The young man in the case is split between two ways of conducting his life, which can make him less suited to both environments.

Of course, being very competitive is not a permanent characteristic of a person, but as mentioned earlier personal characteristics can be hard to change if they have been maintained for a long time, and knowledge-forms such as 'competition' might yield experiences and satisfaction that an individual is reluctant to renounce. Sometimes it might be better to find a context where these default knowledge-forms are suited – particularly if the individual is not adept at judging between and choosing among possible knowledge-forms depending on the situation.

The dilemmas include a double-bind situation (Bateson, 1972) with contradictions, which can only be resolved by a meta-cognitive reflection resulting in the development of new understandings capable of containing the contradiction of the dilemma in a new synthesis. In the first example the social workers might observe the dilemma of the children, but at the same time believe they must obey the rules. However, if they appreciate the challenge of helping the children handling dilemmas, other options are available to them, such as openly raising the conflict between adherence to the rules and keeping secrets. In the second example, the social workers are helping the young man in the first place, but also unintentionally hindering his long-term prospects by showing an unwillingness to accept the 'competition' knowledge-form.

My model of perspectives includes an external perspective. Knowledge-forms such as 'change and re-socialisation' can be so widely held and so firmly defined in pedagogical work that neither social workers nor adolescents can contemplate any other possibility. In the same way, the norms suited for pedagogical treatment can be perceived as universal norms, with potentially deleterious consequences for the adolescents' future lives. The knowledge-form can impede the development of new and different ways of acting, and thus can be a blind spot for the participants in the social-pedagogical fellowship. In this case, the involvement of a third party, perhaps a supervisor or a new member of staff, is necessary if changes are to take place.

Situations as parts of processes

The analysis of residential care using the concept of knowledge-forms considers a single act in a broader context and as part of an ongoing process. It is not merely a question of weighting, for instance, sneaking against following the social workers' norms. It is an act where the adolescents have to manoeuvre in each their life guided by 'corpuses of assertions and ideas' as best they can. In the second example, it is not just a question of the young man not being re-socialised thoroughly enough. It is a question of knowledge-forms that fit in different places. To do effective work, social workers have to be aware of their own (maybe tacit) norms and knowledge-forms in order to see beyond them, if this gives the best opportunities for the adolescent to develop a self without invalidating contradictions. Knowledge-forms suited for pedagogical treatment do not necessarily fit all other contexts. This is a common aspect of development and not particular to residential care.

This analysis tends to regard the knowledge-forms as structures of the situation that set the frames for the agents, but we need also to draw the history of the adolescent into the foreground. Obtaining an understanding of why any adolescent perceives, interprets and acts as they do in a context is facilitated by an understanding of their specific past history. This history should be seen as a history of trying to cope with life given the contexts and knowledge-forms available: that is, within what Hundeide (2004) calls the comprehending-understanding approach.

Returning to the kitchen-alarm example discussed earlier, this episode occurs for each child as part of their participation in several contexts. Each child both carries experiences and consequences from previous contexts to the next, which is the focus of situated learning theories (Nielsen 2008). Likewise the young man discussed earlier has had experiences of success by using the 'competition' knowledge-form in sports, perhaps in his earlier criminal activities, and as a salesman.

While so-called 'scholastic' theories of learning focus on competencies that can be individuated, learned in one context and presumably transferred for use in other contexts, situated learning approaches empirically demonstrate that people sometimes exhibit competencies in one context that they cannot use in another (Dreier, 2003; Lave, 1988; Tanggaard, 2006). If we want to establish an understanding of the way adolescents act in connection with different knowledge-forms, we will have to follow their so-called *personal trajectories* (Nielsen, 2008). The social workers plan for *institutional trajectories*, but each adolescent acts in their life in order to reach the goals they pursue, and through different contexts each forms their own personal trajectory. A similar consideration is represented in developmental theory, where the concept of *developmental pathways* (e.g., Fischer et al., 1997; Hundeide, 2004) articulates the idea that development is more appropriately construed as proceeding along one of a variety of pathways rather than a single line of development. Sroufe (1997, p. 254) describes the possibility of "multiple pathways to similar manifest outcomes" and "different outcomes of the same pathway" as a consequence of multiple developmental pathways. However, the way a person perceives, interprets and acts in a situation depends upon his personal trajectories (Nielsen, 2008) through life since those experiences have influenced that person's cognitive schemes, defence mechanisms, self-regulation etc. as well as the handling of different knowledge-forms in a situation. In other words, the many experiences in an individual's life influence at once that individual's possible interpretations of a given situation, their tendency to adopt some interpretations rather than others, and the possible actions to be taken. This complex web must be taken into account when pedagogical treatment is individualised in the formation of a social-pedagogical fellowship.

Following to situated learning theory, the development of an adolescent in residential care can be characterised as the movement from the position of legitimate peripheral participant (Lave & Wenger, 1991) to that of fully-fledged participant. This raises the question of what criteria social workers are to apply in considering the adolescent 'fully-fledged' – adhering to rules and cooperating alone may not be sufficient for the individual to be able to manage their later life. If the social worker forces norms for the social-pedagogical fellowship, overruling the interests of the adolescent, the adolescent may adapt to these norms without accepting them, and discard these norms when moving to new contexts. This stresses the importance of cooperation within the social-pedagogical fellowship, from which perspective we might construe being a fully-fledged participant ideally as being an individual able to uphold the norms of the fellowship by oneself. On the other hand, acting in accordance with knowledge-forms that are appropriate for life in residential care might not be helpful in other contexts.

This adds another aspect to my model of perspectives, outlined earlier in this chapter (figure 1 and the subsequent analysis). Maria might on the surface accept her relations with her mother as constituting part of the common perspective merely in order to maintain the fellowship, but without agreeing as to its importance. Her development is enhanced if she also agrees to its importance. In this respect, there could be a difference between agreed and accepted common perspective.

Situated learning theories could be strengthened by describing the content of the learning taking place and the dilemmas in a single setting by appeal to the concept of knowledge-forms, as offered by Barth and Stokholm. The risk, however, is that these knowledge-forms are emphasised to such an extent that the individual history of the child is neglected. A common horizon of understanding, or 'common perspective' as it was called earlier in this chapter, is central to the formation of a social-pedagogical fellowship where the social worker can support the development of the child in an optimal way, and this horizon of understanding does not only depend on knowledge-forms influencing the particular situation.

Summary and conclusion

When professionals deliberately influence the development of an adolescent (and his self), the formation of a social-pedagogical fellowship is of central concern. To do this, social workers have to exercise a comprehending-interpreting approach. They can then establish cooperation with the adolescent, and the adolescent can become a subject in its own development, which is central for an approach which emphasises humans as both socially oriented and capable of acting by themselves. A fellowship of this kind includes a common project, which is the life of the adolescent, but its precise configuration is a matter of negotiation between the adolescent and the social worker. During development the social worker gradually hands over an increasing part of this project to the adolescent. This process includes a continuing negotiation about the focus of the fellowship giving the adolescent an experience of being a person responsible for his own life.

A comprehending-interpreting approach can be qualified by analysis of the knowledge-forms in the contexts of the adolescent, where knowledge-forms include understandings, values and possible actions. These knowledge-forms can be used as heuristics in creating an interpretation of specific situations. Knowledge-forms heavily influence the way the adolescent perceives, interprets and acts in a context and therefore they are important aspects of the self construal of the adolescent. In order to form the fellowship and to play his part in its maintenance, a social worker has to be aware of these knowledge-forms. Knowledge-forms are an important parameter in (self-)development and in fact in everyday life in general, so it has to be part of the professional task to teach the adolescent how to handle knowledge-forms too – including how to resolve conflicts between knowledge-forms and choose the knowledge-form suitable for the specific situation. The concept of knowledge-forms facilitates a clearer analysis of how to support social workers in their professional undertakings.

It is important to keep in mind that knowledge-forms are dynamic in the sense that they are maintained by humans applying them, considering the interpretations they facilitate and perhaps acting in accordance with these, but it is nevertheless possible to choose other actions too. That is, knowledge-forms do not determine human actions – they influence them. The way adolescents relate to knowledge-forms in specific situations is affected by previous experiences, and in order to be able to comprehend their attitude and actions social workers have to understand them in relation to their past. Their actions in the present situation are seen as meaningful according to their way of perceiving, interpreting and choosing actions, and the social workers have to identify past patterns in order to access the understanding of the adolescent in the current situation.

In this chapter I have set out to develop concepts for analysing and planning processes of importance for the development of a qualified self in the treatment of adolescents in residential care. This context has made some aspects of these processes more obvious than in ordinary families, where they proceed more smoothly.

References

Bae, B. (1996). *Det interessante i det alminnelige [Interesting topics in the ordinary]*. Oslo: Pedagogisk Forum.

Barth, F. (2002). An anthropology of knowledge. *Current Anthropology, 43*, 1-18.

Bateson, G. (1972). *Steps to an ecology of mind*. New York: Ballantine Books.

Cole, M. (1996). *Cultural Psychology*. Cambridge, Mass · Harvard University Press

Dreier, O. (2003). Learning in personal trajectories of participation. In N. Stephenson, H. L. Radke, R. J. Jorna, & H. J. Stam (Eds.), *Theoretical Psychology. Critical Contributions* (pp. 20-29). Concord, Canada: Captus Press.

Fischer, K.W., Ayoub, C., Singh, I., Noam, G., Maraganore, A., & Raya, P. (1997). Psychopathology as adaptive development along distinctive pathways. *Development and Psychopathology, 9*, 749-779.

Hundeide, K. (2004). *Børns livsverden og sociokulturelle rammer [Children's lifeworld and sociocultural contexts]*. Copenhagen: Akademisk Forlag.

Hundeide, K. (2002). The mind between us. *Nordisk Psykologi, 54*, 69-90.

Højlund, I. (2006). *Gennem flere labyrinter [Through several mazes / On treatment in residential care]*. PhD thesis, Danish University of Education, Copenhagen.

Jensen, M. (2010). *Det ufærdige arbejde [The never-ending work]*. PhD thesis, Aalborg University, Denmark.

Lave, J. (1988). *Cognition in practice*. Cambridge: Cambridge University Press.

Lave, J., & Wenger, E. (1991). *Situated learning: Legitimate peripheral participation*. Cambridge: Cambridge University Press.

Macaulay, C. (2000). Transfer of learning. In V. E. Cree & C. Macaulay (Eds.), *Transfer of learning in professional and vocational education* (pp. 1-26). London: Routledge.

Mathiesen, R. (1999). *Sosialpedagogisk perspektiv [Social-pedagogical perspective]*. Norway: Sokrates AS.

Neisser, U. (1976). *Cognition and reality*. San Fransisco: W.H.Freeman and Company.

Nielsen, K. (2008). Learning, trajectories of participation and social practice. *Critical Social Studies, 1*, 22-36.

Rothuizen, J. J. (2001). *Pædagogisk arbejde på fremmed grund [Pedagogical intervention on alien territory]*. København: Gyldendal.

Sroufe, L.A. (1997). Psychopathology as an outcome of development. *Development and Psychopathology, 9*, 251-268.

Stokholm, A. (2005). *Children in residential care institutions in Denmark. Dilemmas of the everyday*. In Proceedings of Childhoods International Conference, Oslo, June 29th–July 3th, 2005.

Stokholm, A. (2006a). *Anbragte børn mellem kammerater og pædagoger [Children between peers and social workers in out-of-home placements: An anthropological analysis of sociality and identity formation]*. PhD thesis, Institute of Anthopology, Archaeology and Linguistics, University of Aarhus, Denmark.

Stokholm, A. (2006b). Vi er altid en stor flok: fællesskab i børnegruppen på en døgninstitution [We are always a large group: alliances in a group of children in residential care]. In *Mellem omsorg og metode [Between care and method]* (pp. 217-239). Viborg: Forlaget PUC.

Tanggaard, L. (2006) Læring og identitet [Learning and identity]. Aalborg: Aalborg Universitetsforlag.

Tennant, M. (1999). Is learning transferable? In D. Boud (Ed.), *Understanding learning at work* (pp. 165-179). USA: Routledge.

Vygotsky, L. S. (1978). *Mind in society.* Cambridge, Mass.: Harvard University Press.

Wertsch, J. V. (1998). *Mind as action.* Oxford: Oxford University Press.

Manuel de la Mata Benítez
Andrés Santamaría Santigosa
Tia G. B. Hansen
Lucía Ruiz Ramos
Marcia L. Ruiz Cansino

Formal schooling, autobiographical memory and independent self-construal

7

This chapter explores the relationship between autobiographical memory, self, and a type of activity (Leont'ev, 1981; Wertsch, 1985) that is of great importance in modern societies, namely formal schooling. (Cross-)cultural psychology has long been producing considerable amounts of research about the relationship between formal schooling and mental processes (Cole, 1990, 1996; Cubero, de la Mata & Cubero, 2008; de la Mata & Cubero, 2005; Rogoff, 1981). However, autobiographical memory is rarely if ever touched upon in this literature. More recently, a vast and growing field of research about culture and autobiographical memory has emerged. Studies in this field investigate how values about self that predominate in different cultures influence how individuals construe themselves and remember their personal past (Leichtman, Wang & Pillemer, 2003; Markus & Kitayama, 1991; Nelson & Fivush, 2004). This field has, however, given little or no attention to the role of formal schooling in this process. Our chapter aims to integrate these fields to allow the study of formal schooling as a sociocultural activity that contributes to the acquisition and development of specific forms of autobiographical remembering.

The theoretical framework is unfolded in the next section. We describe our 'Sevilla human activity approach', which integrates (1) the study of the relationship between culture, autobiographical memory and self-construal, and the role we ascribe to narratives therein, (2) the influence of formal education on mental processes, and (3) Olson's (1994) ideas about the way in which literacy practices have shaped the modern notion of mind.

We then describe a specific empirical study from Mexico that used this framework to explore the relationship between formal schooling, autobiographical memory and self-construal. The study asked participants with different educational backgrounds (from literacy level to university students) to describe their first memory and analysed these in two ways: using the categories employed in most cross-cultural research linking autobiographical memory and self-construal (Wang, 2001, 2004), and using a narrative coding scheme inspired by Bruner (1990) and Smorti (2004). The incorporation of the narrative analysis is justified both by the role of narrative as a link between autobiographical memory and self and by the relationship between formal schooling and the acquisition and development of literate narrative forms (Brockmeier & Olson, 2002; Bruner, 2002). This analysis also allows discussion of the links between literacy practices such as those carried out in formal schooling, and the development of a notion of subject and mind that is characteristic of Modernity (Olson, 1994, 1997).

The final part of the chapter discusses the results of this study and its implications in terms of our theoretical framework. The results indicated that formal education may promote forms of remembering – and, in general, of self-making (Bruner, 2003b) – that have been described in autobiographical memory research as associated with the cultures of independence (Keller, 2007; Leichtman, Wang & Pillemer, 2003; Wang, 2001, 2003).

The Sevilla human activity approach

Lev Vygotsky's (1978) Cultural-Historical Psychology and Aleksej N. Leont'ev's (1981) extension to Activity Theory set out to overcome biological as well as mentalistic reductionism by accounting for the influence of cultural-institutional factors on the development of mental processes.

This notion of activity was reconceptualised by James Wertsch (1985). For Wertsch, activity is conceived as a socioculturally defined context or *activity setting* where human psychological processes take place. Any activity or activity setting (school, work, sport/play, etc.) is based on a set of implicit presuppositions about the aspects which are necessary for this context to exist and be recognised by the participants. This characterisation of activity settings also resonates with the notion of practice proposed by Jean Lave (1988, 1993).

Our interest in these concepts lies in the fact that they provide access to the relationship between culture and cognition in a fruitful way, as it permits us to analyse how mental processes (including autobiographical memory) develop in everyday activities carried out by specific individuals, overcoming some of the limitations of the studies that define culture from a macrolevel perspective.

Autobiographical memory, self construal, culture – and narrative

Autobiographical memory is defined as memory for the facts and events of one's personal meaningful past (Conway, 1990; Conway & Pleydell-Pearce, 2000; Nelson, 2003; Rubin, 1986). Autobiographical memory is related to the self, and to the experience of personhood: that is, to the experience of enduring as an individual in a culture over time. In fact, Self and autobiographical memory construct each other, as, on the one hand, personal memories are cognitively organised around the self and, on the other, the self cannot exist as a continuous entity across time without the existence of personal memories organised in subjective time.

Both elements, self and autobiographical memory, constitute each other by means of a third element: narrative. Autobiographical memory is the story of our life, the way that we develop a coherent narrative that describes and explains who we are (Bruner, 2003a, 2003b; McAdams, 2001, 2003). One of Bruner's most powerful contributions has been his considerations of narrative as a crucial tool for sense-making and self-making. In this sense, autobiographical memory can be conceived as a self-making narrative (Bruner, 2003b; McAdams, 2003), a narrative in which an individual's life is reconstructed (Nelson, 2000, 2003; Santamaría & Montoya, 2008) in a 'landscape of consciousness' as well as a 'landscape of action' (Bruner, 1986).

Therefore, narrative permits the existence of a memory that is more than a mere collection of isolated facts and events, and of a self that is (perceived as) continuous and coherent. It is, in sum, a discursive construction that is mediated, as is any narrative, by semiotic tools that the individual appropriates across his/her life (Santamaría & Martínez, 2005). The appropriation of semiotic tools is related to the participation in different socio-cultural settings and practices (e.g. formal schooling practices).

Research in the last few years has demonstrated cultural differences in autobiographical memory (Fivush & Nelson, 2006; Leichtman, Wang & Pillemer, 2003; Nelson & Fivush, 2004; Wang & Brockmeier, 2002). One of the aspects to have received more attention is the *age at the earliest memory* (Wang, 2001, 2006; Wang, Conway & Hou, 2004). Evidence shows that, when asked to recall their earliest childhood memory, Asian adults report events dating from more than 6 months later than do Europeans and Caucasian Americans, who remember earliest events occurring, on average, at age 3.5 (MacDonald, Uesiliana & Hayne, 2000; Mullen, 1994; Wang, 2001; Wang & Ross, 2005). In addition, earliest memories reported by Caucasian Americans are more elaborated, specific, self-focused, emotionally detailed, and less socially oriented than those reported by Asian people (Han, Leichtman & Wang, 1998).

The cultural variation in the age at the earliest memory and in the other characteristics of autobiographical memory is thought to stem from different cultural conceptions of selfhood (Markus & Kitayama, 1991; Mullen, 1994; Pillemer, 1998; Wang, 2001, 2003). Differences in the degree to which culture promotes independence vs. interdependence (Markus & Kitayama, 1991) or enhances autonomy vs. relatedness (Kagitçibasi, 1996, 2005, 2007; Keller, 2007; Keller et al., 2004) influence the way in which individuals in these cultures remember their lives. In this sense, Anglo-American and Northern and Central European cultures may focus on the individual, demonstrating an independent self-construal. This independent self is considered as a separate and autonomous entity, defined by a unique repertoire of traits, capacities, thoughts and feelings. Asian cultures, in contrast, tend to emphasise a collective or interdependent self, experienced as a part of a social web (Cross & Markus, 1999; Markus & Kitayama, 1991; Kagitçibasi, 1996, 2005). This relational self-construal that focuses on community rather than agency may de-emphasise individuality and promote social integration and dependence.

Differences in the emphasis on independence vs. interdependence are evident in diverse aspects of the self, such as the experience and expression of emotions, cognitive processes, attributions and moral reasoning, achievement motivation and autobiographical memory, among others (Kagitçibasi, 1996, 2005; Markus & Kitayama, 1991; Wang, 2001). With regard to autobiographical memory, the autonomous self-construal characteristic of Western cultures may drive the early emergence of an organised, articulated, durable memory system for events that happened to 'me'. (Leichtman, Wang & Pillemer, 2003).

Another important aspect of cultural influence is emotion situation knowledge. (Wang, 2003; Wang & Fivush, 2005). Different cultures differ in their understanding of emotions, especially in the consideration of what emotions are appropriate for each situation (also see chapter 4, this volume). In this sense, the emotional meaning assigned to an event affects all memory processes.

The number of studies about the relationship between self, autobiographical memory and culture is, however, limited. In general, they have focused on American and Asian (Chinese, Korean, Japanese) cultures. There are still very few studies with Mediterranean, Latin-American, Muslim or East European cultures (see Rubin, Schrauf, Gulgoz & Naka, 2007 for an exception to this trend).

In one previous study we compared the earliest memory and self-descriptions of college students from Denmark, Spain and Mexico. It is assumed that the Danish culture is characterised by a relatively high level of individualism, and the Mexican culture by a higher level of collectivism, while the Spanish culture can be considered to be at an intermediate level (Hofstede, 1984, 2001).

The methodology and categories of analysis employed in our study were those proposed by Wang (2001, 2004). The participants were asked to write a narrative of the earliest memory and to complete a shortened version of the Twenty Statements Test (TST) (Kuhn & McPartland, 1954). Results showed that Danish and Spanish participants reported their first memory to be one year earlier than Mexicans (43 vs. 55 months, approximately). Moreover, Mexican and Spanish students' memories were more emotional than those of the Danes (de la Mata, Santamaría, Ruiz & Hansen, 2011). Some cultural differences were also observed in self-descriptions, with the Mexicans providing more positive self-descriptions, the Spaniards more negative and the Danes more neutral self-descriptions than the other groups (ibid.; Santamaría, de la Mata, Hansen & Ruiz, 2010).

The results of the study provided support for the link between individualism-collectivism (and independent vs. interdependent self-construal) and some characteristics of the earliest memories of the participants. The differences observed were not very strong, however. From a general theoretical perspective, de la Mata et al. (2011) concluded that there was a need to refine (both in the theoretical and in the methodological domain) the analyses of self-construal to account for, on the one hand, the complexity of the notion, and, on the other, for the variations associated with personal and contextual factors (Brewer & Chen, 2007; Harb & Smith, 2008; Kagitçibasi, 2005, 2007; Santamaría, de la Mata, Hansen & Ruiz, 2010).

For example, Antalíková, Hansen, Gulbrandsen, de la Mata & Santamaría (2011) suggest a trajectory of self development from family over school to friends, based on the temporal distribution of meaningful memories from these three settings. In this explorative study with young Norwegians and Slovaks, memories from school also seemed to represent less relatedness (i.e., contained fewer references to other people) than the other two settings. This preliminary finding is consistent with the suggestion that school is an activity setting for more individual aspects of self development, however, it should be replicated with a bigger sample to allow more firm conclusions.

Formal education and mental processes

The studies described above – like many studies – used college student as participants. This may be an important aspect. Some theorists (Greenfield, 2009; Greenfield, Keller, Fuligni & Maynard, 2003; Kagitçibasi, 2005, 2007; Keller, 2007) argue that education is a cultural experience that promotes the development of autonomy and defend the existence of a close relationship between educational background and the development of a cultural notion of self that enhances the individual's autonomy.

Kagitçibasi (2005, 2007) advocates a view in which the development of 'the autonomous related self' is the result of a combined emphasis both on autonomy and relatedness. From her perspective, this autonomous related self is emerging in societies that are traditionally collectivistic (in which the interdependent self-construal was predominant) as a result of economic development and industrialisation. Formal schooling is an important factor in this kind of development. In a similar vein, Greenfield (2009; Greenfield et al., 2003) has proposed that changes at the societal socio-demographic level, such as the extension of formal schooling, may promote changes in human psychological development towards the model of independence.

It remains to be established, however, how these changes at the socio-demographic level are linked to changes in human development, at the individual level. To establish these links we think that it is necessary to analyse how cultural practices and activities such as formal schooling shape/influence individuals' autobiographical memory and self-construal. Our studies may represent a first step in this direction. And we think that there are reasons to consider analysis of the links between formal schooling, autobiographical memory and self-construal as pertinent and necessary.

First, a considerable volume of (cross-)cultural research has demonstrated the influence of formal schooling on mental processes, such as categorisation, memory, reasoning and problem solving (Cole, 1990, 1996; Cubero, de la Mata & Cubero, 2008; de la Mata & Cubero, 2005; Luria, 1976; Rogoff, 1981, 1990; Scribner & Cole, 1981; Sharp, Cole & Lave, 1979). As a whole, these data have been interpreted as demonstrating that formal education can be conceived as an activity setting (Wertsch, 1985) that promotes ways of thinking called academic concepts (Vygotsky, 1986), theoretical argumentation (Scribner, 1992) or propositional thought (Bruner, 1986, 1990).

Moreover, the influence effectof formal education on mental processes of the individual student does not seem to be the only influence that this institution and the cultural practices associated with it exert.

Literacy and the modern mind

From the social sciences in general, and from psychology itself, it is claimed that literacy and formal education have played a fundamental role in the constitution of the modern subject (Olson, 1994, 1997; Ong, 1982; Ramírez, 1995). So, for example, Olson (1994) claims that the modern mind is constituted after Descartes and authors like Hume, Berkeley and Kant and the ideal of the Enlightenment. These authors emphasised the notion of an autonomous subject, whose acts are governed by reason and reflect the quality of a mind populated with ideas, beliefs, desires, memories, etc. For Olson, these notions of subject and mind are related to the cultural changes that arose in the Western world since the extension of literacy at the beginning of Modernity (linked to the Protestant Reformation and the origins of capitalism). More specifically, Olson claims that literacy and literate practices permitted the separation of things and their representations, so that thinking became an 'autonomous' activity about the world, in other words, an 'epistemic' activity, and mind became an object defined by mental states.

More recently, data from cross-cultural research about independent vs. interdependent self-construals (Cross & Markus, 1999; Markus & Kitayama, 1991; Kagitçibasi, 1996, 2005) may also support this view. As we have highlighted above, some authors state the existence of a relationship between educational background and the development of socio-cultural orientations to the self promoting autonomy and individuality (Greenfield, 2009; Greenfield et al., 2003; Kagitçibasi, 2005, 2007; Keller, 2007; Keller et al., 2004).

With respect to this issue, it is interesting to note the predominance of an independent self-construal in cultures from Central and Northern Europe, where the Protestant Reformation took place. In these locations, a greater development of literate culture has been observed. However, the links between literate culture/literacy and independent self-construal need elaboration both theoretically and empirically.

Some studies from the Sevilla human activity approach have also shown the existence of a relationship between formal education and: 1) aspects of cultural identities (Sánchez, Macías, Marco & García, 2005), 2) attitudes and values (Cala, 1999), and 3) gender identities (Cala & de la Mata, 2004). Coined in general terms, these studies show that the performance of different acts of identification (which possess an argumentative and rhetoric character) depend on the educational level of the individuals. People with more schooling experience use semiotic tools and forms of argumentation based on establishing general relations between classes of objects. The forms of identification of the people with a short schooling experience, on the other hand, are usually supported by narratives of particular everyday experiences. These narratives typically refer to the speaker or acquaintances (Cala, 1999).

Formal schooling, autobiographical memory and self

Despite the existence of research documenting the relationship between schooling and memory (Cole, 1990; Rogoff, 1981; Rogoff & Mistry, 1985) and the link between formal schooling and the cultural model of independence (Greenfield, 2009; Greenfield et al., 2003; Kagitçibasi, 2005, 2007; Keller, 2007), no previous research programmes have examined the influence of formal schooling on autobiographical memory and self. The present study may represent a first step in this direction. For that purpose, we focused on comparing the earliest autobiographical memories of Mexican women and men from three different educational levels. They were asked to orally narrate their earliest memory,

The aim of the study was to analyse the relationship between schooling experience and earliest autobiographical memories in Mexican people. In this analysis, we considered first the characteristics of the earliest memories (age, emotionality, individual vs. social content and specificity). As a second step, we focused on the way in which the self was expressed in the earliest memories, by considering aspects such as autonomy orientation, self/others ratio and agency. The aforementioned research on autobiographical memory and self-construal that documented cultural differences in these dimensions, lead us expect differences associated with formal schooling experience.

Our study also incorporated a narrative analysis, focusing on the two landscapes defined by Bruner (1986): the landscape of actions and the landscape of consciousness. For this purpose, we examined the use of action and mental state verbs, as well as the use of metacognitive expressions (e.g. comments and evaluations about the memory).

Method

Participants. 60 adults (30-55 years old) living in Ciudad Victoria, Tamaulipas, Mexico. The participants varied in gender (30 females and 30 males) and educational background. According to this variable, three different levels were considered: literacy level, with participants that were learning to read and write, intermediate level, equivalent to primary education, and university level. Twenty participants were included in each level.

Procedure. Oral interviews about the earliest memory of the participants were conducted. (Additionally, they were asked to recall three memories from different periods of their lives, but for present purposes only the earliest memory was analysed). The interviews were transcribed literally and analysed with a coding system that considered the aspects outlined in table 1.

Characteristics of autobiographical memories	Self in memory
• Age at the earliest memory (months) • Emotional content • Memory content: individual vs. social	• Autonomous orientation • Other self ratio • Self-descriptions

Table 1. Aspects coded in the first analysis (adapted from Wang, 2001, 2004).

An additional narrative analysis was applied. This analysis was based on Smorti (2004). For this analysis, the transcriptions were divided into sentence units. Each unit was coded into one of the categories seen in table 2. For a more extended presentation of the category system, see de la Mata & Santamaría (2010).

Narrative analysis
- Action verb units
- Mental verb units:
  - cognitive
  - intentional
  - emotional
- Metacognitive units

Table 2. Category system for the narrative analysis (adapted from Smorti, 2004).

To calculate inter-rater reliability, research assistants that were blind to the aims and hypotheses of the study independently coded a sample of memories (20% of the total). For these, kappa-values (Cohen, 1960) ranged from $K = .88$ to $K = .93$ for the 'Characteristics of autobiographical memories' and 'Self in memory' measures, and from $K = .87$ to $K = .93$ for the 'Narrative analysis' measures.

Results

In this section, we present a summary of the main findings of our study. Analysis of Variance (ANOVA) and Chi-square tests were applied. The explanatory variable was educational level. Outcome (response) variables were the measures of autobiographical memory, self and narrative units. Data are presented in three sections: first, we examine some the characteristics of the earliest memories (age at the earliest memory, emotionality, content (social vs. individual) and specificity). Then, we present the results of the analysis of the self in memory (autonomy orientation, self/others ration and agency). Finally, results of the narrative analysis (action verbs, mental verbs and metacognitive units) are presented. In all cases, only the statistically significant differences are presented.

Characteristics of autobiographical memories. With regard to age in the earliest memory, a main effect of educational background was observed ($F_{(2,400)} = 17.99$, $p < .001$, $\eta^2 = .42$). As shown in figure 1, university students' memories were earlier than other participants' memories. No difference was observed between the other two levels.

The next analyses were applied to the content of the memories, considering two aspects: the individual vs. social content, and the specificity (specific vs. general) of these memories (figure 2).

Results showed significant differences in the content (individual or social) of the memories in relation to the educational background of the participants. As content was defined as a qualitative variable, Chi-square tests were applied. Results showed significant differences in the content (individual or social) of the memories in relation to the educational background of the participants. As we can see in figure 2 there was a decrease in the social content and an increase in the individual content of the memories as the educational level of the participants increased ($\chi^2_{(2,57)} = 9.44$, $p < .01$). Finally, a significant relationship between educational background and specificity of the memories was also observed. As the educational background of the participants increased, a higher proportion of specific memories was found ($\chi^2_{(2,57)} = 6.65$, $p < .05$). In these categories, university participants' memories were earlier, more individual and more specific than the other participants' memories.

Self in memory variables. Analysis of variance (ANOVA) was performed for the self in memory measures (autonomy orientation, self/others ratio and agency score). In this analysis, the only statistically significant difference was observed with agency score, and only this variable is reported here (figure 3). The agency measure was calculated by dividing the number of personal self-descriptions by the total number of self-descriptions (personal + social self-descriptions), leading to an index between 0 and 1 where higher scores indicate a higher greater degree of agency. A significant effect of educational background on the agency score was observed ($F_{(2,400)} = 4.33$, $p < .019$, $\eta^2 = .08$). Post hoc (Scheffé) analyses showed a significant difference between university students and literacy level, whereas no significant differences was found between university students and

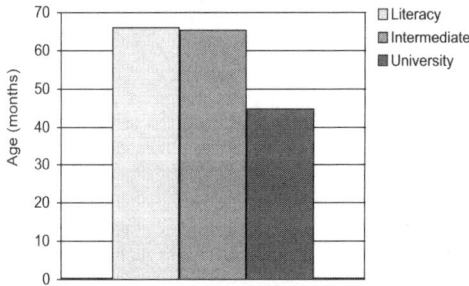

Figure 1. Educational background and age at the earliest memory.

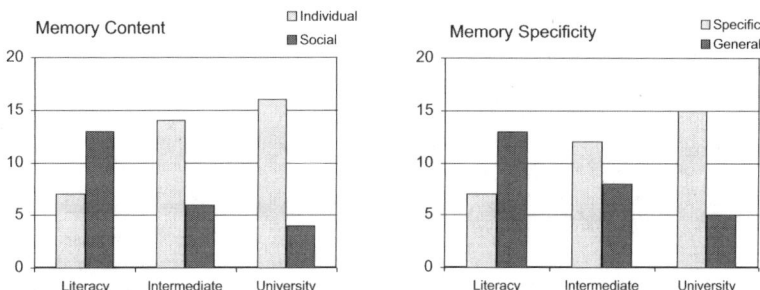

Figure 2. Educational background, content and specificity of the earliest memory.

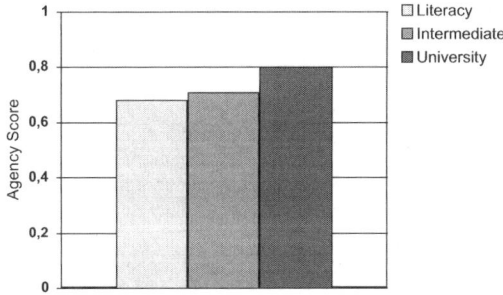

Figure 3. Educational background and agency score.

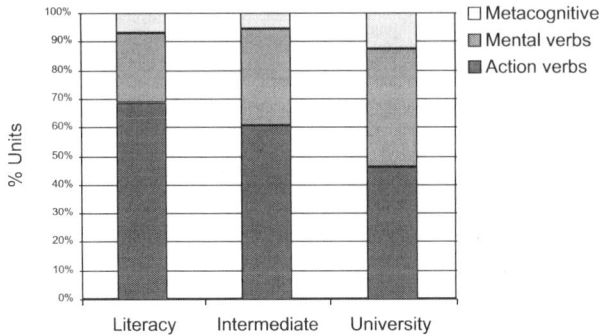

Figure 4. Distribution of sentence units (in percentages) within educational levels.

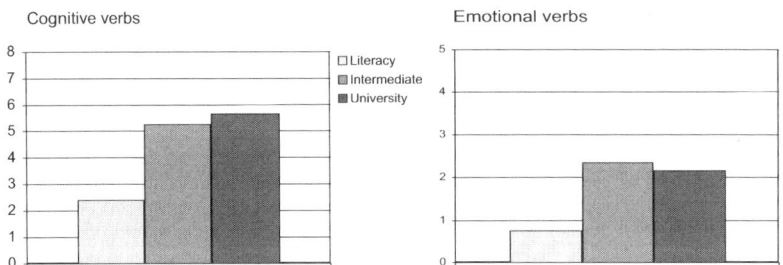

Figure 5. Educational background and mental states units (cognitive and emotional).

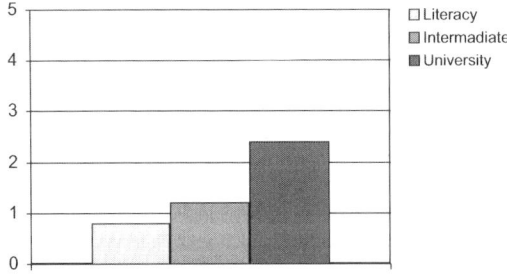

Figure 6. Educational background and metacognitive units.

intermediate level, and neither between intermediate and literacy level.

Narrative analyses. For this Bruner (1990) and Smorti (2004) inspired analysis, the memories were divided into sentence-units and coded as action units, mental states (cognitive and emotional) units, or metacognitive units.

As seen in figure 4, the distribution of verb units belonging to categories 'action' vs. 'mental' varied as a function of the educational background of the participant. While at the literacy level more than two thirds of the units referred to actions, this proportion decreased as the educational level of the participants increased. In contrast, the proportion of mental verb units (cognitive and emotional) increased as the educational level increased, and so did the proportion of metacognitive units. In the case of metacognitive units, we can observe that the increase (from 7.16 to 12.33) was observed in the university level.

Having described the general distribution of units in the different educational levels, we were able to analyse differences between levels within a set of these categories (see figure 5). ANOVA analyses of mental state units evidenced significant differences between educational levels both for cognitive verbs units ($F_{(2,57)} = 7.33$, $p < .003$, $\eta^2 = .23$) and for emotion verbs units ($F_{(2,57)} = 3.58$, $p < .05$, $\eta^2 = .13$). Post hoc (Scheffé) tests revealed that in the case of cognitive verbs, participants from university and intermediate level included significantly more cognitive verb units in their memories than participants from the literacy level. No significant difference was observed between university and intermediate level. For emotion verbs, a significant difference was observed between the literacy level and each of the other two levels, but not between the intermediate and university levels.

The last analysis concerns metacognitive units (figure 6). We observed a statistically significant relationship between educational background and metacognitive units ($F_{(2,57)} = 4.50$, $p < .017$, $\eta^2 = .15$). Post hoc (Scheffé) tests showed that the number of these units was significantly higher in the university level compared to the other two levels. No significant difference was found between the intermediate and literacy levels.

Discussion

The study aimed to explore the relationship between schooling experience and autobiographical memory. For this purpose, samples of Mexican people from three different educational levels (literacy, intermediate level and university students) were asked to orally relate their earliest memory. These memories were analysed to assess some of their characteristics (age at the earliest memory, emotionality and content) and issues related to the self and others (autonomous orientation, agency and social orientation). The results of these analyses showed differences between schooling levels in the age at the earliest memory, emotionality, social/individual content and specificity of this memory, as well as in agency. The memories reported by the participants from the groups with more schooling background, and especially university students, were, as a whole, earlier, with more emotion terms, more self-focused and specific and showing a higher level of individual agency than those reported by the participants with less schooling experience.

Limitations in our study due to sample size should be noted. Analyses of larger samples may eventually serve to check these preliminary results. With that caveat in mind, we suggest the following interpretations.

The differences and the characteristics of the earliest memories of the more schooled participants mirror some of the cultural differences observed in studies about the relationship between culture and autobiographical memory. These studies have shown that adults and children from cultures characterised by an independent self-construal (Europeans, European Americans and Australians, mostly) date their first memories earlier than people from cultures in which the interdependent construal of the self predominates (de la Mata et al., 2011; MacDonald et al., 2000; Mullen, 1994; Wang, 2001, 2004, 2006; Wang, Conway & Hou, 2004). These memories are also more emotional (Han, Leichtman & Wang, 1998; Leichtman, Wang & Pillemer, 2003; Wang, 2001, 2003), more individually oriented and more specific than memories of individuals from cultures of interdependence (Wang, 2001, 2004). As a whole, the memories from independent cultures show a greater degree of autonomy than memories of individuals from cultures of interdependence (de la Mata et al., 2011; Nelson & Fivush, 2004; Keller, 2007; Wang, 2001, 2004).

Our study included a narrative analysis that was inspired by Bruner's (1986) characterisation of the double landscape in narrative (the landscape of action and the landscape of consciousness). In our analysis we have relied on Smorti (2004) and coded sentence units to distinguish between action and mental state verb units. We have also added a new category, metacognitive units, to account for sentences in which the participants reflected about the memory as a whole or about the very process of remembering. This kind of unit was indicative of a way of thinking about the memory as a mental object in the subject's mind. In general, these analyses addressed the way in which the self, as a narrator and as a character, was constructed in the memory, and the salience of the self's mental states in the narrative. The results showed a relationship between schooling experience and the number and proportion of mental state verbs and metacognitive units in the memories. If we analyse in more detail the narratives of the earliest memory at each educational level, we can see interesting differences. The narratives of participants from the literacy level were mostly composed of action verb units. These units represented almost 70% of the total units. The other 30% included mental state verbs and metacognitive units. In these narratives, thus, the reference to mental states was relatively limited (24% of the units) and only 7% of the units were metacognitive.

At the intermediate level we can observe a relative increase in the reference to mental states, which represents 33% of the total number of units and, conversely, a decrease in the proportion of action verb units (60% of the total number of units). These differences in action and mental state verb units were not only relative, but held also in absolute numbers (see figure 5). In the case of metacognitive units, however, there was no difference between literacy and the intermediate level, neither in relative nor absolute terms (see figures 4 and 6).

Finally, at the university level we observed an increase of both mental state verbs and metacognitive units. At this level, mental state verbs represented more than 40% of the total number of units, while action verb units were less than 50% of the total. In absolute terms, however, although the number of mental state verb units was significantly higher in the university than in the literacy level, it was not significantly higher than in the intermediate level. The major difference between the university and the intermediate level was related to the use of metacognitive units. At the university level, these units represented 15% of the total. To summarise, we can say that the memories narrated by the university students in our study were characterised by a predominance of the landscape of consciousness (Bruner, 1986), with many references to mental states and a high degree of reflexivity about remembering, as indicated by the presence of metacognitive evaluations of the memory itself. Conversely, the memories narrated by the participants from the literacy level were characterised by a clear predominance of the landscape of action, with a smaller number of references to mental states and a limited number of metacognitive reflections about the memory. The participants in the intermediate level were in an intermediate location, as they showed a higher number of references to mental states but not an increase in metacognitive evaluation compared to the literacy level.

Our study thus shows that schooling experience is associated with forms of autobiographical remembering that are characteristic of the cultures of independence. Participants with more schooling experience narrated first memories characterised by an earlier date (around three years of age), an emphasis on autonomy, and more references to mental states and metacognitive reflections and evaluations, when compared with less schooled participants. This finding allows us to speculate about the role of formal education as a socio-cultural practice (Scribner & Cole, 1981) or activity setting (Werstch, 1985) that promotes ways of remembering and, in general, of self-making (Bruner, 2003b) that have been described in autobiographical memory research as associated with the cultures of independence (Keller, 2007; Leichtman, Wang & Pillemer, 2003; Wang, 2001, 2003). In this sense, cross-cultural research has demonstrated that formal schooling promotes changes in cognitive processes as categorisation, concept formation, memory and reasoning (Cole, 1990, 1996; Rogoff, 1981, 1990; Scribner & Cole, 1981). From our data we may conclude that it also promotes the construction of a self with specific features.

The latter provides a connection with the theses proposed by David Olson (1994). As mentioned earlier, this author defends the essential role of literacy (and cultural practices associated with literacy) in the development of the notion of individual and mind that is characteristic of Modernity. For Olson, literacy and literate practices made possible the separation that allowed thinking to become an 'autonomous' activity in relation to the world (an 'epistemic' activity) and mind an object defined by mental states that guide the actions of an autonomous and responsible subject. Our results concerning the relationship between schooling experience and forms of autobiographical remembering evince this modern notion of mind and can be considered as supporting these notions. Since school has assumed the task of teaching literate ways of discourse and thinking, we think that it is necessary to investigate in depth the role of educational practices in the construction of modern mind.

Conclusion

There are reasons to assert that formal schooling plays a special role in the development of independent (individualistic) self construals and significant personal memories. Our theoretical framework predicts this, and the findings of our study provide preliminary evidence for a link between increased formal schooling experience on the one hand, and characteristics of autobiographical memory associated to independent self-construal, on the other.

Finally, we must recognize that, albeit promising, the data reported in this chapter only represents a first step in the analysis of the relationship between formal education activities and autobiographical memory. The results suggest that we need to go further in the analysis of the relationship between formal schooling, autobiographical memory and self-construal, including more detailed analyses of the ways by which school practices influence autobiographical memory and self. For that purpose, we think that qualitative analyses of narratives, as well as studies analysing what happens within schools (with a special focus on discourse and interaction in the classrooms), could provide further insight.

References

Antalíková, R., Hansen, T. G. B., Gulbrandsen, K. A., de la Mata, M., & Santamaria, A. (2011). Adolescents' meaningful memories reflect a trajectory of self-development from family over school to friends. *Nordic Psychology, 63*, 4-24.

Brewer, M. B., & Chen, Y. R. (2007). Where (who) are collectives in collectivism? Toward conceptual clarification of individualism and collectivism. *Psychological Review, 114*, 133-151.

Brockmeier, J., & Olson, D. R. (2002). Introduction: What is a culture of literacy? In J. Brockmeier, M. Wang & D. R. Olson (Eds.), *Literacy, narrative and culture* (pp. 1-14). Richmond: The Curzon Press.

Bruner, J. (1986). *Actual minds, possible worlds*. Cambridge, MA: Harvard University Press.

Bruner, J. (1990). *Acts of meaning*. Cambridge, MA: Harvard University Press.

Bruner, J. S. (2002). Narrative distancing. A foundation to literacy. In J. Brockmeier, M. Wang & D. R. Olson (Eds.), *Literacy, narrative and culture* (pp. 86-93). Richmond: Curzon Press.

Bruner, J. S. (2003a). *Making stories. Life, literature, law*. Cambridge, MA: Harvard University Press.

Bruner, J. S. (2003b). Self-making narratives. In R. Fivush & C.A. Haden (Eds.), *Autobiographical memory and the construction of a narrative self. Developmental and cultural perspectives* (pp. 209-225). Mahwah, NJ: Lawrence Erlbaum Associates.

Cala, M. J. (1999). *Género educación y actitudes: una aproximación retórica al estudio de los modos de discurso*. Unpublished doctoral thesis. Universidad de Sevilla.

Cala, M. J., & de la Mata, M. L. (2004). Educational background, modes of discourse and argumentation: Comparing women and men. *Argumentation, 18*, 403-426.

Cohen, J. A. (1960). Coefficient for agreement for nominal scales. *Educational and Psychological Measurement, 20*, 37-46.

Cole, M. (1990). Cognitive development and formal schooling: the evidence from cross-cultural research. In L.C. Moll (Ed.): *Vygotsky and education. Instructional implications and applications of sociohistorical psychology* (pp. 89-110). Cambridge: Cambridge University Press.

Cole, M. (1996). *Cultural psychology: A once and future discipline*. Cambridge, MA: Cambridge University Press.

Conway, M. (1990). *Autobiographical memory: An introduction*. Milton Keynes: Open University Press.

Conway, M., & Pleydell-Pearce, C. W. (2000). The construction of autobiographical memories in the self-memory system. *Psychological Review, 107*, 261-288.

Cross, S. E., & Markus, H. R. (1999). The cultural constitution of personality. In L. A. Pervin & O. P. John (Eds.), *Handbook of personality: Theory and research* (2. ed.) (pp. 378-396). New York: Guilford Press.

Cubero, M., de la Mata, M. L., & Cubero, R. (2008). Activity settings, discourse modes and ways of understanding: On the heterogeneity of verbal thinking. *Culture & Psychology, 14*, 403-430.

de la Mata, M. L., & Cubero, M. (2005). Cultura y procesos cognitivos. In M. Cubero & J. D. Ramírez (Ed.), *Vygotski en la psicología contemporánea* (pp. 47-81). Buenos Aires: Miño y Dávila.

de la Mata, M. L., & Santamaría, A. (2010). La construcción del yo en escenarios educativos. Un análisis desde la psicología cultural. *Revista de Educación, 353*, 157-186.

de la Mata, M. L., Santamaría, A., Ruiz, L., & Hansen, T. G. B. (2011). Memoria autobiográfica, narrativa y concepciones del yo: Un estudio transcultural. *Revista Mexicana de Psicología, 28*, 183-191.

Fivush, R., & Nelson, K. (2006). Parent-child reminiscing locates the self in the past. *British Journal of Developmental Psychology, 24*, 235-251.

Greenfield, P. M. (2009). Linking social change and developmental change: Shifting pathways of human development. *Developmental Psychology, 45*, 401-418.

Greenfield, P. M., Keller, H., Fuligni, A., & Maynard, A. (2003). Cultural pathways through universal development. *Annual Review of Psychology, 54*, 461-490.

Han, J. J., Leichtman, M. D., & Wang, Q. (1998). Autobiographical memory in Korean, Chinese and American children. *Developmental Psychology, 34*, 701-713.

Harb, C., & Smith, P. B. (2008). Self-construals across cultures: Beyond independence-interdependence. *Journal of Cross-Cultural Psychology, 39*, 178-197.

Hofstede, G. (1984). *Culture's consequences: International differences in work related values.* Beverly Hills, CA: Sage.

Hofstede, G. (2001). *Culture's consequences: Comparing values, behaviors, institutions, and organizations across nations.* Thousand Oaks, CA: Sage.

Kagitçibasi, C. (1996). *Family and human development across cultures: a view from the other side.* Hillsdale, NJ: L.E.A.

Kagitçibasi, C. (2005). Autonomy and relatedness in cultural context. Implications for self and family. *Journal of Cross-Cultural Psychology, 36*, 403-422.

Kagitçibasi, C. (2007). Family, self and human development across cultures. Theory and applications. Mahwah, NJ: L.E.A.

Keller, H. (2007). Cultures of infancy. New York: Lawrence Erlbaum Associates.

Keller, H., Yovsi, R., Borke, J., Kärtner, J., Jensen, H., & Papaligoura, Z. (2004). Developmental consequences of early parenting experiences: self-recognition and self-regulation in three cultural communities. *Child Development, 75*, 1745-1760.

Kuhn, M. H., & McPartland, T. S. (1954). An empirical investigation of self-attitudes. *American Sociological Review, 19*, 68-76.

Lave, J. (1988). *Cognition in practice*. Cambridge, MA: Cambridge University Press.

Lave, J. (1993).The practice of learning. In S. Chaiklin & J. Lave (Eds.): *Understanding practice. Perspectives on activity and context* (pp. 3-32). Cambridge, MA: Cambridge University Press.

Leichtman, M. D., Wang, Q., & Pillemer, D. B. (2003). Cultural variations in interdependence and autobiographical memory: Lessons from Korea, China, India and the United States. In R. Fivush & C.A. Haden (Eds.), *Autobiographical memory and the construction of a narrative self. Developmental and cultural perspectives* (pp. 73-97). Mahwah, N.J.: Lawrence Erlbaum Associates.

Leont'ev, A. N. (1981). The problem of activity in psychology. In J. V. Wertsch (Ed.), *The concept of activity in Soviet Psychology* (pp. 37-71). Armonk, NY: Sharpe.

Luria, A. R. (1976). *Cognitive development: Its cultural and social foundations*. Cambridge, MA: Cambridge University Press.

MacDonald, S., Uesiliana, K., & Hayne, H. (2000). Cross-cultural and gender differences in childhood amnesia. *Memory, 8*, 365-376.

Markus, H. R., & Kitayama, S. (1991). Culture and the self: Implications for cognition, emotion, and motivation. *Psychological Review, 98*, 224-253.

McAdams, D. P. (2001). The psychology of life stories. *Review of General Psychology, 5*, 100-122.

McAdams, D. P. (2003). Identity and the life story. In R. Fivush & C.A. Haden (Eds.), *Autobiographical memory and the construction of a narrative self. Developmental and cultural perspectives* (pp. 187-207). Mahwah, NJ: Lawrence Erlbaum Associates.

Mullen, M. K. (1994). Earliest recollections of childhood: A demographic analysis. *Cognition, 52*, 55-79.

Nelson, K. (2000). Narrative, time and the emergence of the encultured self. *Culture and Psychology, 6*, 183-196.

Nelson, K. (2003). Narrative and self, myth and memory: Emergence of the cultural self. In R. Fivush & C. A. Haden (Eds.), *Autobiographical memory and the construction of a narrative self. Developmental and cultural perspectives* (pp. 3-25). Mahwah, N.J.: Lawrence Erlbaum Associates.

Nelson, K., & Fivush, R. (2004). The emergence of autobiographical memory: A social cultural developmental theory. *Psychological Review, 111*, 486-511.

Olson, D. R. (1994). *The world on paper*. Cambridge: Cambridge University Press.

Olson, D. R. (1997). La escritura y la mente. In J. V. Wertsch, P. del Río & A. Álvarez (Eds.), *La mente sociocultural* (pp. 77-97). Madrid: Fundación Infancia y Aprendizaje.

Ong, W. (1982). *Orality and literacy. The technologizing of the world*. London: Routledge.

Pillemer, D. B. (1998). *Momentous events, vivid memories*. Cambridge, MA: Harvard University Press.

Ramírez, J. D. (1995). *Usos de la palabra y sus tecnologías*. Buenos Aires: Miño y Dávila.

Rogoff, B., (1981). Schooling and the development of *cognitive* skills. In H. C. Triandis & A. Heron (Eds.), *Handbook Cross-Cultural Psychology, vol. 4: Developmental Psychology* (pp. 233-294). Boston: Allyn and Bacon.

Rogoff, B. (1990). *Apprenticeship in thinking*. Cambridge, MA: Cambridge University Press.

Rogoff, B., & Mistry, J. (1985). Memory development in cultural context. In M. Pressley & C. Brainerd (Eds.), *Cognitive learning and memory in children* (pp. 117-142). New York: Springer.

Rubin, D. C. (1986) (Ed.). *Autobiographical memory*. Cambridge: Cambridge University Press.

Rubin, D. C., Schrauf, R. W., Gulgoz, S., & Naka, M. (2007). Cross-cultural variability of component processes in autobiographical remembering: Japan, Turkey, and the USA. *Memory, 15*, 536-547.

Sánchez, J. A., Macías, B., Marco, M., & García, J. (2005). Identidad cultural y alfabetización. In M. Cubero & J. D. Ramírez (Eds.), *Vygotski en la psicología contemporánea* (pp. 241-262). Buenos Aires: Miño y Dávila.

Santamaría, A., & Martínez, M.A. (2005). La construcción del significado en el marco de una psicología cultural: el pensamiento narrativo. In M. Cubero & J.D. Ramírez (Eds.) *Vygotski en la psicología contemporánea* (pp. 167-193). Buenos Aires: Miño y Dávila.

Santamaría, A., de la Mata, M. L., Hansen, T. G. B., & Ruiz, L. (2010). Cultural self-construals of Mexican., Spanish and Danish college students: Beyond independent and interdependent self. *Journal of Cross-Cultural Psychology, 41*, 471-477.

Santamaría, A., & Montoya, E. (2008). La memoria autobiográfica: el encuentro entre la memoria, el yo y el lenguaje. *Estudios de Psicología, 29*, 333-350.

Scribner, S. (1992). Mind in action: A functional approach to thinking. *The Quarterly newsletter of L.C.H.C., 14*, 103-109.

Scribner, S., & Cole, M. (1981). *The psychology of literacy*. Cambridge, MA: Harvard University Press.

Sharp, D., Cole, M., & Lave, C. (1979). Education and cognitive development: The evidence from experimental research. *Monographs of the Society for Research in Child Development, 44* (1-2 Serial no. 178).

Smorti, A. (2004). Narrative strategies among early adolescents involved in bully-victim relationships. *Journal of School Violence, 4*, 5-27.

Vygotsky, L. S. (1978). Mind in society. The development of higher psychological processes. Camdridge, MA: Harvard University Press.

Vygotsky, L. S. (1986). *Thought and language* (A. Kozulin, trans.). Cambridge, MA: MIT Press. (Original work published 1934).

Wang, Q. (2001). Culture effects on adult's earliest childhood recollection and self-description: Implications for the relation between memory and the self. *Journal of Personality and Social Psychology, 81*, 220-233.

Wang, Q. (2003). Emotion situation knowledge in American and Chinese preschool children and adults. *Cognition & Emotion, 17*, 725-746.

Wang, Q. (2004). The emergence of cultural self-construct: Autobiographical memory and self-description in American and Chinese children, *Developmental Psychology, 40*, 3-15.

Wang, Q., (2006). Earliest recollections of self and others in European American and Taiwanese young adults. *Psychological Science, 17*, 708-714.

Wang, Q., & Brockmeier, J. (2002). Autobiographical remembering as cultural practice: understanding the interplay between memory, self and culture. *Culture & Psychology, 8*, 45-64.

Wang, Q., Conway, M. A., & Hou, Y. (2004). Infantile amnesia: A cross-cultural investigation. *Cognitive Sciences, 1*, 123-135.

Wang, Q., & Fivush, R. (2005). Mother-child conversations of emotionally salient events: exploring the functions of emotional reminiscing in European-American and Chinese families. *Social Development, 14*, 473-495.

Wang, Q., & Ross, M. (2005). What we remember and what we tell: The effects of culture and self-priming on memory representations and narratives, *Memory, 13*, 594-606.

Wertsch, J. V. (1985). *Vygotsky and the social formation of mind*. Cambridge, MA: Harvard University Press.

Monica Rudberg
Harriet Bjerrum Nielsen

Gender in three generations
Narrative constructions and psychological identifications

8

In this chapter we look into a central phenomenon of social change in our times, namely the emergence of new gender relations. How have processes of rapid social and cultural modernization in the last century been associated with the psychological projects of becoming gendered subjects? Can the similarities and differences between men and women in this period be seen in the styles of their narratives? And what is the emotional history that seems to be simultaneously conveyed in these styles? In order to follow the trace of gendered paths through this historical period, we explore these double aspects of the life historical narratives presented by three generations of Norwegian men and women.

According to Jerome Bruner (2003), narratives could be seen as 'self-making stories' which we do not construct from scratch every time around: We develop habits and some genres accumulate, others get outdated since they no longer fit the situation. The meaning that we experience in any social situation is thus constructed in a two-sided process, both from within and without. Subjectivities will, according to Bruner, change in relation to shifting historical contexts, transmitted through a 'myriad of expectations'. This process can either contribute to or impede cultural change – for instance by providing an inner psychological receptivity or readiness for certain discourses and not for others. People live through the cultural constructions of their times, making themselves as well as being made through the different narratives of gender, class, ethnicity etc. that are predominant in their (section of) society. But how does that which is culturally 'talked about' become individually relevant and desired as ways to talk, as well as ways to live? The challenge is to understand how biographically developed motivations can result not only in adapting to cultural change, but in fact also in desiring such change for oneself. Self-making(s) might be seen as a result of cultural influence, mediated through different micro-social relational scenarios resulting in psychological agency. In our view, culture and psychology should not be understood as separate 'levels' of reality (or self-making) where one determines the other; culture is always psychologically energized and psychology is always embedded in culture. However, to grasp the specific dynamics of cultural and psychological processes, different perspectives and specific vocabularies are also needed. Although self-constructions on a psychological level are not possible to separate from a cultural context, the 'power of feelings' (Chodorow, 1999) involved could represent a psychological impetus to new cultural constructions as well as social organization. Subjectivity is not necessarily lagging behind culture/society; at times society actually has to adapt to new desires.

In the following we will take a closer look at this double construction of narratives making use of memories presented in a three-generational study consisting of both women and men, born (mainly) in the 1910s, 1940s and 1970s. Although our aim is comparative, the focus will be on the men since the women have been analysed and presented in earlier work (Nielsen & Rudberg, 2006). The three generations have lived in a period of rapid modernization from an almost rural society to a post-industrialized, urbanized one. This has involved dramatic changes in relation to economy and social security. While the oldest generation tells us about a childhood where enough food being on the table was a major concern, private consumption tripled in Norway from 1950-1970 (Lange, 1998). During this time the Nordic welfare state was also established with child care benefits, old age pension and sick leave benefits for all. At the same time as the material conditions have become safer, the relational safety net seems to get more insecure, illustrated by a substantial increase in divorce rate. In our own study half of the youngest generation has experienced such family break ups. The historical period is also characterized by shifts in cultural discourses and mentality with a steady decrease of the earlier ethic of work to an intensified focus on the discourses of the psychological self. This process has been described as a change in moral imperatives from 'being of use' to 'finding oneself' (Almås, Karlson & Thorland, 1995; Gullestad, 1996). The cultural change towards increased individualization, reflexivity and emphasis on the psychological self is a general phenomenon of late modernity (Giddens, 1991). Our question in this article is to what degree and in what respects this is also a gendered story. Since social and cultural conditions show both commonalities across and differences between genders, we should expect both similarities and discrepancies in their accounts. What information will such variation give us about the different ways that men and women have become 'modernized'? And how are we to understand these differences in relation not only to social change, but also to the emotional histories involved?

The study

The data stem from a Norwegian sample of 22 female and 12 male generational chains, related to each other in families (Nielsen & Rudberg, 2006). The youngest generation – all born 1971-72 - is the anchor in the study and consists of 22 women and 12 men. They were selected for interviews after a period of observation at two Oslo high schools (academic stream) in 1991, and re-interviewed ten years later. The middle generation (the mothers of the young women and the fathers of the young men) consists of 21 women and 12 men born in the period 1940 to 1950. And finally, the oldest generation (the grandmothers and the grandfathers) includes 14 women and 7 men born 1900-1930. We initially interviewed approximately the same number of boys (25) and girls (32) in the youngest generation, but the follow up with fathers and grandfathers was not as successful as the follow up with mothers and grandmothers. The reason for this was partly psychosocial as fathers were less inclined than mothers to participate, partly demographical as fewer grandfathers than grandmothers were still alive, reflecting the fact that men on average have children at a later age than women, but die earlier. The social composition of the sample varies between the generations, reflecting the social mobility of the chains. There is also some unevenness in relation to gender. The social backgrounds of the grandmothers and the grandfathers are similar, with a dominance of informants from the rural working classes. The social background of women and men in the middle generation is also very similar, with a majority coming from urban working class and lower middle class homes, and approximately 1/3 from the middle classes. The social distribution among the girls and the boys in the youngest generation is somewhat uneven, since there is a higher percentage of boys from working class families (approximately 50 %), and middle class families (ca 40 %) and only 10 % from upper middle class families (both academic and economic) - compared to ca 1/3 of the girls in each of the categories. The reason for this is probably that somewhat different criteria for selection were used: The sample of the boys also included a 'sports class' (due to a researcher's specific interest), which was more heavily recruited from a working class background. Any results regarding class differences in relation to gender must therefore be interpreted with caution.

The interview method employed was a semi-structured approximation of the life historical interview. In the present chapter we focus on the stories women and men gave of their childhood and their relations to parents and other close relatives. Our cross-gendered and cross-generational comparative aim made it necessary to be more directive than is usual in this approach. This implies that the informants have not been completely free in their choice of theme, and this could also have had an effect on the narrative style chosen. However, the informants were given sufficient leeway within the proposed topics to make an interpretation of both content and style plausible.

What kind of historical account can we give, using such data? Memories are dependent both upon what happened before and what happened after the experience was made, as well as on the situation in which the memory is told. Narratives are characterized by selections, interpretations and chosen perspectives (Bruner, 2003; Pillemer, 1998). This should not only be seen as a source of error. The possibility to get substantial information about what happened through such accounts should not be underestimated. The choice of perspective can be just as informative as the experiences that are recalled, since it is part and parcel of the historical period talked about – a period that is often made visible through the contrasting perspectives from later periods (cf. Nielsen & Rudberg, 2006; Wengraf, 2001). Finally, as argued above, just as narrative perspectives open up 'outwards' to social change, they also open up 'inwards' through conveying the emotional meanings attached to such change. In our view it is this intertwining between cultural and psychological dynamics that will result in new versions of gender. For these reasons, we have found it a fruitful approach to combine an analysis of narrative style with a deep-hermeneutic content-analysis (Lorenzer, 1986). We follow here the insight of Ricoeur (1991) that both meaning (content as structure) and significance (content as reference to the world) are vital parts of the interpretation of texts.

Narrative styles in three generations

A first striking feature of the interviews is that both within and across generations there are different 'genres' at work in the ways the three generations talk about the world and their self. Let us start with the way the women present their childhood and youth.

Narrative styles in three generations of women

The grandmothers tend to construct their stories in a rather deterministic 'structuralist' way, as they often say: *"that was the way it was back then"*. They will also give rather broad and generalized pictures of their family life, their activities, and the community in which they grew up in. And yet, it is often detailed enough to evoke a feeling of standing in front of a naturalistic landscape painting.

DEVELOPMENT OF SELF IN CULTURE

> I: "Could you describe your childhood and youth"
> A: "I must say that I grew up in a good home. I must say I did. And father was a carpenter, so we always had skies and ski sticks. I had an awfully long way to school, so in winter we went on our skies, if the snow was good. And we had sleighs, too. We lived close to the railway station, so when we went to school, we had to go all the way down in the valley, and over the river – I think we had a 6 km long walk to school." (Rural woman, working class, born in 1910)

Another recognizable characteristic, especially of the rural grandmothers' way of talking, is this alteration between 'we' and 'I', and the description of parents and other adults as positions more than as individuals: In the above quote, father was a carpenter and that seems to be the most important thing to say about him. This also reveals a clear distance from a modern psychological discourse. Sometimes this represents a sort of cultural collision between the interviewers (who themselves are from the middle generation) and the informants: For instance, when asked whether they ever experienced adolescence as a difficult time, the (rural) grandmothers would typically respond: *"We did not have so many problems back then"* or *"I can't remember that we had like puberty and all that stuff. I can't say I had that"*. This descriptive and rather deterministic perspective is also seen in the grandmothers' evaluations, where nuances and reservations are seldom conveyed: Things were either good or bad – and especially criticism of parents and homes is rare. To say that you are discontent seems in many ways to go against deeply rooted norms of modesty. Only death and illnesses can be openly lamented.

This deterministic sociological genre is more or less outdated in the talk of the mothers. Their self-presentation refers more to a psychological discourse, always problematizing their own motives, seeking the answers in childhood experiences as well as reflecting upon their own reconstruction of memories.

> I: "Could you describe your childhood and youth?"
> A: "When I think back on my childhood, and as a young adult, I must say I think it was unusually good and, well, fortunate. And I know that it is like you often forget things, and you repress bad memories, because nobody is totally happy. I know that. But really, I found this diary, from when I was 17 years of age, and it reads there that 'I am so happy, everything is so good'. So I wrote that there." (Urban woman, middle class, born in 1944)

In this quote we see some of the characteristics of the narratives presented by the women in this middle generation: Firstly, they often provide descriptions of family relations and dynamics. Compared to the grandmothers, there is much less focus on material life conditions or the community in which they grew up. Secondly, their recollections of activities and events often slide into interpretations and evaluations. And finally, psychological concepts have become everyday discursive tools, and psychological models are brought in to interpret their lives and feelings. This also seems to imply the removal of a taboo against talking negatively about others – which often involves blaming parents, especially their mothers. Such statements can now be understood within a legitimate field of analytic and interpretative activity, not as final assertions about how somebody 'really' is. Such a distinction does not seem to have much meaning for the grandmothers.

The youngest generation – the 18-year-old daughters in this study – still makes use of this psychological discourse, but it is often at the same time ironically negated (belonging not only to their mother's generation, but also to a trend of confessional intimacy in media which some of them find ridiculous).

> I: "Do you eat dinner together in the family?"
> A: "Well, mostly we eat at home, but not dinners really. We just have a sandwich system. We make dinners when we feel like it and have sandwiches when we don't feel like it. My mom got quite frustrated. Like every time she had made something I said: 'Ugh, are we having <u>that</u> for

dinner?!' [laughs] 'Ugh, I don't want <u>that.</u> Phew!' If it looked kind of boring." (Urban woman, middle class, born in 1971).

Instead of a 'story' of their upbringing, the women in the youngest generation give us bits and pieces, held together more by the underlying emotional tone than by the actual information or a story line. Media genres promoting irony or black humor seem often to be at work in their talk, just like television sitcoms portraying impossible families come to mind in the quote above. In fact, it can be rather difficult to grasp whether the girls convey actual problems or just put themselves and their family on the stage. In some ways this is a less personalized genre than their mothers' descriptions of family dynamics. Their perspective on the world seems to relate more to 'cultural studies' than to the 'sociology' of the grandmothers or the 'psychology' of the mothers.

Evidently, these generation-specific genres stem from varied sources: the contexts of the interview relation, and the specific life phase of the interviewees. The different genres, however, may also tell us something about historical shifts and how people come to understand themselves in different historical contexts. The material changes that we have referred to earlier seem to be reflected both in content and style of the narrative constructions in different generations. The concentration on the outer world among the grandmothers seems easy to understand in light of the scarcity in their childhood; the relational interest among the mothers could be interpreted as a result of the new possibilities of leisure and self-realization; and finally, the observing, ironic style of the youngest generation would be hard to imagine without their extensive access to media, just as their fragmented stories might be an expression of the actual relational havoc surrounding them. The social mobility of the chains in the study is also revealed in the way they talk: While the oldest generation is predominantly from a rural working class background, their granddaughters are brought up in urban middle class families. The fact that the three generations clearly tend to pick different discourses when constructing their memoirs of youth also makes it feasible to view them as small pockets of history, preserved in the individuals. This becomes quite clear when we look at the men in the same three generations.

Narrative styles in three generations of men

The men use more or less the same narrative styles, but also with some marked differences. Just like the women, the men in the oldest generation construct their stories in ways where different and competing perspectives are not seen as relevant. Yet, the grandfathers are even more reticent than the grandmothers, abbreviating the story to its absolute essentials.

> [Describing his childhood] "We had the essential stuff. So we had some cows, and we had a pig. And hens and we had… since it was rather close to the sea, we could, well we did not fish, but a couple of neighbors did fishing. And then we had some fresh water by the side, so there was a lot of halibut." (Rural man, working class, born in 1900)

The kinship-orientation is also similar. Both men and women in this generation describe other people as positions rather than individuals, and make use of "we" instead of singular personal pronouns. This tendency is also observed in cross-cultural memory research where societies valorizing solidarity and collective norms seem to foster a non-individualistic narrative style (cf. Leichtman & Wang, 2005; Wang & Conway, 2006). However, the grandfathers tend more often to start their tale with the generation before their own – as if in need to place themselves within a larger ancestral network. This might of course be an artefact of the (small) sample, but it could also reflect a stronger orientation towards positions and public matters among the men. That this is both a gender- and generation-specific tendency might be illustrated by the response of the researcher, a woman of the 'middle generation', who finds it rather long-winded and irrelevant to the topic. She makes a note that one of the grandfathers "*tells a long and complicated story of kin*", starting with his grandmother's triplets whom people came from miles around to see. The 'real' story of this grandfather's life begins, according to this researcher, only at page thirteen. This urge to construct long ancestral stories among the men could also be related to studies showing that men tend to construct more linear narratives than women (cf. Gergen & Gergen, 1993).

Otherwise, gender differences in this generation seem more related to the content than the style of their narratives. Not surprisingly, given the rather strict gender division in rural society, the women talk more about family, children and household matters. And even though the grandmothers often are as descriptive in their recollections, the grandfathers' matter-of-factness seems more distant - sometimes even quite horrid events are turned into a 'good story'. Many grandfathers have experienced the death of both siblings and parents. Yet, the tragedy is seldom the main theme; everyday details take over: When talking about a dead sibling, one man quickly recalls all the coffee drinking in his childhood, laughing: "*I have often asked myself if they did not have anything else to do!*" Another one who grew up with a grandmother who buried an aborted embryo in the potato field after a miscarriage, concludes rather laconically: "*But luckily us children were kept out of it*". The matter-of-factness of these stories does of course not exclude emotions, shown both in silences and bravado. Still, the temperature in such family-oriented stories is generally lower than the feelings that are displayed in the memories about work:

> "I though it was a lot of fun. I liked working. I really enjoyed it. /…/ These plates over there, we got them every Christmas. And a big gift, yeah it could be an ash tray. Out there (pointing to the wall on the veranda) there are almost 20 plates. And still I didn't get them all. In the beginning, you know, we worked half day Christmas Eve, as well." (Rural man, working class, born in 1900).

The non-individualistic and emotionally low-key style of the grandfathers is followed up by the working class men in the middle generation, who seem quite embarrassed at the request to describe themselves. However, the middle class men in this generation rather willingly produce more self-focused narratives.

> [Describing his childhood] "I was in rebellion from when I was in 4th-5th grade, so I was a rebel. Against everything, actually. First parents, and that was as it is in that age. So then you had few things to hold on to otherwise. I think I was quite a vulnerable child, and I have it today, too, an understanding of how people are, and can detect it very quickly(…) It may be a bit sentimental, but the image of dandelions growing through the asphalt. Like always the chance to get through as long as you don't stop. But I've also seen myself in this image of being one who climbs upwards a hill of quicksand." (Urban man, middle class, born 1947).

Self-analysis often becomes quite important: One man talks about his childhood and adolescence as times of *"alienation"*, resulting in a lifelong *"insecurity in a masculine milieu"* always being the one *"chosen last for the team"*. Another one talks about his childhood as a *"disastrous time"* where he developed a taste for jazz as a reaction to his religious parents. This whole interview is permeated with self-reflexive comments, also in relation to the interviewer: *"You must just interrupt me, I just talk my head off"*. Like many other middle class men of this generation, the above fathers emphasize that they are creative and non-conformist. And when work is mentioned - which in contrast to the grandfathers is quite seldom - it is usually as a site for possible self development.

The personal softness that is underlined is therefore often combined with a strong sense of being a unique individual with rights to develop according to one's own potential. One of the men, who had a breakdown after a divorce, has now *"become more accomplished in verbalizing emotions"*. He describes himself as open, one who *"dares where others don't"*. And the result of this self-scrutinizing has made him capable of helping others: Women actually call him for help with their emotionally taciturn husbands. There are obviously others involved in this life project, and in contrast to the grandfathers' stories, children are often mentioned as very important. Nevertheless, the impression remains that these men present narrative memories from a perspective of individualization, and that their new self-reflexivity primarily is directed towards promoting personal growth.

The youngest generation of the interviewed men, all 18 years old in 1991, use narrative styles that are both similar and different from the one used by their fathers. At this age (in this culture) they are still their parents' children rather than grown ups in their own right, and this also colours their narratives. Their age evidently fuels a great interest in questions concerning who they are (which could also be seen as a consequence of their child centered upbringing, cf. Wang & Conway, 2006). The most striking feature of the self descriptive narratives in the youngest generation is how willingly and abundantly they are delivered. They are on average much longer than in their fathers' generation – not to mention their grandfathers' shorthand versions of the same.

> [Asked about being young] "The only systematic diary I've written is from the interrail. Well, I did also write before, maybe every other day or something. Got down all what had happened and a bit of my thought and feelings. And I've had some…rounds. I had a bit of an identity crisis in March where I…Well, really felt like breaking away from this ascending education thing. My stepfather has been a sort of model for me, he has gone straight ahead. And then he went to this course in self-development and that was very good. It is like, he really had a confrontation with himself during that week, and understood how much he has lost by just going the straight way following what other people think is what counts as being successful." (Urban man, higher middle class, born in 1972)

Many of these young men describe themselves as being oriented towards relations. The one quoted above calls himself a *"rubber joint"* that smoothens conflicts and creates harmony. The boys discuss many personal and sensitive themes with the interviewer. At the same time as relationships are valued as important, the boys tend – just like their fathers - to enhance their own uniqueness by underlining an explicit outsider status. This status could be related both to a remarkable degree of sensitivity (which might be characterized as a traditionally 'feminine' quality) as well as more or less traditionally 'masculine' criteria like for instance *"a critical taste in music"*, an uncommunicative approach in the classroom or a dream of driving across the American continent. In some cases it is enough to dress in black:

> "No I don't like what is fashionable right now. /.../ I hate it, to be honest. I don't like to be put in a box. You should rather get dressed in what you feel most comfortable with. /Black shirts?/ I like clothes that are different. Maybe it's a protest too, because a lot of people think it looks strange /.../ I don't like to be stereotypical, you see." (Urban man, working class, born in 1971).

Among the middle class boys the psychological perspective is actually more prominent than among girls from the same social background; there seems almost to be a sort of 'cultural lag' at work here. This does not mean that the girls no longer show an intense interest in relational matters. On the contrary, there is a tendency that the traditional 'feminine' care for others is not discarded, but combined with more autonomous strivings and sometimes transformed into a celebration of collective responsibility. This has been characterized as a kind of 'relational individualism' (Chodorow, 1986; Nielsen, 2004; Nielsen & Rudberg, 2006), which could also be seen in the political arena, as values of the welfare state seem to appeal more to young women than to young men (Christensen, 1994; Nielsen, 2004; Nielsen & Rudberg, 2006).

The boys in this study take another route: At the same time as relationships are valued as important, they tend – just like their fathers – to enhance their own uniqueness, which might be indicative of their unresolved struggles to combine old individualism and new relational orientation. This insistence on uniqueness, intertwined with the psychological perspective, might be the reason why there is a relative lack of ironic distance in the boys' narratives – an irony which we as youth researchers rather expected from young men belonging to 'Generation X'. In this study, the boys seem to take themselves quite seriously, actually a bit more seriously than the young women who often excelled in self-ironic commentary.

Narrative constructions and emotional meanings

The narrative styles presented here tell us a generational as well a gendered story.[1] It is a story of individualization connected with both modernized masculinity and femininity. The main shift in perspective seems to take place in the middle generation – although the class differences are important to take into account. The self-reflexive psychological discourse is the main tool for both (middle class) men and women in this process. Yet, this similarity in discursive tools becomes less pronounced when we look at their use and consequence. Women use it to analyze their traditional arena of personal relations more or less extended to a collective responsibility, whereas men add sensitive, personal growth to what could be seen as a traditionally masculine individualization. Both the starting point and the outcome of the psychological perspective have gendered characteristics, which imply that there could be different meanings attached to similar narrative styles. Thus, a reading of narrative perspectives could open up our understanding not only outwards to social change of gender, but also inwards to the subjective processes involved in such change.

In order to grasp this intertwined process, we will take the changes of gender in the family as our point of departure. As mentioned earlier, there have been noticeable and rapid changes in the material and social circumstances throughout the lives of these generations, and this also applies to gender equality. The youngest generation actually lives in a society where such equality is official policy, reinforced by different legislative measures. The 30-year old law on gender equality in Norway (passed in 1979) covers areas like equal right to education, equal salary for equal work, and laws against discrimination on the basis of gender or sexuality. There has also been a promotion of women joining work outside home, both by extended periods of parental leave and guaranteeing public child care above the age of one. The percentage of women partaking in work outside home has gone from 44 % to 78 % in the period from 1974 to 2008, and the great change came in the middle generation of our study. The trend for men is, although slower, in the 'reverse' direction, e.g. from work to home: The use of the 'father quota' of the parental leave (now extended to 12 weeks) has increased from a meager 1-2 % in 1988 to a vast majority of 90 % in 2008 (Holter, Svare & Egeland, 2008).

Thus, there has been a social facilitation of gender change in our society. But how has this subjectively become something that men and women not only dutifully take part in, but even *want* to do? This question may be more challenging in relation to men, since in many ways they have had a lot to lose. Men have – in public debate and research – often been depicted as a rather static gender in regard to this part of social change, in sharp contrast to their role as a driving force in the making of modernity itself. However, there is research that currently tells a different and more optimistic story about 'new men' and 'flexible fathers', practicing gender in 'modern families' (cf. Aarseth, 2009). How has the interaction between cultural and psychological processes contributed to these new versions of gender? Let us take a look at the accounts of our interviewees from this perspective.

Parental identifications in three generations

The family is not only the arena where official policy of gender equality could be 'performed', it is also the site where some of the most potent emotional loadings of cultural constructions of gender are developed.[2] Such emotional meanings partly stem from specific psycho-biographies. Although in-depth interpretations of individual cases are outside the scope of this chapter, it is possible to detect some generational patterns in the subjective meanings attached to gender in change, through tracing the micro-histories of parental identification.

Identification with the same-sex parent

In the grandparents' generation there is a clear pattern of identification with the same-sex parent among both women and men. The rural women hold their hard working mothers in high regard, and the middle class urban women, who experience the first trembling suggestions of cultural individualization, identify with mothers who can be associated with both intellectual capacity and emotional sensitivity. At the same time as these grandmothers identify with their rather competent and/or hard working mother, they have a joint tendency to idealize father: He is the one with time to play or show one the world. As we shall see, this is a tendency among women of all three generations: It is almost always positive to be like your father – while similarity to mother could be a highly ambivalent affair.

In contrast to the urban middle class women, none of the men in the grandfathers' generation mentions emotional sensitivity as a basis for their identification with their father. In need of comfort they almost always went to mother. Regardless of social background, all fathers are depicted as being in touch with the world outside home, even in families where mothers worked. The result is that father often gets an adventurous aura, instigating clear admiration in their sons. One of the grandfathers gives a detailed description of his *"unique"* father, the village tailor who was the recognized social centre of the village, sitting *"like the joker in the deck of cards"*. An upper class grandfather describes an even more 'public' father who took part in the struggle against the union with Sweden in 1905. His family is obviously well off and socializes with men in high positions.

In the grandfathers' stories mother is much less visible than father was in the ones told by the grandmothers. There is only one of the grandfathers who seems to identify with his mother, and as he himself emphasizes, she is clearly an exceptional woman. This is a mother who was left by her husband and managed to take care of all her children on her own. Grandfather recalls that she *"worked like a man"* and actually was *"50 years ahead of these feminists of today"*. But even in this case there is a certain admiration for the deserting father who actually died from syphilis: He was a fantastic singer and at one point he made enough money to buy himself a car! This kind of idealization of a 'useless' father is found, almost word by word, in the autobiographies of other Norwegian men in the same generation, collected by the Norwegian social anthropologist Marianne Gullestad (1996). In other words, father seems to represent the exciting contact with the outer world, even in the rare cases where mother is the main identification figure. Thus, there are two overall similarities between men and women in our oldest generation: Firstly, they both seem to identify primarily with the same-sex parent, and secondly, they both tend to idealize father in their parental memories. Not surprisingly, the majority of both women and men in this generation find 'modern' narratives on gender relations against nature as well as unwanted for themselves.[3]

Identification with the opposite-sex parent

In the middle generation of our study there is also a striking similarity between women and men, but now in a shared tendency to identify with the opposite-sex parent. The ambivalent relationship with mother in the middle generation of women has been amply documented also in other studies (cf. Bengtsson, 2001; Ekerwald, 2002; Hite 1994). On a psychological level the boundaries often seem to be blurred, not least because the daughter in this generation might become their housewife mother's main life project. For the daughter this could imply cherished closeness as well as a constant urge for separation (cf. Chodorow, 1978; Nielsen & Rudberg, 1989). This ambivalence could also be seen as a psychological dynamic behind the rather contemptuous cultural constructions of the housewife of the fifties among some women in this middle generation (cf. Nielsen, 2003). The idealization of the father is at its peak in this generation, since father is seen both culturally and psychologically as a symbol for the freedom that the girl wants to achieve for herself.

While mothers are dethroned by the women, the same thing happens to fathers of the men in the middle generation, although to a slighter degree. This process of gradual approach to mother and distancing from father is also shown in a Swedish study of men born in the 1950s and 1980s (Bengtsson, 2001). But there is one important gendered difference in this opposite-sex identification: The men seem to use less emotional energy in the process. Only two of the men tell us about actual conflicts with their fathers. One of them describes his father as *"tough"*, *"always working"* and *"a somewhat bad psychologist"*, although there was nothing *"really bad in him"*. This informant had a much closer relation with his mother. In the other case, the son also had harsh conflicts with his father who left his wife and five children. The resulting identification with mother is very strong, emphasizing her ability to keep the family together. At her funeral he comments to his siblings: *"Now the chief is dead"*. In spite of this, he is also quite forgiving in relation to his father who fell in love with another woman. He can actually sympathize with his father's choice: *"You know, this is what love is"*.

The new conflicts with mother that we could see among the women in this generation probably stem from different sources. The phase of their life could be important – their mothers are often alive and the conflicts therefore still going on. The more child-centered norms of upbringing that are at work in this generation will also contribute to heightened demands of 'good mothers', and possible failures to live up to these standards will become more evident to the daughters. And finally, the middle generation lives in a time where questions of power are formulated in relation to gender, and where their housewife mothers seem to represent the threat of a bleak future.

But how are we to understand the shift from father to mother as identification object among some of the men? The life phase, the child-centered upbringing as well as the historical context might be important factors in their case as well. Still, as we have seen, there are some important gender differences: As the relative lack of conflictual intensity suggests, the 'push' away from father is never as emotionally loaded and conflict ridden as the push away from mother among the women in this generation. The distancing from father seems often to be associated with his strict work ethic, resulting in a life without freedom and pleasure. The social mobility and new cultural demands for flexibility make father's fixed identity problematic. Or as one of the men says, in an ironic (and somewhat contemptuous) tone: *"My father is the last member of the working class in this country"*.

At the same time, the 'pull' towards identification with the opposite-sex parent is not as strong among the men as it was among the women. This identification does not refer to the mothers' level of competence, which is not so surprising since this is the generation of housewives. But the contempt expressed by many women is never demonstrated among the men, perhaps implying that the threat of becoming *totally* like mother, i.e. ending up in a feminine position, is not seen as relevant by them. What the men themselves emphasize as a reason for the displacement of identification is the closeness they have with mother – an emotional openness which is lacking in their relationship with father. In an earlier Norwegian study, Holter and Aarseth (1993) made a similar observation: It is not father's authoritarian style that makes the sons in this generation upset with him, but rather his lack of emotional presence. And this is also what the men primarily wish to do differently in their own future fathering.

The emotional distance from father has of course often been the case in the earlier generation as well, but now it actually seems possible to make this the main reason for (dis)-identification. Still, the shift towards identification with mother seems hesitant. The men somehow continue to play both sides, and will possibly be kept in ambivalent longing for both worlds (cf. Holter & Aarseth, 1993). The contours of the 'new man' are discernable in this generation, but will he find a comfortable home in the new cultural discourses and practical demands of gender equality? Their ambivalence is shown in the 'in principle' attitude, documented in other studies (cf. Jalmert, 1984; Åström, 1990): Gender equality is a good idea, but it is hard to apply to their personal situation, which is also shown in the statistics reported earlier. The area where the subjective force to change is most prominent concerns the relationship with their children. Will this be noticeable in the generation of their sons?

Asymmetrical identification

The relative symmetry of identificatory patterns (same-sex, cross-over identification) in the two oldest generations is no longer present in the youngest one: Here the women seem to find their way back to mother as an identification figure; the majority describes the relationship as predominantly positive. There are many reasons for this: They take their mothers' combination of family and work as a general model for their own lives – although they may want other jobs, a less stressful life, fewer divorces and more equal division of household tasks. They admire or rather *respect* their mothers almost as much as the grandmothers respected their mothers. The boundaries between the women are clearer in the youngest generation; the daughter is no longer the mother's only life project. A new trend is also that these girls look at their mothers as the dominant figures in the family. Now it is actually father who is often portrayed as the frail and emotional parent, and the girls' relationship with him is quite close. However, this closeness does not threaten the girl's boundaries as an autonomous individual the way the closeness to mother did in the middle generation. At the same time, the father's role as liberator is no longer as necessary, since the boundaries vis-à-vis mother are strengthened; the relative idealization of father is almost vanished when the girls are re-interviewed 10 years later.

Whereas the women in the youngest generation seem to return to a pattern of same-sex identifications, the men present a different picture: In the first interview, father and mother are equally preferred as identification objects. But *most* of the boys insist that they identify with *none* of their parents (this trend is not seen among the girls). The boys who identify with their fathers give nuanced descriptions, with many reservations in relation to some aspects of father's life and personality, like the *"mad career rush"* or *"his managerial character"*. In the few cases where there are open conflicts with father, the emphasis is on his lack of communicative skill and openness, the same complaints their own fathers had against the grandfathers' generation. The identifications with mother are also presented with hesitation: Some of the sons emphasize mother's creativity, her emotional openness as well as her reading the 'right books'. However, there is only one boy who openly *admires* his mother. The fact that identification with none of the parents is now the prominent trend could of course be related to a phase in life when stressing one's own separate individuality is especially important. Still, that would not explain the gender difference, a difference that is also seen in the interviews ten years later. At this point there is even an increase in the insistence among the men that one is identified with 'none' of the parents.

The gender gap is less pronounced in the youngest generation: they want both close relations and autonomy, both families and work outside home. And yet, as we have seen, some important differences remain: Although the young men have strengthened their relational orientation, they still seem to safeguard their individualized position through this identification with 'nobody' which demarcates them as unique. This nobody-identification might not only involve traditional masculine demarcation but also an open-ended and flexible 'freedom' to become anything one wants and where the 'self' is paradoxically more malleable than before. One might think that this would involve some sort of queering, where not only selfhood but also gender becomes more fluid. However, our data show that boys in this generation are quite sceptical to such suggestions, as they unanimously wish to uphold the differences between the sexes, mostly as an erotic trigger to *"keep the excitement alive"*. This difference is usually strictly bodily defined – the activities at home or work are not involved.[4] Gender equality seems to be more or less self evident both as discourse and subjective premise (which does not exclude outbursts against *"hardcore feminists"*).

In Scandinavia, the youngest generation has been brought up within a child centered tradition, as well as a culture and social organization promoting gender equality. That has two implications: Firstly, *mother* becomes a relevant identificatory figure for boys as well, and secondly, *father* is often an emotionally present person in his son's life.[5] Thus, family practices emphasizing emotional closeness and allowing expressions of feelings have probably become more 'gender-neutral', or 'unhooked' from gender. This might be a contributing factor to the more easy-going use of the psychological perspective in the youngest generation of men, as well as to their tendency *not* to choose one parent above the other as the main figure of identification. One consequence is that these boys no longer hesitate to express quite openly their need for emotional closeness. To the youngest generation such openness seems more or less to be a prerequisite for *any* close relationship, with men as well as with women. This is also the case among even younger boys. A new longitudinal study of Norwegian school children shows small boys who can praise and comfort each other, in ways previously more associated with the relations between girls. This new tendency does not vanish as the boys grow older, although gender issues become more important (Nielsen, 2010). Later in life, this might also prove to be part of the motivational basis for taking part in the activities of child care and other practices of gender equality, in a way that represents something else than dutiful adaptation to outer, more or less feminist, demands (Aarseth, 2008).

Narrative constructions, psychological identifications and gender in change

Throughout we have stressed that narrative perspectives could open up both outwards to the cultural patterns involved in gendered and generational change, and inwards to the subjective significance attached to such transformations. Most social and cultural researchers today agree that people use cultural concepts to organize their social world and to constitute themselves in meaningful ways. We have tried to take this one step further through looking at the way such cultural constructions are 'animated' with personal and emotional meaning. In that way a narrative style has to be grasped both in a cultural and a psychological context, which does not just involve a conscious meaning-making subject, but also psycho-biographical processes of a more unconscious kind. When analyzing a narrative, Paul Ricoeur (1991) says, we should always look for the points of support it gets from experience, but also the more unconscious passions that the narrative both expresses and might make more bearable. This is in line with the heightened interest in investigating the relationship between subjectivity and culture that is found in the new psychosocial approach in social science (e.g. Chodorow, 1999; Hollway & Jefferson, 2000; Layton 1998).

Our specific focus in this article has been to analyse how narrative styles and patterns of psychological identification could be seen as dynamic and intermingled processes feeding into each other in the construction of new gender. In many ways there seems to be a close 'fit' between them: Among the oldest informants, the narrative styles were clearly embedded in a culture where practical work and traditions were privileged in relation to an inner world of feelings – and an identification with mother and father in this generation will certainly be adaptable, promoting stability and continuity. In the middle generation the cultural world seems to become more conflictual as well as to 'move inside', and both feelings and words become significant in a new way. The quest for autonomy gives father a special role in the identification process of a girl, at the same time as the quest for closeness is more pronounced among the men, resulting in a hesitant identification with mother. The narrative style of the youngest generation seems to waver between the 'outside' and the 'inside', being both distant/ironic and relational/psychological – recognizing neither the old ways of their grandparents nor the new ways of their parents, as their own. The refusal of the young men in this generation to commit themselves to modelling one parent could be interpreted within a cultural discourse stressing limitless individual possibility, while at the same time the need to integrate relations within this freedom is of paramount importance. For the young women the cultural dichotomy between relations and autonomy might be less psychologically conflictual than it is for the men, partly because it is culturally promoted through gender equality, but also since it is experienced as possible to integrate in the lives of their own mothers.

Thus, men and women can be more or less emotionally attuned to old as well as new cultural patterns, at the same time as both cultural demands and emotional histories are conflictual. It is the dynamic interweaving of these conflicts – rather than any seamless 'fit' between culture and psychology – that is involved in the emergence of new gender relations. This also implies that psychological identifications will not only represent adaptation to (and reproduction of) cultural patterns, but in themselves result in subjective forces towards social and cultural change. The middle generation can be seen as an illustration of such – in no way smooth – processes: The women who struggled for autonomy by idealizing their fathers both strengthened traditional gender narratives and transgressed them, in ways that significantly changed the psychological as well as cultural situation for their daughters. Similarly, among the men, we could discern a rather strong discontent with a cultural pattern of paternal distance, and yet not a strong enough subjective motivation to overthrow traditional gender narratives altogether. Still, the psychological destabilization in this generation seems to have had consequences in one important area, namely their wish for closeness with their own children – a closeness which made possible the 'unhooking' of emotion from gender in their sons' generation. This shows the complex dynamic between cultural narratives and emotional meanings: On the one hand, new narratives can provide tools to strengthen old psychological positions, the way feminism (partly) played along with a psychological contempt for women and the psychological perspective (partly) strengthened masculine individualization. On the other hand, new psychological positions can be ahead of cultural patterns and represent a pressure in relation to cultural change by changing practices in a psychologically sensitive and potent area, creating a sort of 'butterfly effect' in the gender system as a whole.

Notes

1 It is obviously also a story of class, which has been noted throughout in the text. However, the number of informants in each category is too small to make a systematic comparison possible.

2 The suggestion that generational and gendered patterns of upbringing and parental identification are significant mediators in (re)creating gender is not new. Memory researchers have often reported that parents, regardless of gender, have a more elaborative style in talks with their daughters when it comes to emotions and maybe especially sadness. The talk with boys seems to be more oriented towards active solutions to the problems causing the sadness (Fivush & Buckner, 2003; Reese & Fivush, 1993). In relation to our study this might tell us something about the gender-specific readiness to make use of a psychological and emotional discourse.

3 This is not the case for some of the urban middle class grandmothers, who are quite aware of the unjust treatment of women, even cheering the feminists of today. There are also regrets among many of the women connected with the fact that they were denied education.

4 To talk about queering at this stage might be as premature as the talk of gender equality was in the grandfathers' generation. On the other hand, that comparison also goes to show that rapid changes are possible.

5 In a report from a representative sample of 2805 people the percentage of men that feels that father has been absent has decreased in the younger age brackets, from 57 %

among men between 35-49 years old, to 38% among men in the age of 17-24 (Holter, Svare & Egeland, 2008). Even if there is a decrease, however, there is still a substantial feeling of being out of touch with father – which could also be seen among some of the boys in our sample.

References

Aarseth, H. (2008). *Hjemskapingens moderne magi* [The modern magic of home making]. Doctoral dissertation, Department of Sociology and Human Geography, Oslo University.

Aarseth, H. (2009). From modernized masculinity to degendered lifestyle projects. Changes in men's narratives on domestic participation 1990-2005. *Men and Masculinity, 11*, 424-444.

Almås, R. K., Karlsen, H., & Thorland, I. (1995). *Fra pliktsamfunn til mulighetstorg: Tre generasjoner skriver sin ungdom* [From a society of duty to a market of possibilities: Three generations write their youth]. Report, Centre for Rural Studies, University of Trondheim, Norway.

Bengtsson, M. (2001). *Tid, rum och kön* [Time, space and gender]. Lund: Studentlitteratur.

Bruner, J. (2003). Self-making narratives. In R. Fivush & C. S. Haden (Eds.), *Autobiographical memory and the construction of a narrative self. Developmental and cultural perspectives* (pp 210-325). New Jersey: Lawrence Erlbaum Associated Publishers.

Chodorow, N. (1978). *The reproduction of mothering*. Berkeley: Berkeley University Press.

Chodorow, N. (1986). Toward a relational individualism: The mediation of self through psychoanalysis. In *Feminism and psychoanalytical theory* (pp 154-162). Cambridge, England: Polity Press.

Chodorow, N. (1999). *The power of feeling*. London: Yale University Press.

Christensen, A.-D. (1994). Køn, ungdom og værdiopbrud [Gender, youth and changed values]. In J. Andersen & L. Torpe (Eds.), *Demokrati og politisk kultur. Rids af et demokratisk medborgerskab* [Democracy and political culture. Sketch of a democratic citizenship] (pp. 175-210). Herning: Forlaget Systime.

Ekerwald, H. (2002). *Varje mor er en dotter Om kvinnors ungdomstid under 1900-talet*. [Every mother is a daughter. About the youth of women during the 20th century]. Stockholm: Symposion.

Fivush, R., & Buckner, J. P. (2003). Creating gender and identity through autobiographical narratives. In R. Fivush & C. A. Haden (Eds.), *Autobiographical memory and the construction of a narrative self. Developmental and cultural perspectives* (pp 149-167). New Jersey: Lawrence Erlbaum Associated Publishers.

Gergen, M. N., & Gergen, K. J. (1993). Narratives of the gendered body in popular autobiography. In R. Josselson & A. Lieblich (Eds.), *The narrative study of lives* (Vol. I, pp 191-218). Newbury Park, CA: Sage.

Giddens, A. (1991). *Modernity and self-identity: Self and society in the late modern age*. Cambridge: Polity Press.

Gullestad, M. (1996). *Every day life philosophers: Modernity, morality and autobiography in Norway*. Oslo: Universitetsforlaget.

Hite, S. (1994). *Growing up under patriarchy. The Hite report on the family*. London: Bloomsbury.

Holter, Ø., & Aarseth, H. (1993). *Menns livssammenheng* [The life contexts of men]. Oslo: Ad Notam Gyldendal.

Holter, Ø. G., Svare, H., & Egeland, C. (2008). *Likestilling og livskvalitet 2007* [Equality and quality of life in 2007]. AFI-report no. 1/2008. Oslo: Work Research Institute.

Jalmert, L. (1984). *Den svenske mannen* [The Swedish man]. Stockholm: Tiden.

Hollway, W., & Jefferson, T. (2000). *Doing qualitative research differently: Free association narrative and the interview method*. London: Sage.

Lange, E. (1998). *Samling om felles mål 1935-1970* [With joint goals 1935-1970]. Oslo: Aschehoug.

Layton, L. (1998). *Who's that girl? Who's that boy? Clinical practice meets postmodern gender theory*. Hillsdale, N. J: The Analytic Press.

Leichtman, M. D., & Wang, Q. (2005). A socio-historical perspective on autobiographical memory development. In D. B. Pillemer & W. S. White (Eds.), *Developmental psychology and social change – research, history and policy* (pp. 35-58). Cambridge: Cambridge University Press.

Lorenzer, A. (1986). Tiefenhermeneutische Kulturanalyse. In A. Lorenzer (Ed.), *Kultur-Analysen* (pp. 1-98). Franfurt am Main: Fischer Wissenschaft.

Nielsen, H. B. (2003). Historical, cultural, and emotional meanings: interviews with young girls in three generations. *NORA – Nordic Journal of Feminist and Gender Research, 11*(1), 14-26.

Nielsen, H. B. (2004). Noisy girls: New subjectivities and old gender discourses. *Young – Nordic Journal of Youth Research, 12*(1), 9-30.

Nielsen, H. B. (2010). *Skoletid* [School years]. Oslo: Universitetsforlaget.

Nielsen, H. B., & Rudberg, M. (1989). *Historien om gutter og jenter* [The story of boys and girls]. Oslo: Universitetsforlaget.

Nielsen, H. B., & Rudberg, M. (2006). *Moderne jenter. Tre generasjoner på vei* [Modern girls. Three generations on the move]. Oslo: Universitetsforlaget.

Pillemer, D. B. (1998). *Momentous events, vivid memories*. Cambridge: Harvard University Press.

Reese, E., & Fivush, R. (1993). Parental styles of talking about the past. *Developmental Psychology, 29*, 596-606.

Ricoeur, P. (1970/1991). "What is a text?". in M. J. Valdes (Ed.), *A Ricouer reader: Reflections and Imaginations* (pp. 195-199). New York: Harvester/Wheatsheaf.

Wang, Q., & Conway, M. A. (2006). Autobiographical memory, self, and culture. In L. G. Nilsson & N. Ohta (Eds.), *Memory and society. Psychological Perspectives* (pp. 9-28). Hove & New York: Psychology Press.

Wengraf, T. (2001). *Qualitative research interviewing. Biographic and semi-structured metods*. London: Sage.

Åström, L. (1990). Fäder och söner. Bland svenska män i tre generationer [Fathers and sons. Among Swedish men from three generations]. Helsingborg: Carlssons Bokförlag.

Peter Berliner
Line Natascha Larsen
Elena de Casas Soberón

A social action learning approach to community resilience

9

"Our sharing of thoughts and feelings, our respect and trust should be passed on to the next generation"

> *We are not ignorant women, we know what we must expect*
> *and not expect.*
> *We know of oppression and torture,*
> *We know of extortion and violence,*
> *Destitution, disease*[1]

In Paamiut in Kalaallit Nunaat (Greenland) a community mobilisation programme has been launched as a response to a history of violence, suicides, drug abuse, and child neglect. The programme is developed by members of the community through public meetings and interviews of an inclusive sample of community members. The overall goal of the programme is to strengthen community resilience, psychosocial well-being and revitalisation of the culture through promotion of locally formulated values and resources, shared activities, mobilisation of social networks, job opportunities and options for entrepreneurship. One of the main goals is to prevent child neglect through a specific programme for young mothers, who were considered as especially endangered by risk factors in the community – such as social marginalisation, unemployment, alcohol abuse, and being exposed to abusive behaviour. The young mothers who were invited all agreed to participate and all except for one stayed in the group through the duration of the entire programme and continued to meet as a group after the end of the programme.

Paamiut Asasara (*My beloved Paamiut*) is a programme based on the framework of mobilisation for community resilience. The framework of understanding is informed by community psychology and resilience research (Anasarias & Berliner, 2009; Berliner, Anasarias & de Casas Soberón, 2010; Berliner, Larsen & de Casas Soberón, 2012). The applied perspective is on promoting well-being and health through active participation of the citizens in using resources in the community, as well as developing new problem-solving methods for new types of challenges. Through community mobilisation the programme aims to promote changes that increase local groups' active participation in decision-making and in activities that hold the potential to enhance quality of life for the participants.

This chapter describes the development of a new understanding of self and others within a group of young mothers in Paamiut. The group succeeded in developing and enhancing the previous social network system that provided support in cases where the development of the attachment between mother and child was disturbed by risk factors such as alcohol abuse and/or domestic violence. A new understanding of the protection of mothering, of the importance of mutual social support, and a sense of belonging emerged in this group and was disseminated to the local community through public meetings and the local media.

The group was organised within the framework of psychosocial interventions, i.e. supporting a socially endangered group through a shared process of community capacity building (Berliner & Mikkelsen, 2006). The present study is part of the ongoing involvement of research in the development of Paamiut Asasara. Up to now the data collection encompasses 92 individual and group interviews of adult citizens, interviews with 62 young people (and follow up interviews with 18 young people after one year), a survey on values told and values lived (see below), observations from participation in individual and family counselling and supervision of staff (42 sessions + 40 hours with staff), interviews with professionals in health, law enforcement, welfare and education and the collection of statistics on violence and crime from public resources. The total population of Paamiut is 1620 people.

Background

Current research (Christensen, Kristensen & Baviskar, 2008) has identified the need to examine and improve the living conditions for at least 27% of the children in Greenland, 15% having urgent need of support and 12% having some need of support to improve their living conditions. The study shows a wide range of problems for this group of children and demonstrates that alcohol and cannabis abuse, domestic violence (most often violence against the female in the couple, i.e. gender violence) and child neglect form the living context for the most endangered children.

In Paamiut Asasara one of the main goals is to eradicate all sorts of passive or active neglect of children, including sexual abuse and other forms of violence against children. As a part of this process, a comparison has been made to the situation in other parts of the world. Finkelhor (1994) and subsequently Pereda, Guilera, Forns and Gomez-Benito (2009) carried out an overview of the current worldwide situation and concluded that in the 21 countries studied (mainly high- and middle-income countries) at least 7% of females (ranging up to 36%) and 3% of males (ranging up to 29%) reported that they had been the victims of sexual abuse during childhood.

In Kalaallit Nunaat a survey of children's exposure to sexual abuse revealed that 9% of the boys and 28% of the girls report that they have been exposed to sexual abuse (Curtis et al., 2006). Contrastingly, Christensen et al.'s study (2008) shows that mothers report that only 5% of their children have been exposed to sexual abuse. In the same report the mothers also report that an average of 35% of the mothers themselves had been exposed to sexual abuse during childhood.

Even though the figures in Kalaallit Nunaat are higher than the global average, the research shows that the problem of sexual abuse of children is global and that Kalaallit Nunaat does not have the highest rate in the world. Violence against children is a global problem, which has been profoundly summarized by Pinheiro (2006). Pereda et al. (2009) show that a high prevalence of abuse can be found in most countries globally, so every country should be aware of this problem and take action to prevent the sexual abuse of children. In Kalaallit Nunaat there is a widespread and outspoken awareness of the problem and programmes have been launched to prevent and lessen the problem. Unfortunately, the results have been limited and we argue that prevention must rest upon a broader contextual approach which promotes values and supportive communities rather than focusing exclusively on the problem in itself.

Addressing this challenge of launching a broader community-based approach, the town of Paamiut has initiated the 5-year community mobilisation programme: *Paamiut Asasara*. The programme started in January 2008. The population of Paamiut is approx. 500 children/youth and 1000 adults. There is a majority of men in the community, almost 150 more than women. The population consists of families with a long history in Paamiut and families which moved to the town during the process of the closing down of the smaller settlements in the proximity of Paamiut during the last 50 years. Fishing and the fish factory are the main constituents of the economy. The language is Kalaallissut, the Inuit language.

The population is very active in the development of the Paamiut Asasara programme and the citizens address the abovementioned challenges and build attractive alternatives through cultural events, sport, and art. The approach is based on locally defined values and locally available resources. The population does not see itself as victimized, but as a group of people fully capable of changing the situation positively. There is a high level of collective self-efficacy and hope within the community setting.

We assessed the situation and set a baseline in Paamiut in March 2008. This was done through a series of collaborative research interviews with key people in social welfare, law enforcement, health and education, conducted by the first author. The interviewees placed more emphasis on finding solutions than on exact quantifications of the problems – which was, and is, in line with the guiding principles of the Paamiut Asasara programme.

The hospital staff estimated that around one third of the children are born into families where there is a risk of neglect, due to one or more of the risk factors mentioned below. The kindergarten staff estimated that approximately one out of ten of the children in the daycare centres are exposed to some type of neglect at home. Schoolteachers assessed the percentage of neglect at around the same level. The social service and the police estimated that more than 50% of the children and their families were in need of psychosocial support. Specific risk factors for the family include: (1) alcoholism or cannabis abuse, (2) unemployment, poor housing and poor economy, (3) violence or other crime, (4) parents suffering from being exposed to neglect or sexual assault during their childhood, (5) single parent households with less means of protection of the child, and (6) mental health problems in the family.

The Survey of *Living Conditions in the Arctic* (SLICA, 2006) showed that family relationships and social networks in the local community are essential to the quality of life for the citizens in Paamiut. The study was carried out in 2005 with a random sample of 58 citizens of Paamiut and 14 from the smaller settlement of Arsuk, which administratively is part of Paamiut. The results were compared to those obtained in the capital of Kalaallit Nunaat (Greenland), Nuuk. Nuuk is a comparatively big town, whereas Paamiut is seen as a small town with a tight social network in which everybody knows each other to a certain extent. The study found significant differences in the percentage of respondents that reported that they have access to social support and points towards generally low levels of support in Paamiut compared to Nuuk. While only 46% of the respondents in Paamiut reported that they have access to somebody who will listen to them, the percentage in Nuuk was surprisingly high at 73%. Similarly 49% of the respondents in Paamiut reported that they have somebody whom they can confide in, whereas the percentage was 75% in Nuuk. Finally, only 40% in Paamiut stated that they have access to somebody who can give them advice when needed, whereas 74% of the respondents from Nuuk reported this (see table 1).

Questions	Paamiut	Nuuk
How often do you have access to someone who will listen to you?	46%	73%
How often do you have access to somebody who can give you advice when needed?	40%	74%
How often do you have access to somebody, whom you can confide in?	49%	75%

Table 1. Social support.
The figures show the percentage of answers in the two most positive categories, i.e. 'always' or 'very often'.

The study also examined how important a variety of values are to people in Paamiut and in Nuuk. The respondents were asked how much people in the community adhere to the particular values. Then they were asked how much the particular values were important to the respondent herself/himself. A majority of the respondents reported that (1) sharing and helping others, (2) respect for others, and (3) cooperation are important personal values. There is a notable difference between the importance of these as personal values and the importance of these values in the community for both populations; however the discrepancy for 'sharing and helping other' and for 'cooperation' was larger in the Paamiut community (see table 2).

These SLICA findings support the need to mobilise social support in Paamiut. One of the activities in the community mobilisation programme is capacity building for young mothers.

Capacity building for young mothers

Very young mothers, especially single mothers, have been seen as a particularly vulnerable group in the community. They face particular challenges, especially social isolation and a lack of support from the family, but they also have a history of surviving challenges and

	Paamiut		
	Values in the local community[a]	Importance of values for the respondent[b]	Discrepancy
Sharing and helping others	71%	91%	-20%
Respect for others	80%	93%	-13%
Cooperation	74%	93%	-19%

	Nuuk		
	Values in the local community[a]	Importance of values for the respondent[b]	Discrepancy
Sharing and helping others	79%	85%	-6%
Respect for others	76%	95%	-19%
Cooperation	84%	94%	-10%

Table 2. Values.

a The answers are based on the question: *How satisfied or dissatisfied are you with the way your local community promote and support the following values?* The percentage covers the affirmative answers to the categories 'very satisfied' and 'satisfied'.

b The answers are based on the question: *How much do you emphasize the following values yourself?* The percentage covers the affirmative answers to the categories 'very much' and 'much'.

adversities through a range of creative and resilient ways. They may be in need of social support but still, in most cases, they are part of systems of social relations.

The group was established through a capacity building programme with a focus on the protection of the child. The mothers were offered the chance to attend an intervention programme of 7 hours daily for 5 days. The intervention consisted of a variety of activities: relaxation exercises, guided imagination exercises, art and creativity sessions and shared reflections. The participants were invited to participate in the programme by the social welfare service or the hospital. Approximately 30 children are born in Paamiut each year and during pregnancy a nurse visits the homes and examines the mothers-to-be at the hospital. Through this contact the most vulnerable mothers-to-be were selected and invited to participate in the group. The young mothers participated in the sessions during pregnancy and after giving birth. A midwife with experience in conducting groups for mothers facilitated the workshops. The group had ten participants who ranged in age from 18 to 28 years. Most of the mothers were living with a partner. They had all completed secondary school, but only a few had vocational training.

An example of the type of exercise called 'guided imagination' presented in the intervention is briefly described in the following. The participants were asked to imagine the uterus as a tent for the foetus. Through guided imagination they experienced how warmth could shine in like the sun and make it joyful to be in the tent. Then they imagined how cigarette smoke would be felt in the tent. The foetus would start to cough. They imagined how very noisy people under the influence of alcohol and noises of people fighting would impair the feeling of safety in the tent. After the experience the mothers talked about the idea of seeing the uterus as a tent and how the unborn baby will be impacted by the incidents that take place outside its "tent". They talked about how turbulence and loud sounds of violence would make the yet unborn baby upset and that it would start to cry in the uterus. The mothers reflected on how fighting and screaming in between the parents would create fear and insecurity in the baby. Based on their experiences with these group discussions they developed background knowledge and imagined experience that supported their creation of the metaphor of being "neighbours" to the unborn baby and reflected upon how to operationalise this understanding in their activities with the baby as parents.

The goal of the intervention programme was to enhance self-efficacy in how to apply the mother's love for the child in practical behaviour. The objectives were to provide the young mothers with practical communication skills that could be used when communicating with the child and within the family. Furthermore, there was a clear focus that the intervention programme should lead to some kind of sustained social support between the young mothers. The activities were informed by an experiential design for learning and were explicitly open to the inputs and stated needs of the participants.

The language used in the sessions facilitated by the midwife was Kalaallisut (the Inuit language), which is the mother tongue of the participants. Subsequently, the group developed into a sustainable social support network and low-formalised civil society organisation.

Participatory action as method

Participatory action research aims to support the intentions and hopes of the community members to move forward in the direction agreed upon. In this process the participants develop and coin new concepts that capture and reflect the understandings and the desires of the community participants. The concepts are useful in order for the participants to condense and systematise shared experiences. These concepts will be open to new interpretations and new developments. Thus, the research must be open to the new, the unexpected, the unforeseen and the surprising. This requires a philosophy of beginnings, aware that we live in a human universe, which is still in its making, i.e. an open process. In this process people can create new options that were not embedded in the pre-existing understandings. The challenge for community based participatory action research is to study the moments when the shared development opens up new understandings and options.

The study of the group of young mothers encompasses a series of focus group interviews and shared reflections with the mothers. There were 5 interviews and between 7 and 10 participants. The midwife organising the initial intervention programme participated in the first focus group interview. Translation from Kalaallissut was provided by two of the participants in the group. The interviews lasted on average 1.5 hours. The interviews were translated from Kalaallissut to Danish. In the following, the English translations are based upon the Danish formulations conveyed by the interpreters.

The relevance, quality and usefulness of the study were ensured by repeated meetings and dialogue between researchers, the mothers and other participating community members. The focus group interviews and the shared reflections were focused upon the topics which the participants found important to discuss. Two themes of particular importance were developed in this process, namely social support and protection from unwanted interference. These emerged through discussions of the concepts of mothering, family life, protection of the foetus and the infant, sense of community, well-being and social cohesion. The mothers collaborated in the research process and thus turned it into a capacity building activity interlinked with a knowledge generating process. The process also included reflections on the applicability of the new understandings in daily life with the newborn baby and other family members.

The intervention programme provided a space for telling and sharing stories and experience. The group provided an opportunity for the individual narration of stories and for a group reflection. This led to a shared framework of understanding. Through the dialogues and the reflections, the personal meanings of life experience merged into a common framework that was built around a number of key concepts.

Two of the mothers were employed as research assistants and took part in the research planning and the conduct of the interviews. The analysis of the findings was conducted in cooperation with all the participants in the group. The quality of the study was measured by its usefulness for developing the shared discussion in the group and the transfer of its outputs to the life context of the participants. In addition, the group of young mothers participated in reflections on how the results of the research could be applied in concrete activities and programmes in the community.

Results

Some of the young women reported that in the intervention programme, for the first time, they felt free to talk about their resources and problems because they felt that they were being respected and that they were able to establish a high level of mutual trust in the group. They told that they had previously been silent on issues such as loneliness, social stigmatization, sexual abuse, suicidal ideations and substance abuse. Being part of the group opened a space for sharing thoughts and feelings related to challenges in daily life with an infant.

They reported that they used to be alone with their problems. Even though they had company, they felt alone when having problems. Furthermore, they said that sometimes the company was intrusive, unwanted and even abusive.

Through the above mentioned shared reflecting process their concerns were organised into four themes: (1) Isolation, (2) Moving from silence to openness in the group and in the family, (3) Unwanted interference, and (4) Turning to the community.

Isolation

The mothers reflected thoroughly on the relationship between problems and social isolation. They viewed problems as leading to isolation, as they used to be ashamed of talking with others about these problems because they feared that the others would laugh at them or even start to despise them for having unsolved challenges in life. They reported that there was a norm indicating that you should not show weakness as it was considered a sign of inferiority. They reported that it often was difficult to be open about problems and still be taken seriously. One of the mothers said:

> "In the sessions we felt that we were taken seriously and not laughed at and because of that we were able to get out of our solitude and start to work together in supporting

each other. That experience motivated us and made it joyful to be part of this. It gave me a reason for getting out of bed in the morning. It is great that we started with breakfast together and later in the day we had lunch. The structure of the days here was clear to me. I liked that. In fact, I liked that somebody cared for us as I feel that I have been betrayed so many times before."

Another participant said:

"In the beginning it was quite difficult for me really to trust in the others. To have confidence was hard for me. I hardly dared to believe that somebody took me seriously and in the beginning I feared that it would soon stop and then I would be let down again."

Yet another participant reflected on this by saying:

"Through openness, mutual respect, conversations with each other – and when you are welcomed and we talk about the love for our children and about good moments – then the loneliness disappears so that you do not feel alone. You get angry when you feel alone. When you are a single mom you may easily sink into a state of depression."

The group provided a way out of being socially isolated and in some cases even excluded through laughter and mockery. The level of trust in the others was low to begin with, which seems to be considered part of the local social context. To avoid talking about challenges and resources may lead to social isolation and to being alone with the worries about being a mother with the responsibility for the upbringing of the child. The participants managed to break this silence through sharing of worries and reflections.

Moving from silence to openness in the group and in the familiy

The young mothers reflected on how they were able to break the social isolation and the silence that used to be the way they responded to worries. This process of talking more openly with each other, and thus breaking what was considered a long-lasting cultural tradition of not talking about problems, emerged throughout the sessions. One of the mothers in the group said:

> "In the sessions we can talk about our experiences and our problems. We feel that it is confidential and we share experiences and listen to each other. We get inspired to talk about our life when we listen to the others' stories. We are more open now. Maybe it is because our lives changed a lot with the baby. It seems like we are more open to changes now. We are more willing to change our behaviour now, I mean, in this period of life."

Another of the participants reflected on the transfer from the group to the family:

> "If we want to have a healthy family life we need to speak openly about things, so that we are able to discuss things of common concern. To speak together in an open way is important. That is a way to create love and unity and understanding for each other. It is important to express yourself as it makes it possible to express your care, your love and your solidarity within the family."

Yet another of the participants said:

> "Good parenthood requires that we can talk openly about happiness and sorrows. We must have a dialogue about daily tasks and decisions. We must actively create love and togetherness and mutual understanding. This is how support and attachment are created."

Unwanted interference

A particular theme emerged around a need for protection from interference from other family members. All of the mothers had experience of unwanted behaviour that was imposed on them and brought into the family. They experienced huge difficulties in limiting such behaviour because they feared being socially isolated if they did so, or because it was seen as rude to impose such limits on the husband or partner or other members of the family. One of the young mothers explained how she had realised that she had to limit this kind of interference:

> "I have realised that family members under the influence of alcohol, gambling or other disturbances should not disturb my mothering. I will have to protect my newborn child from these kinds of disturbances and interference."

Another mother reported:

> "What I mean by a healthy family is a home without alcohol and drugs and where there is no gambling. It is a home without alcohol and drugs and where people are not under the influence of that. I have experienced that gambling can lead to family disintegration so that the cohesion of the family is broken. Then you feel very lonely. And when the money is spent on gambling, we cannot afford anything. And a family with a newborn baby really needs money for diapers and the formula because I cannot breastfeed anymore as my milk production has ceased because of stress due to money worries. Scratchcards and other types of gambling take a lot of money from our family's budget."

Yet another told the following story:

> "In my childhood my parents were divorced, so I became a pawn between them. I felt like I was being thrown

around between them. Then I went into foster care in another town. When I finished secondary school, they sent me to a larger town to live in a students' dormitory. I feel rootless. I decided that my child should not be exposed to that kind of childhood. So I stopped smoking and drinking when I got pregnant. But my mother still comes around when she's drunk. I do not visit her when she is drunk, but she comes around, even though I have told her not to do that. Sometimes, my boyfriend comes to see me when he is drunk. I have told him that he must go to his own place when he is drunk, but he keeps on coming here. Sometimes he leaves, but then he comes back again and there is some trouble."

It is difficult for the young mothers to protect the child from the interference of other family members, especially in cases of abusive behaviour including violence and sexual violence as well as exposure to gambling and alcohol abuse. The narratives told by the mothers show that they felt insecure about putting a limit to the addictive behaviour of husbands/boyfriends and other members of the family. This problem was described as a repetitive pattern, which required a permanent effort to set boundaries. In the group process they realised that they were becoming capable of explicitly stating the necessary boundaries, but that the challenge was to impose these in a way which would support the social network instead of isolating the young mothers.

Turning to the community

During the progress of the programme the mothers decided to invite the citizens to a community meeting in the village hall. This idea arose from the group meetings and was not planned as part of the programme to begin with. The title of the arrangement was: *Everybody needs somebody to talk with when life is difficult*. The advertisement of the meeting described it as follows: *We will talk about our group of mothers and explain what it did for us and our children. We will talk about how it is to be a single mother, how we can support each other and how the mothers' group has impacted on our lives and opened up new friendships.*

A mother commented on the arrangement in the following way:

> "We arranged the public meeting with PowerPoint presentations about our group and the importance of having a sense of community. We also talked about how we could be more open and talk about our feelings, sorrows, and problems. A lot of people came to the meeting.
> After the meeting we helped to start a new group of young mothers. We have also urged our boyfriends to make a similar group for fathers."

The mothers reported that breaking the silence made it possible for them to develop a social support network that sustained openness:

> "When we meet, we talk about everything: problems, good experiences, kids' clothes and food, boyfriends and a lot of other things. Often we have dinner together. That we have developed a sense of community is the most important aspect of our group of young mothers. If we did not have this sense of community and solidarity our group would not exist. Every Thursday when we have our meeting, we always talk about how important it is that we share our thoughts and feelings and we remind each other that solidarity is an important part of our lives. A sense of community and solidarity are only present in small groups in our community, in families, at work. Before, even when we were together with our families or parents, we did not think of sharing thoughts and feelings, but after the group was established, we found out that this is a very important part of life."

The mothers also developed radio broadcasts at the local radio station, which they named *"The voice of the young mothers"*. In the intervention programme and in the focus groups the young mothers reflected upon how they could break the silence in the context of the community and even beyond that context. One of the mothers reported:

> "We have already made several plans in our group. We have planned to make trips to other places in Kalaallit Nunaat and tell people about our group, how you can organise a group like this and why it is important.
>
> We also visited the secondary school here and told both boys and girls about our group, about contraception and safe sex and how it is to become a parent at a young age. Speaking about boys, in our group the fathers and boyfriends are also welcome.
>
> We have heard that there is a similar group of young mothers in Nuuk. We are planning to contact them. We don't want to be a group of only young mothers. We want to invite all pregnant women in Paamiut to join the group. We have made a leaflet with information about our group and the topics we talk about, when we meet, for instance being pregnant, giving birth, and having a newborn baby. Furthermore, it says that everybody is welcome in the group, and most importantly, that we are open to new ideas. One of our goals is that most of the young girls in town join the group. We feel that our knowledge about sharing thoughts and feelings, the sense of community, respect and trust should be passed on to the next generation."

The four themes mentioned above are illustrated in table 3. The narrative accounts are the stories told by the young mothers. The conceptual framework is the concepts that were coined in the shared reflective process in the group. We have organised the four themes into an overall framework of experience, reactions, responses and intentions (goals). Experience comprises many resources and good moments with friends and family, but also many challenges. The group focused on these challenges as its members wanted to develop a new understanding and new ways of coping. The group members reflected on how they used to react to the challenges in ways which were seen as only partly deliberate as they were thought to be the only possible way of reacting. In the group, other ways of responding to the challenges were developed and applied, both in verbal exchanges and in emotional and practical support within the group and in the social network which emerged from the group sessions. The intentions are the goals and objectives, i.e. the visions of the kind of life the participants want to promote in the community and individually. The conceptual framework collects the components of the narrative accounts into overarching concepts.

	Experience	Reactions	Responses	Intentions
Narrative accounts	Challenges of becoming a mother	Isolation Sadness	Joining the group Continuous participation Supporting each other	A sustained social support network
	Exposure to violence and abusive interference	Lack of self-esteem Alcohol abuse Silence		To have a voice as mothers in the community To give the children a good upbringing
Conceptual framework	Challenges	Symptoms and prejudices	Breaking the silence and isolation though building a supportive social network	Community resilience and individual resilience

Table 3. The framework of understanding developed by the group of mothers.

As a result of this, the group of mothers developed a new understanding of its context and challenges through shared reflections and mutual support. The existing behaviours were challenged as the group developed as a social network through a shared learning process that developed new responses to the challenges. This was accomplished not only through changing the participants' perception of their own capacities, but also by making clear that they could contribute to the development of a new shared understanding of how a social network can be supportive and contribute to the healthy upbringing of children.

Discussion

The group of mothers developed a horizontal social support system that was articulated in the sessions and was sustained through building a social network for the participants that endured beyond the end of the programme. This social support system was established to protect the mothers against social isolation and loneliness in times of adversities and worries. The network and the concepts developed made it possible to see problems as shared rather than individual and unique. The specific problems became visible and with the conceptualisation the mothers developed a clear voice to describe their current situation, their visions and the actions which could bring these into the daily life of the community.

The pattern of vulnerable people tending to isolate themselves when in need of social support has been described in social psychology and community psychology (Orford, 2008). House, Landis and Umberson (1988) reviewed research on social support and health and found that socially isolated individuals are less healthy, psychologically and physically. Social support is a collection of social, cognitive, emotional and behavioural processes that occur in personal relationships and promote the individual's adaptive coping with life's stressors. Dalton, Elias and Wandersman's (2001) review of studies on social support concluded that individuals with strong networks of social support were able to cope well even with high levels of strain. Furthermore, they argued that social support can be divided into specific support and generalised support. Specific support concerns problem-focused coping with a specific stressor in a particular setting such as a school, a workplace or a neighbourhood. Generalised support comprises emotional support and social integration. Emotional support refers to the care and comfort provided within personal relationships, such as in family relationships, while social integration refers to a sense of belonging in a community.

The Cohen and Wills (1985) review of social support made this distinction between specific and generalised social support on a basis of solid empirical studies. They found evidence that social support may protect the individual against stress when he/she is exposed to critical incidents or ongoing straining conditions, a view also called the *buffer hypothesis*. Evidence for the buffering model was found when measuring the perceived availability of interpersonal resources that are responsive to the particular needs of the specific straining event. The review also found evidence for the stress-reducing effect of a more generalised sense of social belonging, i.e. the person's degree of integration in a large social network. Cohen and Wills concluded that both conceptualizations of social support are correct in some respects, but each represents a different process through which social support affects well-being.

The seminal studies of Sarason (1974) and of McMillan and Chavis (1986) relate generalised social support to a sense of community, which is defined as "*a feeling that members have of belonging, a feeling that members matter to one another and to the group, and a shared faith that members' needs will be met through their <u>commitment</u> to be together*" (ibid, p. 9). According to their theory, the sense of community consists of membership, influence, integration and fulfilment of needs, and shared emotional connection.

The group of young mothers provided both specific social support and the more generalised type of social support. In the intervention programme and in the weekly meetings, the young mothers received support in coping with specific challenges of having an infant in the family. The group also provided more generalised support for the individual young mothers as it developed into a social space in which the members felt that they were respected and taken seriously and where they could talk freely and would be listened to.

The development of the group secured another base for emotional and technical support beyond the family. Whereas the family had been seen as the primary base for emotional support and protection, during the intervention, the group became a supplementary space for these. The family as a support system is founded on different roles and generations, whereas the group of young mothers offered a supplementary support system based on similarity and equality. Thus, the support for the young mothers slowly became mediated through horizontal practices of social interaction rather than mainly linked to the vertical structure of family practices. The changes fostered a stronger system of access to social support for the young mothers as well as a feeling of having this support when needed.

The social support was found at a level beyond the family as the young mothers came from different families; it was found 'in between' the family and the community. All participants in this multiple family approach are struggling with similar problems, but may address these problems in different ways. To listen to each other, to reflect on the stories told, and to reflect on possible solutions are the main activities of the group. Through a joint reflection process the overall understandings and behavioural options may be challenged, developed and changed. Multiple family therapies teach that sometimes it is easier to see solutions to problems in other families than in one's own. Even though the problems may be similar, they are not identical, and the families hold a range of varying experiences and ideas.

The young mothers managed to start speaking openly about problems and thus overcame the culture of silence. Through the new understanding that developed in the group they were able to minimize the anxiety of being despised if talking about problems. In this process they also challenged the individualization that isolated each one in her feeling of shame. Instead they created a framework of understanding the problems as contextual and thus partly above the level of the individual's control.

Activity theory (Wertsch, 1985) explains how the self and the identity are shaped in social interaction in particular contexts with political, economic, and livelihood aspects included as mediators. Through the concept of mediators it shows how the individual and in particularly the group is able to change the context and thus change its own identity. The group of young mothers developed into a kind of semi-structured civil society organisation that promoted social responsibility, social support and a sense of community. This was mediated through public meetings, a presentation in the secondary school, radio broadcasts and presentations at the early community meeting in the sports hall as well as through informal contacts with people in the community. The group responded to the conditions set in the context and began a process of changing these conditions. Through the breaking of the silence they moved from being mainly part of a kinship system to becoming a civil society organisation.

The civil society organisation promoted social support through respect for motherhood which included a respect for everybody's basic human rights, including protection from unwanted interference. In their narratives, the members of the group told about continuous incidents of unwanted interference, i.e. abusive behaviour, but still found it difficult to make the other person respect the limits.

The group of mothers started to instil values that applied limits to the abusive behaviour as this behaviour in fact constituted a violation of basic human rights. The group developed a concept of motherhood as a social activity, rather than perceiving it as a natural process. They augmented a discourse of rights against unwanted interference and abusive behaviour.

The social development in the group of young mothers may be understood as a micro-genesis of mutual support in the sessions and in daily living outside the sessions. The reorganisation of the social world includes a practical, behavioural level (sustaining the meetings and the interaction), a discursive level (the concept of protection of children through protection of motherhood), and an economic level (production of art and handicrafts). With the theory of social development, Vygotsky (1978) argued that social interaction precedes development. The social interaction promoted by the group of mothers opened new development pathways for their children and thus also for themselves in a transformative process of social interaction.

The change in the group of mothers was most explicit and observable in the understanding of social support as mediated through horizontal practices of social interaction rather than mainly linked to the vertical structure of family practices. The changes fostered a stronger system of access to social support for the young mothers as well as a feeling of having this support when needed. The success of the group resides particularly in this strengthening of the social support system as it raises the possibility of breaking the culture of silence and thus limiting unwanted interference.

Conclusion

The group developed around concepts of how to overcome social isolation when in trouble, shaping a new identity through breaking the culture of silence, and using the sense of community to establish an order that sets limits to abusive interference.

The group process had a notable impact on the level of perceived social support for the young mothers. Through the efforts of the participants it enhanced a sense of belonging and created the opportunity to talk about problems without being ashamed. Thus it empowered the young mothers to decrease abusive and unwanted interference related to gambling, alcohol abuse and other disruptive behaviour. The group developed concepts that changed their understanding of mothering and the protection of children. It conveyed the idea that it is possible to develop a *culture for the children* rather than just seeing the children as *children of the culture*.

This case study illustrates some wider perspectives for a social action learning approach to community development. In societies all over the world the rights of certain groups are being violated or individuals are being exposed to abusive behaviour because of their gender, age, lack of physical strength or their social and economic role and position. It is the responsibility of rights-based programmes to promote protection of the vulnerable groups either directly or indirectly, and to listen to their wisdom, resources and hopes. We want to emphasize the need to ensure that the voices of all are heard, and we find that it is often those who remain silent that are in greatest need of receiving services – and who hold the key to new solutions to old problems in the community.

Notes

1 The chorus of women, p. 51 in T. S. Eliot (1965) Murder in the Cathedral. London: Faber & Faber.

Acknowledgement

This chapter builds partly upon presentations by Søren Lyberth and the first author at the University of California, San Diego, and at Ilisimatusarfik/University of Greenland, Nuuk. We are grateful to Aaja Chemnitz Larsen, Heidi Jeremiassen and Søren Lyberth, all members of the Board of Paamiut Asasara, for inputs and comments on the text. The research was made possible through a grant from Bikuben Fonden.

References

Anasarias, E., & Berliner, P. (2009). Human rights and peacebuilding. In J. de Rivera (Ed.), *Handbook on building cultures of peace* (pp.181-195). New York: Springer.

Berliner, P., Anasarias, E., & de Casas Soberón, E. (2010). Religious diversity as peacebuilding – the space for peace. *Journal of Religion, Conflict, and Peace, 4*(1). Retrieved 28.7.2011 from: http://www.religionconflictpeace.org/node/79.

Berliner, P., Larsen, L. N., & de Casas Soberón, E. (2012). Case study: Promoting community resilience with local values – Greenland's Paamiut Asasara. In M. Ungar (Ed.), *The Social Ecology of Resilience* (pp. 387-297). New York: Springer.

Berliner, P., & Mikkelsen, E. N. (2006). Serving the psychosocial needs of survivors of torture and organized violence. In G. Reyes & G. A. Jacobs (Eds.), *Handbook of international disasterpsychology* (pp. 77-98). Westport: Praeger Publishers.

Christensen, E., Kristensen, L.G., & Baviskar, S. (2008). *Børn i Grønland. En kortlægning af 0-14 årige børns og familiers trivsel.* [Children in Greenland. Mapping the well-being of 0-14 year old children and their families]. National Research Institute for Welfare: Copenhagen.

Cohen, S., & Wills, T. A. (1985). Stress, social support, and the buffering hypothesis. *Psychological Bulletin, 98,* 310-357.

Curtis, T., Larsen, H. B., Helweg-Larsen, K., Pedersen, C. P., Olesen, I., Sörensen, K., Jörgensen, M. E., & Bjerregaard, P. (2006). *Unges trivsel i Grønland.* [The well-being of young people in Greenland] Retrieved 14.11.2011 from: http://www.peqqik.gl/Publikationer/Rapporter_og_redegoerelser/Unges_trivsel_i_Groenland2006.aspx

Dalton, J. H., Elias, M. J., & Wandersman, A. (2001). *Community psychology: Linking individuals and communities.* London: Wadsworth.

Eliot, T. S. (1965) *Murder in the Cathedral*. London: Faber & Faber.

Finkelhor, D. (1994). The international epidemiology of child sexual abuse. *Child Abuse & Neglect, 18*, 409-417.

House, J. S., Landis, K. R., & Umberson, D. (1988). Social relationships and health. *Science, 241*, 540-545.

McMillan, D. W., & Chavis, D. M. (1986). Sense of community: A definition and theory. *Journal of Community Psychology, 14*, 6-23.

Orford, J. (2008). *Community psychology. Challenges, controversies, and emerging consensus*. Hoboken, NJ: Wiley.

Pereda, N., Guilera, G., Forns, M., & Gomez-Benito, J. (2009). The international epidemiology of child sexual abuse: A continuation of Finkelhor (1994). *Child Abuse & Neglect. 33(6)*, 331-342.

Pinheiro, P. S. (2006). *World report on violence against children*. Geneva: United Nations. Retrieved 14.11.2011 from: http://www.unicef.org

Poppel, B. (2006). *SLICA – Survey of Living Conditions in the Arctic: Paamiut.* Nuuk: PaamiutAsasara. November 2011 available from: http://www.arcticlivingconditions.org/

Sarason, S. B. (1974). *The psychological sense of community: Prospects for a community psychology*. San Francisco: Jossey-Bass.

Vygotsky, L. S. (1978). *Mind in society*. Cambridge MA: Harvard University Press.

Wertsch, J. (1985). *Vygotsky and the social formation of mind*. Cambridge MA: Harvard University Press.

Author list

Peter Berliner • peer@dpu.dk
DPU, University of Aarhus, Copenhagen, Denmark

Jeremy I. M. Carpendale • jcarpend@sfu.ca
Simon Fraser University, Burnaby, Canada

Manuel de la Mata Benítez • mluis@us.es
Universidad de Sevilla, Spain

Marcia Leticia Ruiz Cansino • maricialruiz2004@yahoo.com.mx
Universidad Autónoma de Tamaulipas, Mexico

Carolin Demuth • cdemuth@uni-osnabrueck.de
University of Osnabrück, Germany

Helene Gudi • hgudi@uni-osnabrueck.de
University of Osnabrück, Germany

Tia G. B. Hansen • tia@hum.aau.dk
Aalborg University, Denmark

Mogens Jensen • mogensj@hum.aau.dk
Aalborg University, Denmark

Kristine Jensen de López • kristine@hum.aau.dk
Aalborg University, Denmark

Heidi Keller • hkeller@uni-osnabrueck.de
University of Osnabrück, Germany

Astrid Kleis • akleis@uni-osnabrueck.de
University of Osnabrück, Germany

Line Natascha Larsen • Linelarsen@psy.ku.dk
University of Copenhagen, Denmark

Charlie Lewis • c.lewis@lancaster.ac.uk
Lancaster University, United Kingdom

Harriet Bjerrum Nielsen • h.b.nielsen@stk.uio.no
University of Oslo, Norway

Hiltrud Otto • hotto@uni-osnabrueck.de
University of Osnabrück, Germany

Laura Quintanilla • lquintanilla@psi.uned.es
Universidad Nacional de Educación a Distancia, Madrid, Spain

Lucía Ruiz Ramos • lucyruiz77@yahoo.com.mx
Universidad Autónoma de Tamaulipas, Mexico

Monica Rudberg • m.y.h.rudberg@ped.uio.no
University of Oslo, Norway

Andrés Santamaría Santigosa • asantamaria@us.es
Universidad de Sevilla, Spain

Elena de Casas Soberón • Elenadecasas@hotmail.com
Universidad Cuauhtémoc, Aguascalientes, Mexico